LONGMAN KEY SKILLS
LEVEL 1+2
W O • L P • P S

Barry Smith

Longman

Longman Key Skills

titles available in the series

Application of Number Level 1+2
Application of Number Level 3

Communication Level 1+2
Communication Level 3

Information Technology Level 1+2
Information Technology Level 3

Working with Others (WWO)/Improving Own Learning and Performance (LP)/
Problem Solving (PS) Level 1+2

Working with Others (WWO)/Improving Own Learning and Performance (LP)/
Problem Solving (PS) Level 3

Pearson Education Limited
Edinburgh Gate, Harlow
Essex CM20 2JE, England
and Associated Companies throughout the world

First published 2001

British Library Cataloguing in Publication Data
A catalogue entry for this title is available from the British Library

ISBN 0-582-43218-9

Set by 3 in Sabon and Quay Sans
Printed in Great Britain by Henry Ling, Ltd,
at the Dorset Press, Dorchester, Dorset

Contents

How to use this book   v

Part 1: The Learning Curve

Planning   2
Reviewing and evaluating   19
Group work   22
Problem solving   42
Using the World Wide Web   46

Part 2: The Bottom Line

Preparing a portfolio   56
Working with others   60
Evidence for level 1 (WWO)   62
Evidence for level 2 (WWO)   72
Improving own learning and performance   87
Evidence for level 1 (LP)   91
Evidence for level 2 (LP)   102
Problem solving   117
Evidence for level 1 (PS)   119
Evidence for level 2 (PS)   129

Part 3: Opportunities

Course-related opportunities   142
Art and Design • Business • Construction and the Built Environment • Design
and Technology • Engineering • English • Geography • Health and Social Care •
History • Hospitality and Catering • Information and Communication
Technology • Land and Environment • Leisure and Tourism • Manufacturing •
Mathematics • Media • Performing Arts • Retail and Distributive Services •
Science

Evidence from other activities   203

Creating a webpage • Cooking • Gardening • Working on a school, college or workplace publication • Taking part in a club or event • Study groups • Homework and course work strategies • Outward bound courses and extra-curricular activities • Taking your driving test • Hobbies and interests • What do you want to do next? • Fault finding

Index   229

How to use this book

This book helps you obtain the following three key skills at levels 1 and 2: 'Working with others', 'Improving own learning and performance', and 'Problem solving'. Whether you will be doing your key skills with your other studies in a school, college or at work, this book will help you gain the knowledge, skills and understanding you need to achieve the key skills. This book also offers advice on how to tackle the evidence requirements of the three key skills and indicates where you could look to generate evidence.

The good news about gaining any of the key skills is that you don't always need to do extra work. The evidence for the key skill can be produced while you are doing your normal study and work in the classroom, laboratory, workshop, while at work or even at play.

You can use this book in different ways, it depends on your need. For example, you might not need to read it from the beginning, you may be comfortable with the learning requirements for a particular key skill but need help with the evidence requirements. In this case Parts 2 and Part 3 will be most useful. To get the most out of this book, have a look at the following summary of how it is organised and decide how you can use it best.

Part 1: The Learning Curve

This part of the book concentrates on what you need to know to get the key skill units. It has useful information about how to plan and evaluate your work, how to work effectively with other people and how to solve problems. This part looks at the knowledge, skills and understanding for all three key skills together because there is a relationship between some of the content in the key skills. For example, there are parts of planning and evaluating that relate to all three key skills.

Part 2: The Bottom Line

This part of the book tells you what you must do to gain the key skills units. It explains:

- The words and ideas of the key skills
- What is expected at levels 1 and 2
- What must be in your portfolio of evidence

Part 3: Opportunities

This part of the book is split into two sections. The first section shows you where to find opportunities to create key skill evidence in the courses or qualifications you may be taking. Rather than looking at particular qualifications, this section looks at subject areas and the types of topic they would normally contain which could be used to generate key skill evidence for each of the three key skills.

The second section looks at opportunities to generate evidence for each of the three key skills using non-course-related activities.

Margin

Look in the margin for simple explanations of important words and ideas.

Part 1: The Learning Curve

This part of the book shows you what you need to know to gain your key skills qualification. It deals with the knowledge, skills and understanding involved in planning, implementing and reviewing work. This will be useful for all of the key skills covered in this book.

This part is divided into five sections:

- **Planning**
- **Reviewing and evaluating**
- **Group work**
- **Problem solving**
- **Using the World Wide Web**

Planning

Why have plans in the first place?

A plan serves as a framework for a project and is a useful reference point for everyone involved. It enables you to judge your progress at any time and helps to steer you towards your targets. If kept up to date and amended properly, it can serve as a record of events. In terms of the demands of the key skills unit, it will provide a useful record of your intentions for your portfolio of evidence.

The ability to plan is a transferable skill, which means that once you can plan effectively, you will be able to use it in many different aspects of your studies or work. Regardless of context, planning effectively will let you confront challenges in a well thought out and controlled manner.

People think that planning can be a waste of time and prevents them from getting on with the work. Planning actually saves time by focusing your efforts in more productive ways, cutting down on mistakes and wrong decisions that you could make. Planning helps you to prepare for what you need to do, and prepare for unexpected difficulties. This could end up saving you time.

Getting started

There are two important stages you need to consider before you start. Both stages refer to what you will be doing though both have different levels of detail. The first stage deals with your whole activity in general terms; the second stage looks at the specific detail of what you will be doing. The first stage is establishing your *aim*, sometimes called your *goal*. Your aim should describe in uncomplicated language what you would be trying to achieve.

'Working with others' refers to objectives, while 'Improving own learning and performance' refers to targets

The second stage adds a layer of detail and is far more specific. It deals with the objectives you will need to meet if you are to achieve your aim. Normally people talk about 'aims and objectives' when describing the two levels of detail; however, sometimes this next level of detail can also be referred to as a target rather than an objective. This stage looks at the processes involved in setting clear and feasible aims as well as appropriate and measurable targets or objectives.

Though the key skills don't mention aims or goals, you will find that establishing your aims or setting your aims is a useful first step that will help you to:

- Communicate to others your intentions
- Remain focused on what it is you are trying to do
- Set your plan in context
- Use other techniques to explore the challenges ahead

Defining your aims

To define your aims, it helps to have a clear understanding of what you want to accomplish. The aim should be a well-defined statement of what you are trying to do. You should also give an idea of the overall time constraints and an indication of the types of resources you will need. You could also include a description of how you will know when you have achieved your aim. These statements can be made in broad terms because you will break them down in more detail later.

Identify early on who needs to see your aims, timelines and lists of potential resource needs. This allows others to let you know if your project is unmanageable before you get too involved in the work.

People often forget about this part of planning because they think they understand what needs to be done and just want to get on with it. However, not taking time to think things through properly can mean running into difficulty later. You will lose the benefit of sharing your ideas with others and lose their input if you charge on with the work. You will also be missing out on opportunities to create valuable portfolio evidence to show that you have thought through your work properly.

Setting group aims

When you work with a group of people it is important to have everyone contributing to the aims. This will help each member to feel that he or she is part of the team and encourage everyone to take ownership of the work that has to be done. It also helps to start the process of working co-operatively and reinforces the need for joint effort.

Why have objectives or targets?

Aims are fine for recording your broad intentions. They are a clear way of letting others know what you will be doing overall. However, they are too general to implement as a useful plan because they lack detail. Your aim is too general to allow you to work out exactly what resources you will need, what tasks you need to do and how long everything will take. The aim doesn't really tell you much about the sequence of tasks either. This is why you need to break it down into more detail. By breaking your aim down into a series of precise objectives or targets you can make better judgements about what resources you will need, what needs to be done first and how long different activities should take. This will give you the information you need to produce a clear and detailed plan that will be easy to follow, monitor and evaluate.

Having a clear **aim** is useful for focusing brainstorming sessions and will allow you to create spider diagrams and mind maps

Brainstorming, **spider diagrams**, **flowcharts** and **mapping** are all ways of moving from the general aim to precise targets. See page 10

Setting objectives and targets

It is only when you break your aims down into smaller targets that you begin to get a real impression of the work that will be involved, the resources you will need and the time it is all likely to take. Targets or objectives are basically your aims broken down into a series of smaller statements that describe more precisely what you need to do. Your aims are broader and general, the targets add a layer of detail and precision to your work and are specific and task related.

Setting targets also gets you to think about the sequence of your work, making you consider what preparation needs to be done before you start the work. This is useful in helping you to organise in your mind an order for your activities. It will also be very useful in helping you to devise and monitor your plan.

There are five key characteristics to consider when identifying targets or objectives:

- Specific
- Measurable
- Achievable
- Realistic
- Time-sensitive

Specific

Try to provide enough detail to prevent any misinterpretation or un-certainty about what you intend to do. One of the main mistakes people make when setting targets is to be too vague. This won't help you when you need to establish how well you've done, so break your aim down into precise, small, measurable targets.

Don't go for vague, general statements like 'Do better in English'. Focus on specific areas, for example, use an aim like 'Improve my grammar', or 'Make fewer spelling mistakes'.

Measurable

It is always helpful to have actual evidence of having completed targets. Evidence and proof are two very powerful words when doing courses like key skills. Assessment depends on your being able to demonstrate that you have met the requirements, so work on having targets that can be measured or are easily proved.

Build into your plan ways of showing how your work is progressing or what you actually achieved when you reached the end of a stage. Treat this as a cut-off point and try to find some way of recording or acknowledging what you have done. If one target has been to read a chapter of a book about something, once you have reached the end, spend some time writing down from memory what you learned. This will not only record the fact that you actually read the chapter but will also give you a clear indication of how much you took in and understood while you were reading it. You can use this to judge whether you need to go back and re-read something or take notes on work you have not understood. Alternatively, if one of your targets has been to use the Internet as a resource, keep evidence to show how you used search engines and were able to find the information you needed. Your evidence could be printouts of your search results and copies of the information you found.

Achievable and realistic

Always consider whether or not your targets are possible. Be aware of both your own and other people's abilities and limitations. Consider carefully whether you are going to be able to meet the challenge you have set yourself.

A common mistake is to be too ambitious when you set your targets. Before you commit yourself to anything make sure you consider:

- The resources you will need
- The time it will take
- The training or skills you need
- The support or help you will need

Then you can consider:

- If the resources are available to you
- Whether you have enough time
- Whether you have the skills you need or can get the training necessary
- Whether the support is available

Cost factors must also be considered. Remember, although an aim is achievable it may not be workable because it will cost too much or take too long.

Time-sensitive

Time is a critical factor. Are you going to be able to do what you say you can do within a reasonable time frame? Think carefully about the amount of time you will need to do the work successfully and the amount of time that is available to you. Start to allocate rough timelines to targets and tasks. This should begin to give you an idea of whether or not your proposal will be workable.

Feasibility studies

Before taking your initial ideas much further, it is worth doing a feasibility study to establish whether or not you will actually be able to meet your objective or targets. Carrying out a feasibility study will not only help you to determine whether your ideas are going to work, it will also provide some useful evidence showing that you have thought through your early target setting.

Start by writing up your aim in as much detail as possible, clearly explaining what you intend to do. Then, if you have the time, leave it a day or two, come back to it fresh and check the aim against the five SMART criteria. Draw up a table with two columns and put the positives down one side and the negatives down the other. The table overleaf shows you an example of a possible layout.

PLANNING | **5**

	Positive	Negative
Specific		
Measurable		
Achievable		
Realistic		
Time-sensitive		

RECAP

Once you have your general aim, techniques like brainstorming, spider diagrams or mapping can be used to help you create smaller, more precise targets or objectives.

Work up your targets or objectives and put them through the SMART test.

Once you feel confident about your targets or objectives and are clear about how long it could take and the resources you need, you can start putting your plan together.

The sunshine method

One way of helping to identify the objectives making up your aim is to use the 'sunshine method'. This is a very simple technique. Draw a circle in the middle of a page large enough for you to write your aim inside. Once you have written your aim inside, try to identify the various objectives that need to be achieved or targets that need to be met to reach your aim. Each objective should be put at the end of a ray of sunshine.

This is a very basic method that can be a useful way to get you started. You could work up your ideas more fully using other techniques. This method is like drawing a simple spider diagram.

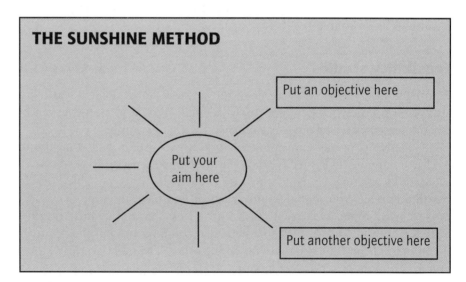

THE SUNSHINE METHOD

Put your aim here

Put an objective here

Put another objective here

The plan itself

You need to consider what form your plans will take and how you are going to represent targets, time, decision taking and resources. Flowcharts can be a useful way for outlining the whole process and can also be used to focus on particular targets in detail. This is one useful way of representing the sequence of stages in your plan. However, flowcharts may not be the most effective way to help you to show your timelines.

You can find out more about **flowcharts** on page 14

Action plans are a very useful way to keep track of group and individual work. When you work in a group, everyone can receive the same blank action-planning sheets and be asked to show their own individual targets and responsibilities. Once you have written out your action plan, check that it takes you through all the tasks that need to be done in order to achieve your objectives or targets. If you are working in a group you need to make sure all the action plans fit together and will achieve the group aims or objectives. Group action plans shouldn't conflict with each other or repeat work.

You can organise your action plan either to show the tasks that you need to do in sequence or to show how you prioritise your work with the most important tasks at the top. The example overleaf – a template for an action plan, showing work priorities – shows the type of plan you could use, but you are free to design one that is more suited to your work. If you create your own action plan using a computer, put it on the 'landscape' page setup and make sure you leave enough space for the important details. Consider creating a template that others can use and leave it on the disk that others can access and use. If everyone working on the same project uses the same template, it will be easier to follow and you will be able to spot conflicts and problem areas more easily when the action plans are compared. Keep in mind that a good action plan:

- Makes reference to the overall purpose (your aim)
- States the target or objective that it relates to
- Includes time to be taken and important deadlines
- Is laid out in a clear and logical manner
- Is updated and amended as changes are made
- Will be dated or have a draft number to show it is the current version

Hint: use the table function in your word-processing software to create an action plan

Changes to your plans

There are two particular ways to prepare for and deal with unforeseen circumstances that risk disrupting your plans. The first involves adopting a *flexible* approach to planning, the second is *contingency planning*.

Flexibility in planning

You can keep plans flexible and be able to respond to changes in circumstance by building in review stages. When you finish a task, review the work done, commenting on or evaluating your progress and check if the planning decisions you made for the next stage are still appropriate. If there has been a change in circumstances you can then adjust your planning.

1. Name			
2. My objective or target:		3. My final deadline	
4. The action I need to take to meet my objective or target			
What I need to do	When I need to do it Start Finish		The resources I need
1.			
2.			
3.			
4.			
5.			
6.			
5. People who can help me			
Name How they can help			When they can help
1.			
2.			
3.			

A simple action plan layout

Action Plan for ... *Put the target or objective here*				Date
Aim: *Put the overall personal or group aim here*		**Details of target or objective**: *Put a brief explanation of your target or objective here*		
Person/people responsible:		Others involved:	Resources needed:	
Priority no:	Action required:	Start date	End date	Evidence or proof of achievement

A more detailed action plan layout

Every time you meet a target, achieve an objective or complete a task, take a 'time-out'. Think about the work you have just completed and look at how much closer it has taken you towards your goal. Think about how you worked and try to identify how you could improve. As well as reviewing the work that you have just done, check how well prepared you are for the work that lies ahead. Ask yourself 'Is my plan still relevant or does it need to be changed?' You can work out if your plans are still relevant by asking a few more focused questions like:

- Is the goal still the same?
- Are my targets, objectives or work responsibilities still the same?
- Have any decisions been taken that affect my work?
- Are the resources I need still available?
- Are there any other changes in circumstances?

Try to keep a written record of these review stages as you check your plans and keep evidence of any changes you make to your plans. Of course changes or difficulties won't always happen at convenient times for you, for example, when you're taking a 'time-out'. They cause problems because they happen when you are not expecting them. To help you to deal with problems whenever they happen, spend time during the planning stages thinking about what things could go wrong and how you would deal with them if they did go wrong. You could go a stage further and have a contingency plan ready in case something goes wrong.

Contingency planning

A contingency plan describes the steps you will take if something doesn't go according to plan. It attempts to address what could go wrong before it does and gives you an alternative course of action and a way to keep your work on schedule. Contingency planning is all about spotting problems that might occur and preparing for them if they do.

One useful technique is to look at your plan and ask a series of WHAT/IF questions. Go through your plan and assess what could go wrong and ask yourself 'What will I do if this does go wrong?' Focus on important stages of your plan first, then look at the resources you need and work out what you would do if you are not able to get what you need.

You could create a two-column table and put the 'What/if' questions in the left-hand column and your contingency arrangements opposite in the right-hand column. For each resource you need you could also identify a suitable alternative method or piece of equipment that could be used instead. Things rarely go as planned, so contingency planning can be a useful way of dealing with the unexpected.

Monitoring your progress

Once you start acting on your plan you need to gauge your actual progress against your intended or planned progress. If there is a difference you need to be clear why this is the case and take appropriate action to make any necessary adjustments.

One technique that can help you to monitor your progress is to establish interim targets. These are targets that break down your main targets into smaller stages of partially complete work. The value of interim targets lies in their relationship with your timescales. They help you to monitor your progress closely and alert you to any adjustments that you may need to make. By setting yourself mini-targets you will have a greater sense of achievement and this may help to keep you motivated.

One of the main problems you will have is finding an appropriate way to record how to monitor your work. Consider using a diary or journal to keep track of your progress and perhaps produce a brief progress report when you reach an interim target. The report could be used to inform other group members, a teacher or supervisor.

See the section on **'Reviewing and evaluating'** to learn about assessing your planning and performance

WHAT MAKES A GOOD PLAN?

1. Your plan should always have a workable end result.
2. Your plan should be full and detailed enough to get the job done but simple enough to understand and implement.
3. It should be logical so others can follow it.
4. Have backup plans ready to help you cope with unexpected circumstances. Make decisions that are realistic and take account of the circumstances. This will mean your plan is more likely to work, because it will be well thought out and feasible.
5. Be as specific and detailed as you can when it comes to time, cost and resources.
6. Keep your plan flexible with appropriate review stages built in. By continually reviewing your plan in terms of your overall purpose and the progress you make, you will be able to adjust and adapt your work to respond to changes in circumstances. You will also keep on track!

In a group or team situation a plan should include ideas from everyone who has to carry it out.

Planning techniques to get you started

This section introduces you to some of the common techniques used to help to generate ideas and help to plan and solve problems. The techniques can be used to help you to think about your work and help you realise what might be involved in it.

This section looks at:

- Brainstorming
- Spider diagrams
- Flowcharts
- Mapping out ideas

Brainstorming

This is a useful technique that tries to use creative thinking to generate as many different ideas as possible about how to do something or how to solve a problem.

When brainstorming in a group you need to help create a non-threatening environment where people feel their opinions and ideas will be valued. If people feel uncomfortable and don't want to take part, perhaps because they feel they will be ignored or made fun of, then they will not contribute. This means you will not be using the group to its full potential and the best ideas or most appropriate solutions may go unmentioned.

Think of how you would like your contribution to be received and ensure that this is how you receive the contribution of others. During brain-storming sessions there should be no criticism of ideas. You must not stay on any one idea too long. The point is to get as many ideas down as poss-ible. You can go back and analyse the results and shortlist the best ideas afterwards.

Brainstorming is a great way to come up with different ideas about how to solve problems, start action plans or to think about contingency plans. Establish a few ground rules to ensure the discussion goes well and appoint someone to record the ideas.

Begin by making sure that everyone is focused on the main idea or aim that you need to discuss. Try to record all ideas that are offered. Using a board, overhead projector (OHP) or flipchart is a useful way to record ideas because you may find that, by seeing ideas, other ideas will follow. You may find that having a group leader is a useful way of getting every-one started on the right lines. Leaders should define the problem and go over the ground rules for everyone. Organise your group seating to get the most from the discussion: you want to get everyone involved and inter-acting with each other. A circle is a good group layout; however, if some-one is taking notes for the group using a flipchart or OHP then a horse-shoe shape is better.

Keeping the proof

You need to find some way of recording the brainstorming session that lets you use it in your portfolio of evidence. You should keep your own notes and thoughts on the session anyway, but work out how to make a copy of the group effort. Make sure that the person recording the notes for the group isn't tempted to start editing out ideas. You need a record of the whole event. Other things to consider include asking the people taking the notes (especially if they are not group members) to write up the notes or enter the ideas on computer and copy the information to everyone. Include the time and date of the discussion and how long it went on for. You may also find it helpful for an outsider to sit in and feed back their thoughts on the session to help you to work on improving the process in future.

Another common form of proof is a witness statement from someone who watched the group in action. You might even want to consider recording the group using a video or audio cassette. However, make sure this isn't going to stop people taking part. Have the video set up at the back of the room on a stand; don't be tempted to have someone wander around with a camera. The audio cassette can be a useful and discrete way of recording the occasion and can be a cheap way to ensure that every-thing is recorded.

Leading a brainstorming session

There are a few simple *dos and don'ts* to follow if you are to ensure that a brainstorming session is successful. As leader you will be the person responsible for keeping the environment friendly and supportive. The rules are given in the following table of dos and don'ts.

Do	Don't
Define the problem to be solved for the group	Don't allow too much time to be spent on one contribution or idea
Encourage an open, friendly, enthusiastic and uncritical attitude among group members	Don't abuse your position by speaking too much
Encourage everyone to participate	Don't allow the person recording the session to edit and choose their favourite ideas
Help people finding it difficult to make a contribution by creating an opening for them	Don't let people spend too long making one contribution
Keep everyone focused on the subject	Don't let the session drag on if everyone has dried up
Have a fixed time limit for the session to help focus minds	
Ensure that records of all contributions are being taken	

Recording a brainstorming session

If you are chosen to record a brainstorming session, you need to follow a few simple rules. Firstly, don't edit or be selective and record only some ideas. Record them all. This will make sure that nothing is missed and people will see that their contributions are all equally valued and are being noted. Secondly, ask people to repeat points if you are not sure what was said or if they were speaking too fast. Finally, try to do a little preparation work beforehand by finding out how best to record the contributions. If you are taking notes, prepare some paper with a column for the contributor's name and one for their contribution or have a prepared list so you record each idea numerically as they are made. If you are using a flipchart remember to use a dark-coloured pen, write on one side of the paper only, number your pages and try to keep each person's contribution on the same page. Make sure you know the names of everyone taking part.

Reviewing your brainstorming session

There are two types of review worth doing if your are using brainstorming as a technique to generate ideas related to key skill work. The first is an evaluation of the results themselves.

You need to sort out the suggestions made and identify some way of assessing them to see which are the best or the most workable. This means looking at the difficulties you have (for example, time, resources, quality) and working out which ideas or suggestions are the best and are likely to bring success. To do this you could get a blank sheet of paper and draw a line down the middle, top to bottom. On one side put a positive (+) or the word 'FOR' on the other side put a negative (−) or the word 'AGAINST'. Then go on to list the advantages and disadvantages of each idea or suggestion made during the brainstorming session. Rank them using numbers if you want.

The second type of evaluation involves the brainstorming session itself. Spend a little time looking at how the session went and assess what went well, what went less well and try to think why this was the case. Look at the different factors that make a brainstorming session successful and measure how well your session went against these factors. This way you'll know how to improve in future.

Spider diagrams

When thinking about problems or plans people can get bogged down in detail very quickly and then begin to lose sight of the overall goal. A spider diagram can be a useful way of sketching out the main features of a problem or issue before you get too heavily involved in one particular aspect of it. It can be a quick way of getting the key features down on paper as they come to you and is a useful written record of your initial thoughts on a subject. A spider diagram can be drawn in this way:

- **Step one:** Turn your paper side on (landscape)
- **Step two:** Write the main issue or problem in the centre of the page (the body of the spider)
- **Step three:** Think about what is involved in your central issue. Then link each idea you have to your central issue by a line (the legs of the spider)
- **Step four:** Each idea can be broken down into smaller issues or themes also attached by lines.

Drawing the diagram as in the example shown, grouping related themes, and using colour to show connected associated ideas can help you to get a better picture of what is involved.

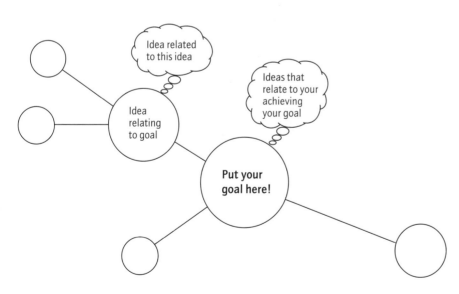

Example of a spider diagram

Spider diagrams can be used to begin to link ideas with action. For example, once you have identified all the key points relating to the central idea or problem (step 2), use step 3 to establish what activities need to take place to make each point happen. Having identified all the related tasks go back over the diagram and prioritise it by numbering the sequence to help you to develop an order for your plans.

Spider diagrams are normally drawn freehand. This allows you to quickly sketch out your thoughts without having to interrupt your flow too much.

Flowcharts

A flowchart is a useful graphic way to help you and others figure out and understand the sequence of steps involved in your work and the key decision points and consequences. A flowchart consists of a series of different standard boxes and symbols, connected by flow lines that show the major stages and decisions involved in carrying out a task or solving a problem in sequence. You should begin to construct your flowchart early on and keep adding to it and changing it until you have an accurate picture of the actual stages involved. Once you have a completed flowchart that accurately shows the steps involved in your work it can be used to show others.

Constructing a flowchart can be a useful way to get a clearer picture of what will be involved in a task. It can be a useful way of uncovering hidden or unexpected difficulties and can prepare you for what lies ahead. The diagram in the margin shows the main flowchart symbols, and their definitions are given in the table. However, there are many more symbols used in flowchart work than those shown here. If you think this might be a useful way to help you plan, find out about the other symbols that can be used. This will help you to produce more detailed flowcharts.

Shape	Meaning	Explanation
Rectangle	Process step	This symbol is used to represent a single action, stage or step in the flowchart
Diamond	Decision point or question	These can contain 'Yes/No' options or other types of decisions that need to be made
Oval	Starter or terminator	Used at the beginning and end of a flowchart with the word 'start' or 'end' inside
Arrow	Flow line	These are used to indicate the direction of the flow
Circle	Go to	Used when flowcharts get too big for the page and need to be continued on another one. It can also be used when your flowchart gets complicated and you want to avoid arrows crossing over each other or to 'go to' a sub-routine. If you use it for this then you need an exit point (e.g. Go to A) and then an entry point (e.g. a circle indicating where you should re-enter the flowchart with A written inside it)

Keep the flowchart clear and simple, as shown in the diagram below. To begin drawing flowcharts get to know the symbols and their meaning, find yourself an appropriate starting point and an aim or target as an appropriate end to the process. Then beginning at the start of the process ask yourself what needs to be done first and what happens next. Work your way through each step putting in any decision points and the outcome if the decision goes one way or the other.

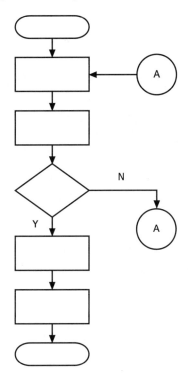

Example of a flowchart

At first, stick to the major steps in the process and major decisions. You can then go back over the flowchart and add further layers of detail. You can create separate flowcharts that break down large processes further to show the detail of exactly what is involved in a particular key stage.

Decision points
Decision taking using the 'diamond' symbol is straightforward. Normally when there are two or even three options they are shown leading off corners of the diamond as in the diagram below.

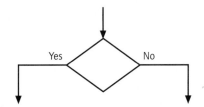

Simple two-option decision

Drawing flowcharts

There are a few simple rules to follow in order to produce clear and effective flowcharts:

1. Draw flowcharts on white, plain paper using one side only
2. Use a template to draw the symbols in your final version
3. Print the contents of each box to make them easier to read
4. The flow is from top to bottom of the paper
5. Arrowheads indicate the direction of the flow

Produce a simplified plan using a flowchart that shows only the main tasks and decision points. More detailed flowcharts can be used for specific targets. The simplified chart may be useful to share with others, while you can use the more detailed work to plan your progress. The process of drawing the detailed charts will also ensure that you confront what lies ahead and will help you to realise what will be involved.

Mapping out ideas

Mapping out ideas on paper is a useful way to develop them further. It's a little like brainstorming on paper although your thoughts are organised in a more structured manner. Mapping does this by getting you to start thinking about the relationships between different ideas. Although the process of creating a map is similar to creating a spider diagram, it is a more thorough and comprehensive attempt to explore the main idea being mapped out.

Mapping could be a useful exercise at level 2

Start by taking a blank sheet of paper then write your idea or main aim in the middle of the page. Then write any related ideas or concepts as branches radiating from your central idea. These will be smaller tasks or related ideas that make up or relate to the main one. Each time you get a new idea start another branch and follow it through until you have exhausted the thoughts you have on it. Branch off any related points you have to consider. Try not to interrupt your flow too much by stopping and thinking about one point for too long. Concentrate on getting it all down on paper first. The point is to get you to start thinking about how the ideas relate to the central aim or meeting the main targets. Try not to edit: concentrate on getting it all down first. Once you put something down, look at it to see what it will involve, and try to unpack it a little further.

Mapping will take practice to do well. It is worth trying and even your first attempts will be useful as a record of your early thoughts for your assessor, and they can also act as a reminder in case you forget something.

Some advantages of mapping as an exercise include:

- Mapping helps you to clearly define your main idea
- It allows you to see all your thoughts and ideas on one page
- You can always come back to review your map so it makes recall and reviewing easier
- It makes figuring out the links between key ideas easier and lets you begin to see the relationships between ideas
- It can help you spot, at an early stage, any problems like contradictions, conflicts or gaps in your work

Once you have a map you can begin to see complex relationships between ideas and judge the relative importance of each. This can be a useful starting point for planning your work and target setting.

Mind mapping is a technique devised by Tony Buzan. Check out his great website at www.mind-map.com. You can also try a Web search using his name or "mind mapping" as your search phrase

Techniques to use when you map

There are a few simple techniques that can be used to help you get started and to organise your work. The table below explains some of these techniques.

Technique	Explanation
Branches	An idea may lead to other closely related ideas and these can be shown branching off the idea they relate to
Arrows	Used to show links and relationships between ideas
Clusters	Related ideas or branches can be grouped together when you create a second draft
Lists	Some branches may lead to a list of things you want to come back to later
Colour	Using the same colour for related ideas can be helpful. Again this might be a useful second draft process to go through

HINT

Once you have a map you are happy with containing all the key points (even points that are unlikely to be acted on), copy it. Use this copy as evidence for your portfolio. To make it a better piece of evidence write comments on it using a different colour of pen to explain what you were thinking about as you created the map. This will be a very useful way to show your early thought development and planning process.

Most people try to go from the initial mapping straight into planning. However, you should take time to look at your map once you have exhausted all your initial thoughts and try to organise them a little before you finish with this stage. By reorganising your initial map as a second draft it will become easier to follow and may make drawing up the plan a little more straightforward.

In your second draft, group related ideas together to give your thoughts a little more order and structure. Do this by drawing circles around related ideas or tasks, or by highlighting them with the same colour pen when you look over your first draft. Then recreate your map. You may want to take this opportunity to think about what you put down and to edit out ideas that may no longer seem relevant. Keep your original map to refer to just in case there is something that you rejected but may need to come back to. It is also an important piece of planning evidence for your portfolio.

The second draft will make a better starting point for drawing up plans and it is at this stage that you should begin to introduce a time frame. Take sections of the map and try to set some timelines. There may be different activities that need to be done together so you need to start thinking about how you need to co-ordinate your efforts and how you can keep track of your progress.

Reviewing and evaluating

When you 'work with others' you are expected to review the activities and report on how your methods of working and working relationships could be improved. 'Improving own learning and performance' has a section on reviewing your achievements and progress, and 'Problem solving' will involve reviewing the approaches you take to solving problems. This section will look at ways you can review and evaluate work whether you are working in a group, working individually or problem solving.

One common fault people often make is to leave evaluation until the end, once the work is done. Evaluation should be a dynamic and ongoing process. It should take place as a natural part of the way you work.

There are a few simple things you can do to make reviewing your work a little easier to do. The first thing is to keep a journal or a diary. Write in it regularly. You will find that just by writing down your thoughts they become a little clearer and you begin to see things differently.

Another way to help you reflect on your learning and performance is to increase the amount of useful outside information available to you about your work and progress. The thoughts and observations of others you trust or respect will be a useful source of feedback. People who know your work or are familiar with your situation can offer invaluable insights and can be good objective sources of information. Even people who don't know you particularly well may have experience or expertise that you could find useful. This input can be added to your own thoughts and help you to establish how best to improve or proceed.

Be careful not to be too harsh on yourself. Even if you get some negative feedback that may be harsh or blunt, try to look for messages or information that you can use and then move on.

Feedback

Feedback can be a chance to give or receive important information about how you are doing. This will help you work out how you can improve your performance based on someone else's thoughts and opinions. You will get a chance to help others develop and improve by offering them feedback and in turn you will be able to benefit from their points of view.

People may see this as an opportunity to settle scores or to get their own back by being unnecessarily negative. There is very little anyone can

Constructive: being helpful, positive or useful

do with negative feedback. It stirs up bad feeling that can unsettle and damage team relationships. Try to be fair and honest. Treat others as you would like to be treated yourself. The watchword for giving feedback is 'constructive'. You must always try to limit your feedback to either positive remarks or constructive comments that help others understand their work or behaviour better.

Giving feedback

Keep the following factors in mind when giving feedback:

- Be honest but tactful. Try not to be blunt, emphasise the positives in others' work and be sensitive to their feelings
- Try to be specific rather than vague or general. Try to make sure that they get the message and can relate what you are saying to actual events or work
- Avoid the temptation to speak for others. Let people know how you feel but don't get involved in rumour or gossip. Keep it work-related and report on how you thought things went from your point of view. Avoid the 'I thought you were great but I know such and such thought you were terrible' syndrome
- Don't be embarrassed about giving praise, thanks or showing appreciation when it is deserved. Explain why you feel this way and how their work or attitude was a positive influence on your own

Remember, once you are clear about the kind of feedback you want to receive then you will also be clear about the type of feedback you will give to others. The key words to aim for are:

- Constructive
- Honest
- Tactful
- Objective
- Useful
- Friendly
- Encouraging
- Supportive

Consider how best to give the feedback. The person may appreciate a paper copy of your comments because it may be useful as evidence. Try to always create a hard copy to give as feedback. This will mean that you need to think about what you write, and the extra time it takes means that you are giving the matter appropriate thought and will influence how you phrase the feedback.

Look for opportunities to use the feedback you give as evidence for your own portfolio. Giving feedback on someone else's work might be useful as evidence in 'Working with others' or 'Problem solving'.

How to use feedback

There are a few simple steps that you can take to help you make effective use of any feedback you receive:

1. Check that you understand what the feedback means and try to understand why you received it, i.e. what made the person make each comment in particular
2. Don't be afraid to ask follow-up questions on the feedback to help you clarify something
3. Identify what the important issues are. (Issues that will mean making changes)
4. Identify what the minor issues are. (Issues that will mean slight adjustments or just mean taking more care or time)

Asking follow-up questions on feedback you are given can be a good way to get the most out of the people around you. This can be useful if these people have skills, expertise or experience relevant to your work.

LOOK ON THE BRIGHT SIDE

You will find that many people have a tendency to focus on the negatives like what went wrong and whose fault it was. In times of crisis or failure people focus more on 'blame-storming' than trying to sort problems out.

Try to be positive and help others to be positive by focusing on the problems or issues at hand rather than on individuals. Try to provide positive comments alongside any suggestions for improvements.

Helping others to comment on your work

Make it easy for people to comment on your work by producing it on computer. Set the line spacing to double or 1.5 spacing and leave large margins left and right. (This makes it easier for others to write comments on your work at appropriate points.) Use a simple, straightforward typeface that is easy to read like Times New Roman or Arial and use a font size that is easy to see, for example, font size 12. Make sure you have page numbers and always include a title.

Make sure that the person commenting knows you are expecting feedback and let them know when you need it by. Remember to be polite and give them advance warning and plenty of time to comment. If you need to remind them, send them a friendly note to jog their memory.

Font styles
- Times New Roman
- Arial
- Courier
- Tahoma

Group work

At the heart of group work or teamwork is the commitment shared by those involved. You should experience a number of benefits when working with other people. By looking at the benefits you get an idea of what you should expect from others and what others will expect from you. The main benefits include:

- The ability to share ideas
- The chance to gain different points of view
- The opportunity to benefit from other people's experiences or abilities
- Help and encouragement to keep focused and get the job done

You will also get the opportunity to learn to deal with criticism, develop the ability to give constructive criticism and gain the skills needed to deal with conflict and disagreement. These skills and abilities are all vital and will be of benefit in a variety of different circumstances.

PLANNING

Planning is a key part of the process of working with others successfully. Make sure you read through the section on planning that starts on page 2 for help and guidance on how to create a team plan and set appropriate objectives.

Dealing with people

People act and react in many varied ways. Sometimes people have a tendency to adopt ways of behaving that are more self-protective than open and co-operative. People also tend to forge alliances with friends that can frustrate others and may detract from the group and its purpose. Two things to keep in mind are who to work with and how to try to keep everyone focused on the task. The best way to deal with these issues is at an individual level by making sure you strive to be open and co-operative, and at a group level by discussing how to create an open and co-operative atmosphere.

Even when you are working with others, you need to keep in mind that it is **your own individual portfolio** that will determine whether you achieve the key skill. Even if the group is not as effective as it could be and some work or targets are being missed, you need to show that you can work with others. Even if some of the others are not able to work with you or with the rest of the group, show you can do what is required of you in a group situation. This means showing that you have acquired the necessary skills and have evidence of them in action. Such evidence will show that you can be open and are able to communicate and work effectively with others.

The two main factors that will show a group's success are *tasks* (how the group's performance is measured) and *relationships*.

Group leaders v. self-managing groups

When you form a group to carry out a certain task you may want to consider whether the group needs a leader or whether you will all manage the group. Deciding which organisational method is most appropriate really depends on what you want to achieve. Larger groups facing a difficult challenge tend to work best with a leader who, if nothing else, acts as a focal point. Smaller groups with a clear focus work well as self-directed groups. In self-managing groups there are no formal leaders and group members work together to organise and carry out the work.

If you decide that a leader would be beneficial for your group then you need to remember that there is a difference between leader and boss. The 'Working with others' key skill credits people who demonstrate that they can work together. This requires leaders to be more like facilitators who help the decision-making process to happen at meetings and not someone who dominates the group and gives orders to others.

It doesn't have to be as clear cut as having or not having leaders. Establish what functions need to be handled by individuals (e.g. a chairperson for arranged meetings) and consider sharing these roles around the group so everyone gets a chance to be carry them out.

You will need to discuss five key areas when you begin working with others in teams. These are:

- Organisation and ground rules
- Establishing objectives
- Agreeing working arrangements
- Monitoring progress
- Evaluating the work

Organisation and ground rules

Although it may feel a little awkward, you should spend time discussing rules or guidelines for the type of behaviour the group wants to encourage. This spells out for everyone, right at the beginning, the type of behaviour expected. You need to establish early on how decisions will be made, how you will work and how problems or differences will be resolved.

When you discuss the topic of decision making you need to consider whether or not you will take decisions by:

- Majority voting
- Consensus (where everyone can reach an agreement about what to do)
- Compromise or
- Delegating decision-taking responsibilities to one or more individuals directly involved in that particular work

Perhaps the best approach is to be flexible and to keep your options open. Particular decisions may be more important than others and your group may decide to choose a method of decision taking that is appropriate for each type of issue that arises. If this is the case then set out a few examples of the decision taking that will be used for different issues. For example:

- Seeking consensus will be used for important whole group issues like setting aims and objectives
- Delegated decision taking will be used for small-scale everyday events
- Subgroups in charge of a specific area of work could have responsibility for decisions in their area

However you choose to take decisions, make sure that there is some way of reporting them that keeps the whole group informed of events. This will also help to ensure that smaller groups or individuals don't get carried away and exceed their authority.

Your aim should be to make sure that all members feel that they are an important part of the team and that no one feels left out. If you notice someone who seems to be left out from a conversation or discussion, try to involve him or her by asking that person to comment. Not only is there a team responsibility to involve everyone, there is also an individual responsibility on everyone to play their part and to ensure they do their best to help others participate. Remember there are two ways to do this:

See the section on **brainstorming**, **spider diagrams** and **mapping** to find out how to generate ideas, (page 10)

- By behaving in a way that encourages others to participate
- By actively helping others to participate

Establishing objectives

Teams need to identify and agree what their aim is. You need to establish why the team exists and what purpose it is to serve. This helps to make sure right at the beginning of the process that everyone is clear about why they need to work together and will also help to clarify specific tasks that need to be carried out. Hopefully people will feel greater commitment to the group effort if they are clear about why the group exists. When members participate in setting the group aims, they become more committed to ensuring the aims are achieved.

The group will need to break down their aim into objectives and the related work to be carried out. A key part of objective setting is ensuring that objectives can be measured in some specific way. You will need to be able to determine whether you met your objectives and judge how well you did. Try to establish performance standards for your work and how progress can be measured. This way not only will people know what the group must do but they will also know the standards expected of them. As well as establishing how to measure your group objectives, you also need to begin to establish a time frame for all this work and begin to discuss the resources you will need.

When you establish your own role within the group you should turn this into a set of objectives with criteria to measure your performance. You need to make sure these tie into the overall group targets and on completion will have helped the group reach its collective aim. Also identify review points where you can assess your progress and consider when you need to share information with or update other people, when you will need information from other people and when you may need the group to help you to make decisions.

Your individual work must relate to and involve the group. Don't be tempted to get your work allocation, then go off on your own and come back when you have completed everything. This is not working co-operatively. Make sure you identify timelines for your individual efforts that fit with the overall group deadlines.

See also **target setting** on page 4

Agreeing on the working arrangements

You will need to spend time discussing how the team should be organised. Decide whether or not there will be a leader, or whether the group will be able to work without one. Effective teams are made of committed individuals working together towards a common aim with each playing an important part in ensuring the team's success. So your group will need to address how it will be organised and how the work will be shared among the group members.

Establish how the group will make decisions and report progress. This may mean deciding about how and when the group needs to come together and meet. You need to arrange a programme of meetings, establish how long you think they should last and decide how participants will be notified.

Groups can communicate through meetings. This may involve one or two members working together on a specific project or a larger group discussing ways of sharing important information, taking key decisions and monitoring progress. Effective meetings take time, commitment and planning and need a purpose. Without these ingredients they can often be a waste of time.

Learn more about **holding meetings** on page 28

Monitoring progress

How is your group going to keep each other up-to-date on progress? Who needs to know what? Consider how the group will communicate with each other and share information. Businesses use memos and email; how do you intend to do it? Though sending memos or email may be seen as a chore, remember that it is not just a useful way of keeping others informed but also represents useful forms of evidence of your involvement in the work.

The key is to communicate effectively regardless of how you choose to do it, so discuss it with the team. If you are sending memos or email, discuss what should be sent and who should receive copies. It can be useful to appoint someone as an information person who gets copies of everything to keep in a central file that anyone can access. This helps create an open atmosphere and serves as an information base for the whole group.

Effective group environments

See also **Creating a good atmosphere** on page 39

You need to build a group environment that encourages people to participate. This helps generate enthusiasm in the group members. You can do this by setting appropriate standards of behaviour for yourself then trying to encourage them in others. You need to try to avoid creating hostile environments where participants would be reluctant to speak or to contribute ideas. This would demotivate people and problems will start to emerge as communication breaks down.

As an individual group member try to:

- Co-operate rather than compete
- Involve everyone in decision making
- Share your information and update people on your progress
- Be open and receptive in group discussions
- Make sure you are not the one making it difficult for others to take part

Maintaining good working relationships

The main ways to keep good working relationships are to be open, receptive to the contributions of others, supportive, friendly and communicative. You need to make sure you do your best to help others to perform their tasks and meet their objectives successfully. Share information about your work and progress. Aim to find out how best to communicate with others, when to communicate and what to communicate. Find the balance that leads to appropriate levels of communication, don't swamp others with unnecessary information or keep them in the dark, guessing what you are up to.

Resolving conflict and arguments

Conflict can lead to the breakdown of working relationships and thus deflect the group from its purpose. Often, given time and space, people can think about a difficult situation and return to it with a more positive and constructive attitude. So sometimes a break and a little space can benefit all concerned.

Resolving conflict is not easy, but by considering a few points and acting appropriately you might be able to rebuild a positive working relationship.

- Keep in mind why the group has been formed
- Try to think and act rationally
- Avoid the temptation to take sides if matters become heated
- Keep talking, listening and stay open and approachable

Remember that conflict is resolved by **building** bridges not burning them

Remember that any initial response you make to a comment or situation will set the tone for the following conversation so try to avoid an over-reaction or a confrontational response. Keep your side of any exchanges open, receptive, genuine and respectful. You can be assertive without being aggressive. Try to be patient with others and try to understand what could be upsetting others.

Generally, conflict is a result of disagreement about work or personality clashes. Work differences become the responsibility of the whole group to try to resolve. The group could mediate between the two disagreeing parties and try to reach a satisfactory solution for everyone concerned. This could be done with a group leader, an individual in the group that both parties trust and respect, or with an appropriate outsider. The point is to resolve differences for the good of the group in a way that both parties can agree to.

The other way to resolve conflict is to use the group to arbitrate either at a meeting or in a less formal place. In arbitration both parties present their positions or points of view and the group decides how best to sort things out. The responsibility is on the group to give each person a fair hearing and to make fair decisions. Group members can take some of the potential heat or bad feelings out of the situation by finding and commenting on the good in both sides.

In this type of situation you want to try to prevent making matters worse. If you are involved in the conflict or are trying to resolve it, try to be sympathetic to the others' position and think about why they feel the way they do. Come prepared to listen, reason and resolve the difficulty fairly. Other steps to consider include:

- Behaving responsibly and judging the argument on its merits. Try not to show favouritism
- Looking for ways to create a compromise that everyone can agree. Identifying the common ground that might exist between the people arguing can help do this
- Ask each what they like or don't like about the other's position
- Try to use friendly language and a soft, low tone of voice to take some of the heat out of the situation. Be objective, fair and tactful even if faced with irrational behaviour or arguments

Personality clashes are harder to deal with. This type of conflict is often best dealt with outside the group by drafting in help from an appropriate third party.

If all else fails, agreeing to disagree on an issue can often be a useful strategy to resolve conflict. However, try not to bear grudges.

Holding meetings

Meetings will generally involve sharing information and decision taking. They can be used to focus a group's attention on particular issues or tasks and help generate ideas to act on. They also provide an opportunity to review progress and take appropriate action if things are not going to plan. Meetings can also be a useful place to review and monitor the success of your plans.

You will find that by having meetings you will get the chance to show your ability to meet many of the evidence requirements for the key skill section on agreeing objectives and working arrangements.

Making the most of meetings

You may decide that 'one-off' meetings will be more appropriate than a regular meeting set at the same day and time each week, fortnight or month. Either way make sure you will have a record of what is said and discussed. This will be useful evidence for your portfolio. Establish whether you need a chairperson to help run the meeting, decide how you will record the meetings and how this information will be distributed to the group afterwards. Rather than appointing one person to chair the meetings and someone to produce minutes, consider rotating these responsibilities around the group. This approach will provide more varied evidence for everyone's portfolio. Also discuss whether you need someone to chase progress for the group and report back. Always make sure everyone is clear about why you are having a meeting and that they know what the group needs to achieve by having the meeting. Then everyone can try to play their part in achieving it.

All meetings should have a clear agenda, given to group members well before the meeting. This gives everyone a chance to prepare appropriately. Make sure at the end of a meeting you spend a little time agreeing what needs to be discussed at the next meeting. Ensure that you discuss:

- Any issues that should be on the agenda
- Any key reporting issues that need to be addressed
- The time, date and venue of the next meeting

Try to involve everyone in meetings: this will help to make sure that everyone feels that they are part of the team.

Agendas

Be clear about the purpose of meetings and work out in advance what subjects will be discussed. You can do this by preparing an agenda for the meeting. An agenda is a formal notification of all the important information about the meeting and it is sent or handed out to those attending. It needs to contain the time, date and place of the meeting, what will be discussed at the meeting and the order of topics to be discussed. This makes the meeting run more smoothly. When you come to draw up an agenda put the most important issues at the beginning of the meeting.

KRUGER FRIGHT CLUB

Friday, 13 July 2000, 2 p.m.

Room 8
Basement, Jason Building, Kruger College

Agenda

1. APOLOGIES FOR ABSENCE

2. MINUTES OF LAST MEETING

3. MATTERS ARISING

4. TREASURER'S REPORT

    i. New memberships
    ii. Account balances

5. PROPOSALS FOR HALLOWEEN FUNDRAISING

    i.   Disco   Paper ref.: BOO/001
    ii. Fete   Paper ref.: BOO/002
    iii. Raffle   Paper ref.: BOO/003

6. FILM SHOWINGS

    Martin Storie to report.

7. ANY OTHER BUSINESS

8. DATE OF NEXT MEETING

Example of an agenda

The outline of the agenda should be easy to determine if you have a good plan of action. Depending on the progress made, you should be able to identify items that need to be discussed. If this is not the first meeting of the team, then there will be matters to discuss from the previous meeting, updates to be made and you should have a list of items previously raised that need attention. You will also be able to refer to the overall plan of action and get some further ideas.

Normally on agendas there is a section called 'Matters arising'. As in our example, this usually appears after the agenda item for the minutes or notes of the previous meeting. 'Matters arising' covers anything that is outstanding from the previous meeting's business shown in the minutes or notes. This is the first opportunity to check on progress. You can report the follow-up work done as a result of discussions made at the previous meeting.

The agenda could also contain updates on progress in key work areas, with the person responsible for the area updating the rest of the group. You may want someone to provide an overview of progress in all aspects of the work, it really depends on what would be the best way to monitor developments in meetings.

Key roles in meetings

As effective members of the group, everyone has a role to play in meetings. You will be able to share information, update others and update yourself on how others are doing. There may also be decisions requiring your participation. You should certainly prepare for the meeting by reading through the agenda and previous minutes and seeing whether you are expected to contribute anything to the various items to be discussed and how you can help others to do so.

In more formal meetings it is usual to have someone chairing and someone taking notes (minutes).

The role of chairperson

A chairperson (Chair) introduces the meeting, saying a few words about the context of the meeting as well as handling any organisational issues. The Chair should be clear about the meeting's objective and the results or decisions that need to taken at the meeting. It is always a good idea to talk about this up front. The Chair needs to ensure that the agenda is directly related to the objectives of the meeting and lays out a clear path to achieving them.

They are then expected to lead the group through the agenda and control the meeting, making sure people who want to speak get a chance to, keeping the discussion on track. They are responsible for ensuring an orderly meeting that addresses all items and issues that need to be dealt with.

The Chair is usually responsible for overseeing the production of the agenda for the meeting and needs to have a clear idea of how much time they are prepared to spend on each agenda item. They also need to review any supporting material that needs to be sent out to accompany any agenda items, for example, the minutes of the previous meeting, any copies of reports or presentations that will be given at the next meeting.

The Chair should sit where he or she can see each member of the team so as to be able to direct the meeting. Try to end the meeting with an upbeat summary of the successes so far.

GUIDANCE FOR CHAIRING A MEETING

- Enforce rules
- Keep everyone involved
- Keep everyone informed
- Maintain a positive approach throughout

Minute taker

The group needs to decide in advance what kind of minutes should be taken at their meetings. You may want full minutes of each meeting, or perhaps a brief note outlining key issues discussed, decisions taken or contributions made will do. The example overleaf shows the general format of minutes, but the important thing to remember is that you must all be clear about what you want to achieve and the minute taker must know what is expected of them.

The minute taker normally sits beside or near the Chair. This allows them to quickly confer if they need to.

GUIDANCE FOR MINUTE TAKERS

- Don't leave it too long after the meeting to write up the minutes. Do it while it's still fresh in your mind
- Use the agenda headings as headings for the minutes
- Work out an appropriate numbering and referencing system beforehand
- Include a list of those attending
- Refer to people in your minutes by their initials

ROTATION

Consider rotating the role of Chair and minute taker at each meeting. This way everyone who would like to can get a chance to experience the roles. Appoint each role for the next meeting at the end of the current meeting.

Agreeing who does what

When it comes to allocating tasks for group members you need to try to work to people's strengths and ensure you get the best out of everyone. This is more likely to guarantee success. You must try to avoid allocating tasks to people who are reluctant to do them or are not really well suited

MINUTES OF THE JERSEY YOUNG ORNITHOLOGISTS CLUB
31 August 2001

Present: Ms J. Wren (chair)
Mrs L. Goosey (secretary)
Mrs C. Licken
Mrs H. Penny
Mr D. Duck
Mr B. Finch
Mr H. Martin

In attendance: Mr T. Cat

1. APOLOGIES FOR ABSENCE
Apologies for absence were received from Mr C. Robin.

2. MINUTES OF LAST MEETING
The minutes of the meeting held on 15 June 2001, previously circulated, were passed as an accurate record of events.

3. MATTERS ARISING
CL reported that the problem reported at the last meeting had been resolved.

4. WINTER MIGRATIONS
HM presented a paper (ref: JYOC/001) proposing a survey of migratory species during the month of September. After discussion, the club agree to the proposals asking that the results be reported at the next meeting.

5. BIRD TABLE SURVEY
TC attended for this item.

i. Survey results
TC presented the results of the survey to the group reporting that 35 people had taken part in the local area with 17 different species recorded.
ii. Continuation of the survey work
BF asked if the survey was to continue. TC replied that the plans were to continue monitoring the tables through the winter. There was a discussion on the need to include more appropriate winter food on the tables as well as a range of feeding devices. TC agreed. The club thanked TC for his hard work and asked that he continue to keep the club informed of the survey. TC agreed.

6. RAPTOR WATCH
DD and HP presented a paper (ref: JYOC/002) about the local raptor populations expressing concern about increased numbers. Discussion followed. Members agreed that increased numbers of top-level predators were indeed a concern and agreed to remain vigilant. The club thanked DD and HP for bringing the issue to their attention.

7. AOB
HM reported that he would be out of the country until May and unable to attend meetings until then. He asked that he still be sent JYOC papers. HM to liaise with LG.

There being no further business, JW thanked the members and closed the meeting at 4pm.

8. DATE OF NEXT MEETING
It was agreed that the next meeting would be held on 7 October 2001 at 2pm.

Example of the minutes of a meeting

to them. When it comes to dull or boring chores, be fair and share them out evenly.

You need to ensure that everyone is clear about the working relationships and their individual and joint responsibilities. This will help avoid unnecessary duplication of effort or confusion. The minutes of the meeting can be a useful way to remind people of their responsibilities and should be circulated well in advance of the next meeting.

Playing your part at meetings

Look at your own role in meetings and see how you can work towards becoming an effective participant as an individual and team player. The first thing you can do is to be prepared. This is regardless of whether you have something on the agenda that you need to talk about or not. You may be responsible for updating people about your work; even if you don't there is still work to be done. You have a duty as a team player to ensure that the meeting is effective and the team aim is a little clearer, easier to achieve or closer to completion as a result of your presence at the meeting. This includes taking part in discussions and decisions, listening to other team members and making appropriate comments.

If you are presenting some information at a meeting, try not to talk for too long and remember to let others participate. For example, don't be tempted to give some information, highlight a decision that must be taken then go on to make recommendations about what that decision should be. Stop after you have presented all the necessary facts and figures and invite others to comment. Acknowledge their suggestions, and along the way offer your own. Once you have a full range of possible solutions try to round up the agenda item by suggesting to the Chair what would be the best solution from your point of view.

Before meetings, study the agenda and work out what points you would like to bring up and when to discuss them. Work out what you personally need to get from the meeting to make your team role easier to achieve and note down where it would be appropriate to discuss this. If there is something that you need to discuss that's not covered, draw it to the Chair's attention. Many agendas have a last item that handles any other business (AOB); this might be the appropriate opportunity to discuss your issue. The Chair could mention the topic in their introductory remarks to give people prior warning that it will be discussed.

During meetings your main priorities should be to:

- Get involved without being too bossy
- Be open to the views of others
- Take notes on major decisions or issues raised

After meetings don't wait too long before you look at your notes of the meeting. Deal with them while they are still fresh in your mind and take the appropriate follow-up action.

Taking part in discussions and team meetings

No doubt you already discuss different topics with friends, family or colleagues, and this section aims to help you develop these abilities, allowing you to take part in discussions regardless of who else is in the group. It will also help you to keep focused on the topic under discussion as well as show you how to help others get what they need.

Contributing to discussions and meetings

In an ideal discussion, everyone will want to participate and no one would say anything silly or irrelevant. All the contributions made would be useful and the discussion would be a worthwhile experience for everybody.

When you are having a discussion you may find that some people will talk far more than others, perhaps even taking over the meeting. Some may make irrelevant contributions or comments or wander off the topic, while others may say nothing or very little. Participants need to think about their role and behaviour in discussions. You also need to keep in mind that you will gain far more information and opinions if everyone is involved and contributing.

The first thing to keep in mind is that contributions should not be long speeches. You aren't giving a presentation; you are taking part in a group exercise. Talking for a long time, preventing others from making contributions or interrupting others are all signs that you are failing to participate effectively. The reverse is also true. Just showing up, sitting quietly and hoping that no one will notice you will also mean that you are failing to play your part.

Types of contributions

Any of the following count as making a contribution to a discussion:

- Making a point

SUGGESTION TO GET YOUR GROUP STARTED

Meeting 1

Meet at an early stage and have someone chair the meeting to ensure all the points are covered and that everyone gets a chance to speak. Someone should take notes on the main decisions taken and points made. Talk about the work you need to do and how to best organise yourselves to do it. Deal with the organisation, decision taking and ground rules first. Try to get down on paper:

- A description of what you will be trying to do
- Why you are doing it and the results you expect
- A rough timetable illustrating completion times of each main phase
- What you will need to do the tasks, and
- Who would like to do particular tasks

If you manage to do all this you will have had a successful first meeting. If you don't manage to cover these topics, discuss how you will. Then make sure everyone in the meeting receives a copy of the notes. Consider asking the person who chaired the meeting to obtain feedback from someone appropriate, asking their advice on the suitability of the decisions taken.

By the end of this meeting everyone should be clear about the group's purpose and working arrangements.

Meeting 2

After a short period of time, when everyone has had a chance to read the notes of the meeting and has thought about how it went, meet again. Update everyone then go back over all the decisions that were taken about the group organisation and the work discussed to see if everyone is still in agreement. Try to refine the decisions a little more. Concentrate on adding more detail making everything clearer.

Everyone should be aware of the purpose and format of the meeting so they can make appropriate contributions. By the end of the meeting try to have completed a thorough statement that firms up the objectives, how they are to be measured, the resources needed, timelines and each team member's role in their attainment.

At this point you should be clear about your own individual responsibilities and how they relate to the team aim and the responsibilities of others.

- Expressing opinions
- Explaining something
- Asking and answering questions
- Presenting an agenda item
- Sharing some results
- Encouraging others

Concentrate on making a relevant contribution each time you speak. Don't just make one contribution then keep quiet; get involved in the discussion. When you do make a contribution show that you can adapt what you say to suit the needs of the group and the situation. For example, show that you can recognise whether the discussion is formal or informal and act accordingly or whether a point needs to be made firmly or a word of encouragement is needed. Remember that politeness is always appropriate regardless of context.

Be prepared to take brief notes during discussions or meetings. Writing down the key points made, decisions reached or who said what could be helpful when it comes to referring back to something. It is always good to correctly attribute what is said to the person who said it first. It can be a kind of compliment and shows that you are paying attention. Your notes will also become a useful record and evidence of your involvement in the discussion. The notes will also help you to check any minutes that were taken for accuracy and this helps you spot if there are any differences between your interpretation of events and other people's.

You could start your notes by jotting down the names of the people taking part, even quickly putting them into rough seating arrangements. This will help you to remember who's who. For example, look at the brief sketch in the margin; that is all it would take.

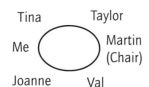

Keep your notes brief because you need to be looking at those contributing and not persistently looking at your papers. Making eye contact with others when they talk is encouraging for them.

Always

- Be aware of your surroundings and the people in your group when you make your contributions
- Be polite
- Speak clearly
- Wait for others to finish making their points
- Try to be supportive

Never

- Shout or raise your voice
- Be rude
- Get angry
- Dominate the discussion or fail to participate

Active listening

The point of a discussion or meeting is to exchange information and ideas with others. This involves giving and receiving information. The simplest way to show someone that you are listening is to look at him or her, and to jot down any key points you think are important.

There is a difference between *listening to* and *hearing* someone. You can be looking at someone and not really listening to what they are saying. You hear the sound of them talking but you're not really paying attention. People can usually tell because your eyes have glazed over, and such signs can be really off-putting. They may even notice your attempts to fight off a yawn, especially one of those 'closed mouth' yawns. To the rest of the group and to anyone watching (like the teacher assessing you) this is just like your saying 'I'm only interested when I'm talking' and reflects badly on you.

Make sure you are actually listening to what is being said. The word that typifies a good listener is *attentive*. This means using different listening techniques to let others know you are taking an interest in what is being said. There is a range of verbal and non-verbal techniques that convey to others that you are paying attention and you will be surprised how important these are to the people talking to you. Just imagine how you would feel if no one looked at you when you talked. In fact, not looking at someone can be a sign of disapproval.

Look at the table overleaf for common examples of these techniques.

Attentive: to be alert, careful, pay attention or be observant

---

EXPERIMENT TO SHOW THE IMPORTANCE OF VERBAL ENCOURAGEMENT

Try this exercise to see how important verbal encouragement or reassurance can be to those talking. When someone chatty calls on the telephone and starts to tell you something at length, make sure you keep quiet and say nothing, make no noise at all. Not even a grunt or a 'yeh!', nothing at all. See what kind of reaction you get from the person on the other end of the phone. They will probably find it disconcerting and will keep checking that you are there and are following what is being said. This is because you are not giving any clues to show you are listening and taking in what is being said. The point is that even when you are not talking, sometimes people still need to hear the odd indication of reassurance.

When you are not under the spotlight and are in a normal conversation or discussion with family or friends, you are probably already an expert at using these types of gestures anyway. What you might need to develop (practise) is the ability to maintain them without being inhibited when you do your key skills assessment.

Making sure you understand what has been said

Test your understanding by rephrasing statements and repeating them to the person who made them. It should then be clear that you have understood what was said (and that you were listening). If you haven't understood, they will correct you and clarify what was said.

Asking questions and responding to others

Questions and answers

When you are taking part in question and answer sessions, be aware of what you don't know. This means recognising beforehand your

Techniques for active listening

Facial expressions	These can give the person talking important clues as to how their contribution is being received. For example, looking puzzled can encourage them to explain or elaborate more about a point they are making
Body movements	Nodding in agreement can be encouraging, as can shaking your head if it matches what the speaker is saying
	Having your arms crossed could be taken as a sign of being defensive, while a slightly tilted head can show that you are listening. Maintaining eye contact shows the speaker they have your attention
Verbal encouragement or reassurance	The occasional word or noise of approval can be a useful way of offering support to someone speaking. Repeating the message back to the speaker is a useful technique that not only shows you were listening but allows you to check your understanding. This involves using phrases like:
	'So, what you're saying then is . . .' 'Let me get this straight, are you saying . . .?' 'Am I right in thinking . . .?'
	Affirmative verbal sounds are the noises or words you use to show that you either agree or understand what is being said. These are useful ways of supporting or encouraging others during their contributions
Probing for further information	You can ask a speaker to go into more detail about what is being said by focusing on one point they have made and asking for more information or by asking them to expand on something. For example, consider using the following phrases:
	'Is there anything else we need to know about . . .?' 'What do you feel is the most important . . .?' 'What led you to this conclusion?'

Affirmative verbal sounds: these are the sounds of agreement or understanding that you make in conversation, for example 'uh-huh' 'mmm', 'OK'

limitations in terms of knowledge in certain areas or topics. When you are asked something you don't know the answer to, you should do one or more of the following:

- Admit that you don't know
- Say how you could find out the answer
- Ask if anyone else knows the answer

HANDY HINTS

- Refer to the questioner's name in you answer
- Repeat the question before you give the answer. This is an especially useful tip to remember for larger groups. It allows you to make sure everyone has heard the questions and it also 'buys' you a little time to think of your answer
- Never try to make others (questioner or person answering) feel silly or awkward, even if their question or answer is irrelevant or confused. Try to be positive and helpful

Helping others participate

Creating a good atmosphere

One of the best ways to encourage others to participate is to help ensure the atmosphere suits discussions. This means making sure that people don't feel intimidated or worried about participating. Others will feel this way if the atmosphere is threatening and they think that they are likely to be ridiculed, made to feel silly, likely to be confronted, faced with aggressive behaviour or with being ignored. Play your part in helping to ensure that the atmosphere is light, friendly, receptive and non-threatening and show that you are *receptive* to other people's ideas, comments and suggestions.

Receptive: willing to listen to new ideas or suggestions

Sensitivity

Try and be aware of how others might be feeling when you participate in discussions. The key word that describes the quality you should strive for is *empathy*.

Empathise by imagining yourself in the other person's position, trying to understand what they are thinking and how they might be feeling about how the discussion is going. You could try to help them feel more comfortable or confident by using some of the different techniques mentioned already.

Empathy: the ability to be aware of, and understand how others are feeling

How you behave and the tone of your voice can affect how others will react or participate. When the topic is serious, don't be *flippant*. Be positive, supportive and friendly, and choose an appropriate tone of voice that will help create a good atmosphere and encourage others to feel confident and able to take part.

Flippant: treating serious things lightly, being cheeky or disrespectful

Encouraging others to take part

Show you are able to help others to take part in the discussion. If someone is finding it difficult to make a contribution because they can't seem to get the group's attention, invite them to make their point. Create an opening for them by inviting them to speak. However, don't turn the spotlight on someone who won't be comfortable with this attention.

You can ask 'follow-up' type questions to help get someone more

GROUP WORK | **39**

Elaborate: the ability to expand on something said by explaining further about it or going into more detail

Alienate: in this sense it means to make someone feel that they are not a part of what is going on and are deliberately not included

Resolute: determined, firm or purposeful

Overbearing: dominating or bossy

involved in the group discussion by asking them to *elaborate* on or explain some of the comments they have made. Ask them in a supportive way, showing that you are interested. This would be a good way to get others more involved, as long as you are sure that the person would want to make further contributions. Don't add to another person's stress or worries by getting them to be involved if they don't want to be. This is where empathy comes in. Try to judge if the person would be comfortable making further contributions. If you think they wouldn't, then don't press them on the matter.

Using language that doesn't offend or exclude anyone

When you discuss something or present a topic you need to be careful not to *alienate* certain people in the group. You need to be aware that your gender (male or female) can influence the way you think and speak.

When you make an effort to explain concepts or ideas, you need to make sure that you do not use examples that are familiar only to you. Try to avoid using examples aimed at a particular gender. Replace these examples and phrases with more 'neutral' ones. This will show that you are aware of the potential danger of alienating those listening to you and that you are trying to involve everyone and are trying not to offend anyone.

The risk of being culturally specific is similar. Basically, it means that you have failed to take into account the potentially multi-cultural nature of your group or those listening to you and are using terms that may mean something to your own cultural group but mean nothing to others. Again, the danger here is in leaving out or even offending others.

The answer is to review your work to make sure you have been sensitive to the situation by trying to make sure that what you say is understood by all.

Firm but fair

Being assertive does not mean being stubborn or aggressive. It involves being clear, concise and firm in what you say, do, or want to see happen, showing you are confident in what you say. Try to get your point of view across resolutely without being overbearing. If others can follow your reasoning, and appreciate the fairness of your line of argument then they are more likely to respect your opinion.

Dealing with arguments

When you are involved in discussions or meetings you will find that people will disagree with your opinions. People will offer alternative viewpoints to your own but you should remember this is a sign of a healthy discussion. You need to learn how to handle disagreements without having them build up into arguments that become a major problem for the group.

Try to look at alternative suggestions or disagreement positively and objectively, and identify the value of what is being said. Also look objectively at your own views. The temptation is to become defensive and to stand your ground. You need to consider what others think and review your own thoughts in light of other people's reactions. Remember you are trying to show you can participate effectively in groups, not that you can win arguments. You must learn to accept and acknowledge differences of opinion and be able to reach agreement or consensus when there is disagreement.

Sexism or racism

There is no quicker way to alienate part or all of your group than by using sexist or racist language. This is a sign that you have failed to take into account the feelings of the people you are talking to.

Make sure that prejudice and discrimination do not feature in your own behaviour, and don't encourage or put up with it in others. Play a part in making it clear that this type of behaviour is unacceptable and has no place in your group work or discussions.

As a rule, racist or sexist language or comments and any other type of language that deliberately offends people are not acceptable in any type of conversation and have no place in work with others.

Try, wherever possible, to use gender-neutral words and avoid stereotypes. The most common oversight is the use of the *masculine* terms to mean men and women, for example using 'man' or 'mankind' instead of 'people' or 'humankind'.

Check beforehand, whether your remarks could cause offence. Ask yourself if they could offend someone on the basis of:

- Gender
- Age
- Race
- Disability

You are basically making sure you are not going to say anything that will alienate or offend someone or will be inappropriate. This is something you also need to remember if you are using humour or telling a joke, which should never be made at someone else's expense.

You have a right to work without feeling harassment, discrimination or intimidation. If you feel any of these three pressures you must bring it to the attention of an appropriate person in a position of responsibility who can support you and help you take the correct steps to deal with the problem. Schools, colleges and the workplace are places that have rules, regulations and guidelines that can help you deal with these types of unpleasant behaviour. You need to find out who is best to talk to and can offer advice, e.g. schools and colleges will have a guidance or counselling team.

'WORKING WITH OTHERS' POWER WORDS

- Patience
- Empathy
- Tolerance
- Consideration
- Supportive
- Open
- Communicative
- Considerate

Problem solving

Making decisions

The decision-making process in problem solving is very like the decision-making process you will use when working with others. This will mean keeping an open mind, being receptive and aware of the opinions and information that surround you. There are many dangers in thinking there is only one possible answer to a problem or only one right way to proceed.

Consider all sides of a problem, explore all your options and try to form a complete picture of the situation. The more information you have or are able to gather, the more effective your decisions will be. When dealing with others, consider all sides of an argument and weigh up each on its merits. That way you will be able to have an informed opinion or draw appropriate conclusions.

You must learn to separate out a range of factors that could influence your decisions or cloud your judgement. This will help you think more clearly and reason more effectively. Emotions can often get in the way of sound judgement and can influence people's ability to reason effectively. However, feelings can be important: how many times have your 'instincts' or 'gut reaction' been proved right. You should never underestimate your feelings but also try to learn to realise the role and effect they may be having on your decision process.

When it comes to decision making, another real pressure can be the need to act quickly. Very often, quick decisions are more about your emotions or snap judgements than about carefully considered or reasoned thought. Think of the phrases used to describe decisions taken quickly:

- 'Knee-jerk reaction'
- 'Heat of the moment'
- 'Act first, think later'
- 'Snap decisions'

None of these sounds particularly positive.

You should try to take and use time effectively in decision making. This will allow you to sort out your thoughts, consider the thoughts of others, and consider all the facts or arguments and form a clear picture. Then you can act, knowing the likely consequences of your actions.

Of course, very often you will have to take a quick decision. By developing your reasoning skills you will be able to operate under this type of pressure more effectively.

What's your problem?

You need to clearly identify the main issue and then break it down into its various smaller parts. By breaking it down the problem may look less formidable and intimidating and therefore easier to solve. However, first you must be clear about what the problem is. By being clear in your own mind what the problem is you can avoid being distracted by minor or secondary issues. You can keep focused on what is really the issue. Too many distractions can mean that you lose sight of the key problem and become overwhelmed. You need to prioritise and focus on what is really the issue; this way you can go on to find an appropriate and effective solution.

By breaking the problem down into smaller parts, you may find that it is not as complicated as you first thought. However, you may find that it is more complex. Either way, you begin to get a clearer idea of what it will take to solve the problem. Whether it is simpler or more complicated, by breaking it down you make it more manageable. This allows you to take one step at a time.

How will you know if you have solved your problem?

You need to find a way of showing how well you have dealt with the problem or how effective your solution is. This means thinking about the actions, evidence or information that can be interpreted as proof that it you have found a successful solution. You must look to create standards that will help you show you have been successful, that you have achieved your aim and the solution you put into work has been effective. These standards will also be useful in terms of keeping you focused on your targets and they will provide you with a useful way of judging your progress.

Techniques to get you started in problem solving

There are some techniques you can use to help generate ideas, help plan and solve problems. These techniques can be used to help get you thinking about your work and what might be involved in it. The techniques looked at here are:

- Skills audits
- SWOT analysis

Make sure you also look at the sections about brainstorming (page 10), spider diagrams (page 13), flowcharts (page 14) and mapping (page 16). These techniques could also be useful in exploring problems, the consequences involved in choosing different options and in helping you to plan to find a solution.

Skills audit

Audit: to examine or take a look at something
Skills audit: checking how ready you are to meet the challenges that face you

A skills audit is a self-evaluation and doesn't need to involve the views of other people. It is a useful way to identify the strengths you bring to a challenge and also helps you realise potential weaknesses. Though it sounds a little negative to spend time identifying weaknesses, by coming to terms with any areas that need to be strengthened you become more comfortable and confident about dealing with them or discussing them with others. You can turn the identification of weakness into a plan of action to build these up and develop necessary skills.

Start by looking at what you do well or have done successfully. Then think of the skills needed to do this work. You are starting to identify strengths. Don't just focus on academic achievements. Then begin to narrow these down a little, looking at the strengths that are appropriate to the challenges that you face.

Consider repeating the process of looking at areas of weakness, and then see if any of these will be needed for your challenge.

SWOT analysis

S Strengths
W Weaknesses
O Opportunities
T Threats

SWOT analysis is a way to identify your own strengths and weaknesses and to examine the opportunities and threats you face in a more thorough way. It is a way of analysing what you do and don't bring to a problem or situation and the chances and challenges that await you.

SWOT analysis can be a useful way to quickly identify where you stand in relation to a problem and can help you begin to realise what might be waiting for you in the form of further challenges and opportunities.

It can also be a helpful way to work out how well prepared you are and where you may need support. To carry out a SWOT analysis you need to be honest about yourself and the knowledge and skills you possess and be realistic about the challenge that confronts you. The two risks that could upset the process are overconfidence or, alternatively, being too modest. It also helps to have done a little research about the problem you want to solve or the project you intend to carry out. This way you can be more fully aware of what you are up against and this will help you conduct a better SWOT analysis. This means it might be best to do a SWOT analysis after you have explored what could be involved in a problem or project.

Carry out a SWOT analysis by asking questions like those shown in the table. Try to be as objective as possible when you answer these types of questions. To help you do this, think not only of how you might answer the questions but also of how someone else who knows you might answer them.

Strengths	Weaknesses	Opportunities	Threats
What suitable skills do you have?	Are there any skills you don't possess that will be needed?	Is there any training available?	Is there anything working against you, preventing you from being successful?
What do you do well?	What do you do badly?	Is guidance and support available?	Do you have conflicting work demands?
What useful contacts do you have?		Are there people around that have dealt with similar issues?	
What have you got working in your favour?			

Other questions like 'How much do you know about the situation?', 'How much time do you have?', 'What resources are at your disposal?' could have answers that turn out to be a strength or weakness, opportunity or threat.

Using the World Wide Web

This chapter looks at how to find out information on the World Wide Web (the www part of web addresses). Learning how to access information held on the web will be useful because you can learn more about areas covered in the other parts of this book.

The web can be an important resource, helping you to find information from anywhere in the world or from just around the corner. You need to learn how to use search engines to find information efficiently and effectively. Otherwise you can waste time sifting through numerous, unhelpful websites. Learning how to make effective use of search engines and how to do searches will help you find what you want quickly and help prevent your wasting time.

The table gives you a few ideas about how the web can be used as a resource in each key skill.

Working with others	*Improving own learning and performance*	*Problem solving*
Find out more about:	Look up reference sources like:	Find out more about techniques like:
• Body language and non-verbal communication • Minutes or agendas	• www.britannica.com • www.howstuffworks.com • www.bbc.co.uk/education • www.gcse.com • www.learnfree.co.uk	• Mapping • SWOT analysis

The Internet is also an important link with the events and resources available in your own community. People often forget that although you have access to the World Wide Web, you can also use it to search for information closer to home.

CRASH COURSE

What is the World Wide Web?
Basically, it is a huge group of files of information stored on computers around the world. The information is held in different websites and each website has its own web address (for example www.nj.com).

What is a web browser?
A web browser (or browser for short) is a software program that helps you look at files of information on the World Wide Web. It helps you access webpages. The two most common browsers are Microsoft's Internet Explorer and Netscape Navigator.

What is the Internet?
The Internet is the route web pages take to get to your computer. It is an interconnected network of computers that allows information to come from anywhere on the web to your home computer.

How does it all work?
A web browser gets hold of information through a connection to the Internet. The connection is made using a modem, a telephone line and an Internet Service Provider (ISP).

In a nutshell
Your web browser can help you get to a website using a web address and accessing it through the Internet. You access the Internet over your telephone line using a modem to send and receive data and an ISP to link you to the Internet.

Accessing the web

You will probably access the Internet via an online service like AOL or an Internet Service Provider (ISP). An online service has its own software package connecting you to the Internet, allowing you to search for information and send and receive email as well as offering a range of other facilities, e.g. news, chat rooms, buddy lists, etc., all under one roof. The illustration overleaf shows you an example of the main menu from an online service. You can see the range of different facilities including searching the web. They attempt to simplify and organise the Internet for you.

Some online services
AOL
CompuServe
MSN (Micosoft Network)

BE QUICK!

Get on the Internet in the morning before the USA wakes up and logs on. Your searches might be a little quicker without all the traffic from US users slowing things up.

Some ISPs
BT Internet
Freeserve
Claranet
Virgin Net

ISPs provide you with a connection to the Internet, making use of the software already on your computer to enable you to send and receive email through software like Microsoft's Outlook Express. You can also

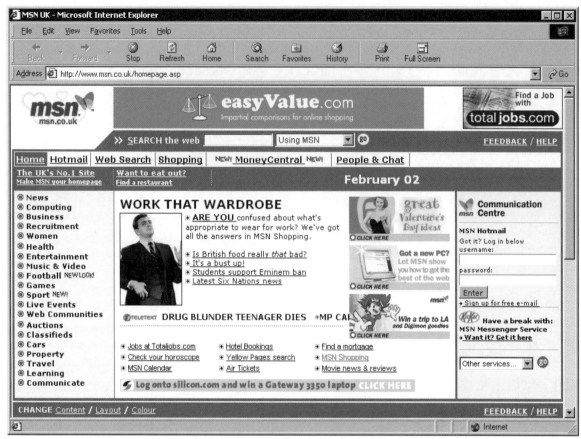

A typical web 'portal' page

'surf' the web using web browsers like Microsoft's Internet Explorer. The other common software also used by ISPs is Netscape Communicator, which combines searching and email. Explorer and Netscape can be seen in the illustration opposite.

You need to explore the Internet access options available to you either at home, work, school or college. Internet cafés may also be an option or a local library may provide access.

Using a browser

Most browsers work in a similar way and have a banner along the top of the screen that displays the different commands. This is sometimes called the 'standard toolbar' or 'navigation tool bar'. The main commands are described in the table opposite.

Search engines

Click the Stop button if the connection is very slow and try again later

The Internet links a chaotic world of information, with no one person or company responsible for organising it. Search engines are tools to help you cut through this huge amount of information. They can quickly sift and

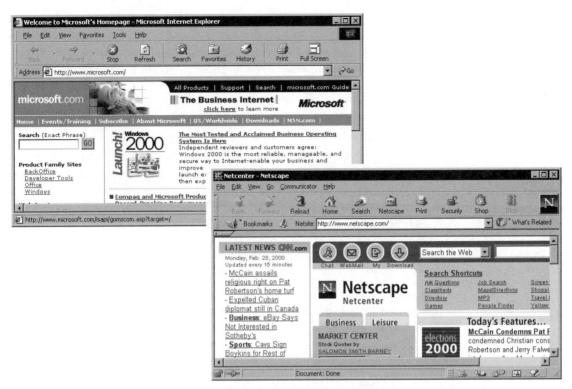

Internet browsers: Internet Explorer and Netscape Navigator

Main browser commands

Icon	Effect when clicked
Address or Go to	Allows you to enter the address or name of a website
Back	Takes you to the webpage you just visited
Forward	Moves you to the webpage you just came from
Stop	Halts loading the current page
Refresh or Reload	Loads a new version of the current page, updating it with the most recent information. This is also useful if a page only partially loads the first time you access it
Home	Takes you to the page seen when your browser opens. You can customise this home page to one of your choice
Search	Begins options which search by key word
Favorites or Bookmarks	Shows you the list of websites you have entered in the past and are worth returning to
Mail	Connects to email
History	Shows you the list of websites you visited recently
Print	Prints out the webpages shown on screen

deliver to you the information you need. They let you explore databases that contain information from millions of webpages. They present to you the results of your search as lists of pages that match your search request and when you decide which one is most interesting or relevant you can click on it and a link will take you straight there.

Hits: lists of matches for your search

The more accomplished you become at using search engines the better quality information you will find and, most importantly, the more relevant it will be. How to access relevant information is key. Otherwise you will waste time sifting through long lists of websites that contain information that may or may not be useful. You need to develop searching skills that will help you tighten up your searches giving you smaller amounts of more appropriate information to work with.

There are several search engines that you could use and the best not only provide you with search functions but also have directories that you can browse for information on any topic.

The importance of key words or phrases in searching

The trick to any effective searching on the web is to identify the key words and phrases that will get you *hits* on sites that contain the information you need. You will be using these words to differentiate between the websites

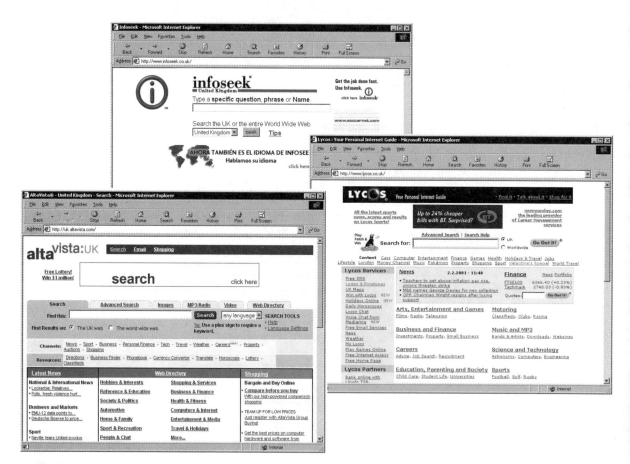

Typical search engine home pages

that you do want and the ones that you don't. This means the better the keywords or phrases you use, the more irrelevant sites you will avoid.

Regardless of what you are looking for, think of the best word or phrase that is specific to what you want to find out about. Don't choose something general, be as specific as you can. For example, if you are interested in the Manx cat (a breed of cat without a tail) don't search using 'cats' because you will get a huge number of hits about everything from the animal to the musical. Don't even use Manx because you will get lots of hits about the Isle of Man generally. Instead use the phrase 'Manx cats'. This filters out all the sites about other cats and about the Isle of Man, leaving you with results about Manx cats.

Rather than look for key words or phrases in the text of webpages, you can also search in just the titles. This will mean you are more likely to get pages dedicated to your subject rather than pages where the phrase happens to appear in the text. You would enter your search phrase like this in a title search:

Some search engines need you to put key phrases in inverted commas, e.g. "Manx cat"

- Title: "Manx cats"

Different search engines may have different procedures. This is why it is often best to learn about one particular search engine in detail, once you have found a favourite.

You can set 'Learning how to use a search engine' as one of your targets or objectives in your key skills work. As you develop the relevant skills you can keep the evidence of your improving Internet abilities by printing out the results of your searches.

Searching in plain English

By far the easiest way to search for anything on the web is to use plain English searches. Plain English searches are the best to use if you are relatively new to using the Internet. Many search engines allow you to type in what you are looking for as a simple question. They then will try to match your question to websites that may have the answer. Plain English searches can generate a lot of hits; however, the most appropriate will normally be near the top of the list.

One of the easiest plain English search engines to use is *Ask Jeeves* (Jeeves is a cartoon butler who will give you help in finding the answer). You can find it at **www.askjeeves.co.uk**. When you ask Jeeves a question he will tell you where you might find the most appropriate answer. The search engine shows you how well suited the sites are to your original question. This search engine also offers directories and reference sites to help you find the answer you are looking for.

The illustrations ask and answer the question 'Where can I find out about problem solving techniques?' as an example. Knowing what problem-solving technique you wanted to find out about in particular would mean a more accurate search.

The smaller illustration shows a question entered into the Ask Jeeves. Don't worry if your question is too big for the box. Just type it in and the search engine will make room in the window. For example, the full

USING THE WORLD WIDE WEB | **51**

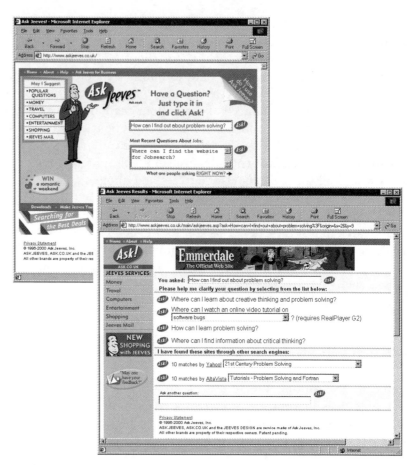

What do you need to know? Just 'Ask Jeeves' for his response!

question typed in for the search shown was 'Where can I find out about problem solving techniques? The larger illustration shows the 'Jeeves' response. You can see that it does three things. Firstly it finds answers either to my question directly or to similar questions. Then it provides webpages that may have potential answers for me. Lastly, it offers me a list of sites that might be useful that can be found in other search engines.

By clicking on the downward pointing arrow in the shaded box on the right you can see the list of pages that have been found. You can then select an appropriate one (AltaVista's 'Problem Solving Techniques' has been selected in this diagram), then click on the 'Ask!' button and these pages will be called up.

Excite and Infoseek also provide good plain English searches.

Using advanced search techniques

There are a few simple techniques that can be used to help narrow searches down and will result in a list of hits that should be closer to your needs. These advanced search techniques involve using 'Boolean' operators. The three most useful search operators involve using:

Hint: you can print off the search results and appropriate webpages and keep this for your portfolio

For the Internet enthusiasts

- AND
- NOT
- OR

Search engines may also have a menu of options that ask you how your keywords should be treated in the search.

- **Using AND**

  You can search for two or more keywords and make sure that they all appear in the results by using AND. This will dramatically cut down the number of hits you could receive if you search without using AND. Without it you would get a far larger range of results that contains each key word on its own and in combination with the other key word. For example, if you wanted to search for information on Celtic Art and just used the key words Celtic and Art you would get a host of hits for Celtic (the people and the football team) and a massive response to the word Art. By entering Celtic AND Art your search would be reduced dramatically and the results would be closer to what you are looking for. Remember, the other way would be to use inverted commas and type in "Celtic Art". You can also use the plus symbol (+) instead of AND; in some search engines, for example, you would enter Celtic + Art.

- **Using NOT**

  NOT is used to exclude one word from the search. This is a way to avoid the search engine calling up hits that you know will be irrelevant. For example, if you want to learn about cooking spice, the last thing you want is a huge number of hits on Spice Girls webpages, so you would use Spice NOT Girls and save a lot of pain.

- **Using OR**

  OR searches are likely to give you more results than AND searches. This is because the command tells the search engine to show all the hits that have either word or phrase in them. However, they are useful for dealing with searches that involve topics that could be referred to in more than one way.

If you look at the illustrations showing advanced search pages on Yahoo! and AltaVista, you will see that each offers a number of ways to focus your search. AltaVista even allows you to specify where to look, e.g. the UK web or World Wide Web, what dates to cover and how to sort your results. You will find a click on link or tab that takes you to advanced searches on the main search page.

AND, NOT and **OR** are also called Boolean search operators

> ### HINT
>
> Most online services and web browsers have a 'Favorites' file or 'Bookmarks' where you can store your favourite website addresses. You can go straight to this file and access your favourite site directly without having to find it again or type in its address. Find out how this function works on your browser and keep useful addresses stored here. You can add to and delete addresses from your list of favourites.

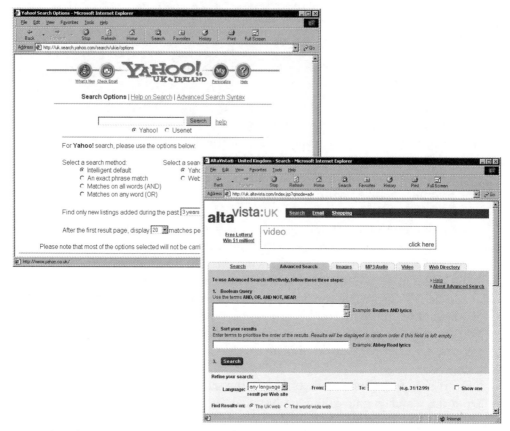

Examples of advanced search options (Yahoo and AltaVista)

The Internet addresses of some of the more common search engines are:

- Yahoo www.yahoo.co.uk
- Ask Jeeves www.askjeeves.co.uk
- Lycos www.lycos.co.uk
- AltaVista www.altavista.com
- Excite www.excite.co.uk
- Infoseek www.infoseek.co.uk

Information on the World Wide Web

Dictionaries, directories, maps and images can also be accessed on the Internet

Because there is no regulation of the content on the web, you need to be careful about the information you access there. There is no guarantee that the information is correct. You need to consider where the information has come from (is the source reliable and trustworthy?) and when it was last updated. Information from reputable organisations will be reliable but always check what you are reading.

Part 2: The Bottom Line

This part of the book shows you what you must do to gain your key skills qualification. It will show you:

- The words and ideas of the key skills.
- What is expected at levels 1 and 2.
- What must be in your portfolio of evidence.

This part starts with an introductory section **Preparing a portfolio**, and then looks at the actual evidence requirements for each of the three key skills:

- **Working with others** (WWO)
- **Improving own learning and performance** (LP)
- **Problem solving** (PS)

Each section will cover what you need to do and the knowledge, skills and understanding you need to demonstrate at level 1 and at level 2. The section then goes on to look at the key skill evidence requirements. Sometimes, it can be difficult working out what the key skill specification actually wants you to do so this part of the section looks at what you need to do and tries to explain the key skill requirements in plain English. In case you are still a little unsure, it explains the requirements again putting them another way.

Each section finishes with some handy hints for collecting evidence, and some suggestions about what might be in your portfolio of evidence at the end of each stage of the key skill.

Qualifications and Curriculum Authority

The key skills specifications are published by the QCA, and are widely available through schools, colleges, training establishments and awarding bodies. They are also available on the QCA website (www.qca.org.uk).

Preparing a portfolio

The secret of success

Each key skill tries to encourage you to take greater responsibility for your work and your own actions. They are all about helping you to think more clearly about what you have to do (regardless of what it is) and to plan how to do it. Then they get you to implement your plans as you work towards your goals. When you are finished, each key skill gets you to think about what you did and how you did it.

The more you take responsibility for your own learning or show that you can work responsibly and sensibly, the better you will meet the key skill requirements. The real goal is ownership. The key skills are either trying to get you to take ownership of group targets and the process of working well with others (Working with others), or more ownership of the process of learning (Improving own learning and performance), or ownership of problems and their solutions (Problem solving).

The more responsibility, ownership and control you are able to show either individually or as a group, the better you will do.

Key words and phrases

Who is an 'appropriate person'?

The key skills often mention using an appropriate person, appropriate people or 'others' for support, guidance, permission or advice. Generally speaking, anything that concerns the amount or type of evidence you collect or relates to the quality or suitability of your work, e.g. targets or plans, should be discussed with your tutor or whoever is responsible for assessing your work.

Discussing these issues with the person who eventually assesses your work will also help them become familiar with what you intend to do. They can offer advice on what they would expect to see in your portfolio of evidence. Also consider people with relevant experience or expertise as useful sources of support and feedback.

To judge whether someone is an appropriate person to talk to, you need to find someone who is able to give help or advice because:

- They have experience that relates to what you are doing
- They have expertise or skills that would be useful to you
- They are in charge or responsible for the equipment or resources you need to use

As part of the early planning process for any key skill you should establish the people you need to contact and consult. This is absolutely essential when health and safety issues are involved. Think carefully about any health and safety issues at the start of your work and make sure you get the correct health and safety advice.

You may also need permission to do or use certain things. Again, seek the appropriate advice and guidance from the right people. If you were doing something career related like training and development, then a careers adviser or line manager would be appropriate. If you were intending to use equipment, you might need to discuss what could be borrowed with a technician or teacher. If in doubt, your tutor or trainer will be able to advise you on who best to speak to.

Portfolio of evidence

All the key skills in this section are assessed using the evidence you produce in your portfolio. Your portfolio is the place where you record and keep all your evidence to prove that you have met the evidence requirements. It holds the work that you have done to prove you can do what the key skill requires. You will need this proof to get final key skill certification. You will find more details and guidance about putting together a portfolio of evidence in the section called 'What about your portfolio' on page 58.

DEFINITIONS

- **Evidence** is the proof that you can do what is required in order to get the key skill. It is proof that you have learned about the key skill and that you can use and apply what you have learned
- **Evidence requirements** are shown in the key skill specifications under the heading 'What you need to do'. They are statements telling you what you are expected to do and show in order to get the key skill

---

What's meant by straightforward?

Dealing with *straightforward* activities is a key feature of the level 1 and 2 work. The word *straightforward* is used to help identify the standard expected of you at these levels.

Straightforward activities will involve objectives, targets or problems that are easily broken down into smaller, manageable tasks. There is no need for anything complicated. Straightforward activities can involve familiar situations, and don't have to involve anything out of the ordinary. You should be familiar with the books, equipment or other resources you use and there doesn't have to be anything unfamiliar or unknown about what you plan to do.

Class work will provide you with a range of suitable straightforward activities, as will work experience or employment. Hobbies, interests or other types of leisure pursuits may also be suitable if they give you an opportunity to generate evidence. Always discuss ideas about how you

intend to go about building your portfolio with your tutor or key skills supervisor. They will be able to advise you on whether your plans are suitable or not.

OTHER WORDS FOR STRAIGHTFORWARD

Here are some others words that can also mean *straightforward* to help you get an idea of the standard of topic you are required to do and what straightforward means:

Simple, uncomplicated, clear-cut, not confusing, routine and **elementary**.

What about your portfolio?

Building your portfolio of evidence

A key skills unit is quite a large amount of work and it may take you quite a while to collect enough evidence to show you can meet all the requirements. To help you keep track of your work make sure your portfolio is well organised and that the work inside is clear and easily understood.

The simplest approach to collecting and keeping your evidence is to have it in a separate folder. This is by far the easiest way to organise your work and to keep a record of what has been done and what's still to do. Consider using the following handy hints as a way of organising your work:

- Have an index page that you keep updating as you build up your evidence. This should show where evidence can be found to meet each part of the key skill requirements
- Keep records of when you collected your evidence and where it came from (e.g. which GCSE or Vocational GCSE unit)
- Use titles that copy the different sets of evidence requirements you are covering in your chosen key skill to break up and organise your evidence. For example, if you were doing 'Improving own learning and performance' you could have 'Confirming my targets', 'Following my plan' and 'Reviewing progress and achievements' as the different subheadings for each task you do
- Copies of work are acceptable if the actual key skills evidence is part of another course
- Keep a checklist of all the things that you must cover in your portfolio (e.g. group work and one-to-one in 'Working with others', study-based and practical activity learning in 'Improving own learning and performance')
- Annotating work to show how it was produced and how it meets specific parts of the assessment can also be helpful
- Put dates on your work

Evidence matters

Examples of evidence include items you have made, material you have written, computer printouts and diagrams you have created. Artwork, photographs, audio and video recordings are also acceptable as evidence for your portfolio. Records of performance evidence can also be used. This may be in the form of testimonies or witness statements from people like a teacher or someone else who has watched you perform the tasks. You may be able to get a statement from an employer about your ability to meet aspects of the specifications.

You need to discuss with your teacher or assessor the kind of evidence you are likely to produce and the forms this evidence might take in your portfolio. It is always a good idea to make sure the person assessing your portfolio is comfortable with the types of evidence they are likely to find in it. This also gives you the opportunity to make sure you know exactly what will be expected of you. This is especially important if you intend to submit observation records and checklists detailing your performance.

The person assessing your work will be trying to answer three simple questions when they look at your evidence:

- Is it your work?
- Do you actually meet the evidence requirements?
- Is there enough evidence?

If you keep these things in mind as you build your portfolio you will prevent problems later.

Remember that the same piece of evidence could be used for more than one key skill. For example, you may have evidence from your problem solving that will also show how you were able to work with others. In these types of situation you need to check that the evidence does actually address both key skill requirements in an appropriate way. Then you need to ensure that it appears in an appropriate place in each portfolio of evidence.

> **Quantity** is not a measure of **quality**

The Bottom Line

Working with others

Deciding which level to do

What's the difference between level 1 and level 2?

You need to be clear about what level of key skill you intend to collect evidence for. This is because each level has its own particular set of evidence requirements. The crucial differences between the level 1 and level 2 'Working with others' key skill evidence requirements involves the amount of control and responsibility you are expected to take over the work.

Evidence that shows you can work with others can be collected from your GCSE work, Vocational GCSE work, or another qualification. You could use work experience or a hobby or interest you share with others as well. For example, you may want to use work experience as a way to show you can work in one-to-one situations and class work to show you can work in a group.

What is level 1 all about?

At level 1 you will be given the objectives you need to work with others and be expected to show you can:

- Understand what it is you need to do in order to meet your objectives
- Carry out the work you need to do to meet your own responsibilities
- Say how well you did in meeting your objectives and suggest ways to improve

You must show you can work in both a group and a one-to-one situation.

How is level 2 different?

At level 2 you are expected to take more responsibility for and control over your work and need to show you can identify and set your own objectives and plan how they will be met. You are expected to work much more closely with others as you:

- Identify your objectives
- Clarify who does what
- Agree how you will all work together
- Organise yourselves

- Analyse what went well and what didn't and discuss how you can improve your group work

At level 2, the evidence requirements are more demanding and expect more of you in terms of how you perform as a group member or 'team player'.

Frequently asked questions

What is one-to-one work?

Both levels require you to show you can meet the standards set out in a group and in a one-to-one situation. One-to-one means working with a work partner, colleague, friend or customer to meet your objectives.

> **IMPORTANT NOTE!**
>
> Be careful when choosing a partner in one-to-one work. The other person cannot assess your key skills work as well as be your work partner. So if you are going to work with your tutor or teacher someone else will have to assess your WWO key skills work.

How big should a group be?

The best size of group really depends on what you intend to do. Too large a group or to small a group can cause problems. For example, if the group is too large:

- It will be difficult to control and organise
- Finding time when everyone can get together will be a problem, e.g. for meetings
- Communication with everyone could be difficult
- Keeping everyone involved and motivated may be more difficult
- Work might get duplicated

However, if the group is too small:

- You may find it a struggle to meet the evidence requirements
- You may miss out in developing a range of group working skills
- There could be too much work to go around

Think through the type of work and challenges you want to set and use this to help determine an appropriate group size. Think who would be interested in working towards the same objectives as you. Then make sure your teacher or assessor is happy with the size of group that you propose to work with.

Evidence for level 1 (WWO)

At level 1 there are basically three types of activities you need to do that relate to working with others. You will need to show you can:

- Confirm what needs to be done
- Work with others to try to meet your given objectives
- Identify the progress you have made

At level 1 you must provide at least two examples of meeting the evidence requirements for each section of the key skill. The easiest way to go about generating evidence is to carry out two separate tasks: one where you work with a group, and one where you work with only one other person. Make sure each task is big enough to allow you to carry out all three parts of the key skill. This way you only have two pieces of work to do and show evidence of in your portfolio. One example must show that you can work in a one-to-one situation, and one example must show you can work in a group situation. Try to organise your portfolio of evidence to show both types of 'Working with others' evidence separately. This will make it easier to organise and easier for others to read and understand as well.

Confirming what to do

What the unit expects

Do you understand what you need to do?

Your teacher or key skills tutor, supervisor or some other appropriate person will give you your objectives for working with others. You must make sure you understand them. Make a written record of the objectives and take some time to think about them. If you have any questions about them, write these down and then ask the person who gave you the objectives. Make sure you record the answers they give you. Once you are completely sure you understand the objectives you can begin working out what you will need to do to meet them.

Records of the questions and the answers you got in reply can be used as evidence to show you checked that you fully understood the objectives you were given. So keep copies of any questions and answers you had along with a copy of your original objectives in your portfolio of evidence.

Making it happen

You need to identify what needs to be done in order to achieve your objectives. You need to discuss with the person or people you are working with:

- What tasks need to be carried out
- What resources you need
- What your deadlines are

Consider holding a 'brainstorming' session to get everyone participating as you work out what is involved in meeting the objectives. Remember to keep the brainstorming notes and copy enough for everyone's portfolio.

See the section on **brainstorming** on page 10

Tasks

You need to try to work out all the jobs that need to be done in order to meet your objectives. This means breaking down the objectives into a series of smaller targets or tasks that need to be done. You can use techniques like drawing a flowchart to help you work out which order to do the tasks in. Alternatively, you could use an action plan like the one shown on page 8.

You can find out more about **flowcharts** on page 14

Resources

You need to work out what equipment, materials, tools, books or help you need to meet your objectives. The resources you need depend on the objectives and tasks you have to do. If you need to use tools and equipment you also need to consider how to get access and appropriate supervision. Include where you will be working as one of the resource issues you need to consider.

You also need to consider any training or practice you will need to learn how to use the resources properly. If you need to practise using tools or equipment or need to learn how to handle materials correctly, you need to build this into your plans.

Resources can include:
Materials
Tools
Equipment
Money
People who can give advice
People who can offer support

PEOPLE WHO MIGHT PROVIDE USEFUL SUPPORT OR FEEDBACK

- Subject teacher
- Tutor
- Supervisor
- Health and safety officer
- First aid officer
- Trade union representative
- Audio-visual technicians
- Caretaker staff (e.g. janitor)
- School or college management
- Local businesspeople

Time

One of your first questions when you were given the objectives might have been 'When do we have to do this work by?'. You need to find out what your deadlines are and plan how you can get the work done in good time.

Time doesn't just mean your final deadlines. You need to plan when you will do your work and how it fits into the overall group deadlines.

The Bottom Line

Who is going to do what?

You need to work out how you can help achieve the objectives. How are you going to play your part? Is there anything you are particularly good at or are keen to do that will help meet the objectives?

Rather than wait to be asked, play an active part in helping to meet the objectives. Volunteer to take on some of the tasks that need to be done.

Try to match the tasks to be completed with the best people in the group to do them. Try to make good use of your group members' talents to ensure the best people for particular jobs or responsibilities are actually doing these tasks.

CHOOSING WHO DOES WHAT

Try to agree different tasks and responsibilities by considering each member's:

- Relevant experience or knowledge
- Particular skills
- Enthusiasm for particular tasks
- Relevant personal qualities (e.g. patience)

Once you have decided how the various tasks will be shared out, take a little time to think about your own role and responsibilities. Even write them down clearly and try to work out a time frame for your work and who you need to keep informed of your progress. You may have to share particular tasks with someone. This will mean working closely with them to ensure you don't repeat each other's work or get confused over who was doing what.

Once you have a record of what you have to do (and by when), share it with the others. This way they are all clear about what you will be doing. If you have misunderstood something then hopefully others will spot it and put you straight.

Make sure that by the end of the process everyone is happy doing their tasks. No one should feel pressured into having to do something they don't want to. This would be a sign of the group's failing to work effectively. Play your part in making sure the different tasks are allocated fairly.

Working arrangements

You need to be clear about who does what and ensure all the tasks that need to be done are allocated. Everyone needs to know how you will work together, where you will work and when you need to work. This means discussing if you will all work in the same place at the same time, or if you will work another way. Regardless of how you will work, you need to make sure that everyone:

- Understands the working arrangements
- Knows what decisions need to be made, and how they will be made

- Is clear about how to keep in touch with the rest of the group
- Is clear about what is expected of them and by when
- Knows who to speak to if they need help

By the end of this stage of the key skill everyone should:

- Feel they played a part in planning how to meet the objectives they have been given
- Have contributed to deciding who does what
- Be clear and comfortable with their own role and responsibilities
- Be clear about the roles and responsibilities of others
- Understand the working arrangements
- Be familiar with the deadlines

Collecting evidence

Remember you have to provide at least two examples of meeting the evidence requirements (one must be in a one-to-one situation, the other in a group situation).

WHAT YOU NEED TO DO

Look at the objectives you have been given for working together. Make sure you clearly understand what they mean and identify and discuss what needs to be done if you are going to meet these objectives.

Suggest ways you can contribute to the work.

Finally, once you have agreed who will do what, make sure you are clear about your own responsibilities and the working arrangements.

Evidence requirements in a nutshell

Whether you are working in a one-to-one situation or as a group, you will be given a set of objectives for working together. You need to show that:

1. You are clear about what these objectives mean
2. You can break these objectives down into a series of tasks to be completed
3. You can suggest ways you could help carry out some of the work to help meet these objectives
3. You are clear about your own work responsibilities and the working arrangements

HINTS WHEN CONFIRMING WHAT TO DO
- Organise your portfolio to show your one-to-one and group work evidence
- Identify early on who will be a useful source of help and advice if you need it
- Keep written records of the original objectives you were given

- Get everyone to write down their own individual responsibilities
- Check that all the individual responsibilities, if carried out on time, will (a) cover all the work that needs to be done, and (b) mean that the objectives will be met
- Find some way of showing how all the tasks fit together so everyone is clear. A simple flowchart, for example, would do this
- Keep a diary, journal or log so you can note down thoughts as you do the work

What might be in your portfolio at this point

1. An index and dividers showing where your one-to-one evidence and where your group work evidence will be
2. A copy of the objectives you were set
3. A record of any questions you had about the objectives and a copy of the answers you received
4. A record of your own responsibilities (and perhaps copies of other people's responsibilities as well)
5. Diagrams that show the sequence of tasks (flowcharts) or notes about how you worked out what needed to be done (e.g. from a brainstorming session).

A 'working with others' journal or diary

A diary is a good way to keep a record of what is happening in your group work and can be used as evidence in your portfolio. You can record your work and also keep notes on how you think the work is going noting down what worked well and what didn't. This will be a useful reminder when it comes to meeting the last part of the 'working with others' evidence requirements about 'identifying progress'. You don't have to buy a diary or journal. Just use a note-pad and remember to always enter the date before you write anything down.

A well-kept diary or journal could contain some important evidence and could eventually become part of your portfolio of evidence for the key skill.

KEEPING A LEARNING JOURNAL OR DIARY

As you confirm what needs to be done and who should do it, your diary or journal should have records of:

- The people you are working with
- The objectives you have been set
- The different tasks that need to be done
- The tasks you will do and the resources you need
- Deadlines for the objectives
- Deadlines for your tasks
- A note on how you thought the decision taking went when you broke down the objectives into tasks and when you allocated the tasks
- 'To-do lists' and reminders to help keep you on track

Working towards your objectives

This is where you start to make it happen. You have worked out what needs to be done, how you are going to work together, what your contribution will be, and you know what the deadlines are. Now you need to get on with it.

Get hold of the resources

Hopefully you will have identified and made a list of the resources you need in order to carry out your tasks. You need to organise the resources you need by:

- Getting the right people's permission, if needed
- Arranging appropriate supervision, if necessary
- Gathering whatever else you need in terms of equipment, tools, materials or support

Make sure you are able to use the tools, equipment or handle the materials properly. If not, you need to learn how to use your resources before you go any further.

Working safely and responsibly

You must work safely and responsibly preventing any harm or risk to yourself or to others. This means you need to make sure you avoid:

- Accidents, by learning how to take the necessary precautions
- Health risks
- Offending, upsetting or disturbing others

You must make sure that you use tools and equipment appropriately, handle materials correctly, follow instructions, and conduct yourself in an appropriate manner.

Regardless of whether you are working with tools, equipment or with other people (for example, customers or visitors) you must show you are able to conduct yourself in an appropriate manner and prove that you can work responsibly, safely and with consideration for those around you.

If you have been given a set of instructions relating to working methods, behaviour (for example, a code of conduct), or have been shown the correct way to do something, show you can be trusted to follow these instructions carefully.

Asking for help or advice

There are two key features in asking for help. These are:

- Knowing who to ask
- Knowing when to ask

- **Who to ask**
  Who to ask for advice or feedback will depend on what you need help with. A guidance teacher may help you with problems within your group (for example, people 'falling out' with each other), while

EVIDENCE FOR LEVEL 1 (WWO) | **67**

a health and safety officer or design and technology teacher can help with advice on how to use equipment. Basically, you need to show you can seek help and support from appropriate people.

- **When to ask**
  This is linked to acting responsibly. You need to show you can seek advice, help or support when you need it. This means acting in a timely way and not leaving things until it is too late. When you think you need help, you should get help.

Think ahead a little and try to identify when you might need help and who would be an appropriate person to ask. You could even let them know when you will need to talk to them and what you will need to talk to others about. This gives them time to prepare.

Support others in the group

You should also offer your support to others. You need to decide whether you can help someone else out and, if you can, offer your assistance. You may have information or resources they might find useful, or perhaps you have some experience they might be able to benefit from.

Try to support others who are in difficulty and may be struggling with something or may have difficulty meeting a deadline. Offering this type of support is what being a good team player means.

You want people to see you as friendly and approachable. This way they will feel more comfortable about asking for your help. Let others that you work with know you are willing to help if you can.

Collecting evidence

Remember you have to provide at least two examples of meeting the evidence requirements (one must be in a one-to-one situation, the other in a group situation).

WHAT YOU NEED TO DO

Work with others towards achieving your objectives by showing you can:

- Carry out tasks to meet your responsibilities
- Work safely, responsibly and carefully following the working methods or instructions you have been given
- Ask for help when you need it
- Help others if they need it

Evidence requirements in a nutshell

As you try to meet the objectives you have been set as a group, you each need to provide evidence that shows you can do the following three things:

1. Play your part – you can do this by carrying out the tasks you are responsible for
2. Be safe and responsible at all times – this means following the

working methods and the instructions you have been given accurately and always working in a safe manner

3. Give and get help and support – ask for help or support when you need it and offer your support to others if they need it

What might be in your portfolio at this point

1. A list of the resources that you need for your specific tasks
2. A copy of any working methods or instructions you have been given
3. A record of any questions you had about the working methods or instructions
4. A copy of the answers you got to your questions
5. Notes about any special safety requirements for equipment or tools you are using or materials you are handling
6. A note of the health and safety risks or hazards you must avoid
7. An explanation of how to avoid risks and hazards

Identifying progress

This section could be called 'How well did you do?' because that is basically what it is about. You need to look back at how you worked with others, at what you and the others did, how you worked together and what you might have done or might do differently in future.

What went well?

Look back on your work and try to identify what has gone well. You could comment on:

- How you were able to support others
- How others supported you
- Successful ways you carried out tasks

- Targets, objectives and timelines you were able to meet

Try to explain why you think something has gone well.

What difficulties did you deal with?

You also need to explain any difficulties you faced as you tried to meet your work responsibilities. Once you have identified these problem areas, spend time describing what you did about them. Things to consider include:

- Problems you faced when carrying out your tasks
- How you managed to overcome disagreements within the group
- Problems with any of your resources

Could do better?

Consider how you could improve working relationships and your working methods based on your experiences. Think about how everything went and consider what could have been done differently to avoid some of the problems you had. How could you have made the work go better or more smoothly? Consider things like:

- Could the tasks or work have been done in a different way?
- How could the group have worked better together?

You are trying to show that you have learned from your experience and that you can build on what you learned next time you do group work. You can ask yourself the following questions to get you started:

- Should I (we) have done things differently?
- If I had to do it all again what changes would I make and why?

Hindsight: the ability to understand something after it has happened

You have the benefit of hindsight and you need to try to show how you would learn from your mistakes and build on your successes. This is where having a diary that you kept up to date would help you remember what went on during your work.

Collecting evidence

Remember you have to provide at least two examples of meeting the evidence requirements (one must be in a one-to-one situation, the other in a group situation).

WHAT YOU NEED TO DO

Look at the work you did with others as you tried to meet the objectives you were given and describe what went well. Then describe the difficulties you had when you tried to carry out your responsibilities and explain what you did to try to deal with them.

Finally, look back on the work and suggest ways to improve how you worked.

Evidence requirements in a nutshell

1. Identify what worked well or was a success in your work with the others
2. If some things went wrong or you had any difficulties, say what happened and how you dealt with it
3. If you had to do the work again, what would you do differently? What lessons have you learned from your experience that would help you improve how you work together?

HINTS FOR IDENTIFYING PROGRESS

- Spend time thinking about your own role and responsibilities as well as thinking about how the group did
- Statements from other group members can be used as evidence of how well you performed as a group member
- If you are asked to give feedback on how someone you worked with performed, be fair and considerate

---

See the section on **feedback** on page 19

The Bottom Line

What might be in your portfolio at this point

You could produce the evidence for this part of the key skill either by doing a short presentation, writing a brief report or by having a discussion with your teacher that covers all the points. If you make a short presentation to the group or take part in a discussion about it, take notes so that you don't forget anything than you need to cover. Use 'what went well', 'what caused difficulties' and 'how you think you could improve' as headings for your notes. Keep the notes in your portfolio as evidence. Alternatively, you could use these same headings as sections for your report on how the 'working with others' went. Keep a copy of the report for your portfolio of evidence.

You could even record your thoughts on each of the areas on tape and keep that in your portfolio. Make sure you keep the notes that you read from or used to jog your memory along with the tape. You might also have statements from other people about how you helped them and a record of people who were able to help you.

KEEPING A LEARNING JOURNAL OR DIARY

If you have a diary or journal, remember to enter things like:

- When your tasks and responsibilities finished
- When you all finally met your group objectives
- Any difficulties you were having with other people or resources

---

Evidence for level 2 (WWO)

What is level 2 all about?

At level 2 you will see that there are basically three types of evidence you need to generate. You will need to show you can:

- Plan your work
- Work towards the objectives you identified, and
- Exchange information on your progress

This particular key skill asks that you provide evidence to show you can work with other people: group work and one-to-one. Take this into account when organising your portfolio and when tracking your evidence as it builds up. Though the following guidance is written as if you were working as part of a group, most of it applies to your one-to-one situation as well.

The guidance also assumes you are involved in tasks big enough to allow you to generate evidence for all three sections of the key skill. This will be by far the easiest way to generate evidence and to organise your portfolio. By being involved in major group tasks from start to finish, you will find it easier to comment on your original plans and your working methods in light of your experience.

Group evidence v. your own evidence

One important issue that relates to group work is the separation of your work and performance from that of other people's in the same group. Discuss this issue as a group and work out how you will tackle it. The records of the group decisions and your role in them could be used as evidence and it will help you and the person assessing your portfolio gain a better idea of how you met the key skill requirements.

The issue as far as you're concerned is 'What group records do I need for my portfolio?' and 'What records of my own individual performance will I also need?'. Keep in mind that although you may be working in a group, key skill attainment is a personal achievement and your portfolio of evidence should reflect this. You need to prove that you have personally met the requirements and you should construct your portfolio with this in mind.

Keep thinking of what you need to have in your portfolio of evidence to help show that you actually met the key skill requirements. There will be three types of evidence that you will have to manage and discuss with other group members:

1. The evidence relating to group work or your work and interaction with others
2. The evidence associated with your own individual responsibilities within the group
3. The evidence collected by other people showing their own individual responsibilities

Though you may be involved in a group activity you must think about your own evidence needs and plan accordingly. Consider asking a teacher, tutor, assessor or other appropriate person to speak to the group and offer advice about how best to manage this process.

What your evidence might look like

You need to consider what form your evidence will take. Consider including in your portfolio evidence like reports or notes describing the activities and outcomes of the planning process. Make sure you have clear statements of objectives and group members' individual responsibilities. You also need to have evidence explaining the time frames, how the work is shared and organised and how you will take decisions.

Planning work

What the unit expects

You will find that actually writing a plan gives everyone something to focus on for discussions and decision making and can be a useful way of making sure everyone agrees to the group objectives and time frames. Having a plan will provide a record of the decisions and agreement processes that went into meeting this aspect of the key skill for the group working together. You should also work together to agree contingency plans and interim targets and begin to discuss how you can monitor and review your progress.

Identifying your objectives

The group needs to be clear about why it is working together and what the end results are expected to be. Then you will also be able to identify and agree clear and straightforward objectives that everyone can understand.

Suggestions for possible objectives could come from your tutor or supervisor, or you may be able to decide appropriate objectives as a group. If you are setting your own objectives, keep them realistic, measurable and feasible.

Not all the objectives need to be related to the work. Consider some that relate to the group performance and working process. These can be

objectives that feature as individual targets as well as targets for all group members. These types of objectives could relate to:

- Maintaining co-operative relationships
- Active participation in decision taking
- Encouraging others
- Communicating effectively with others in the group

Everyone should participate and feel that they have made a contribution to the overall group objectives. This way each member will feel a sense of ownership of the group objectives and will work more effectively as a group member, feeling like they are a part of the team. You must play your part and encourage others to take part.

Tasks, resources and timescales

Once you have a clear idea of what the objectives are, you need to build up a complete picture of what it will take to achieve them successfully. The three areas you need to address are the tasks to be done, the resources you will need and the time it will all take.

You can find out more about **brainstorming** on page 10

Consider using brainstorming as a technique to help the group work out what might be involved in meeting the objectives. Use the three issues to consider (tasks, resources and time) as headings for your brainstorming session.

- Tasks
  This is where you decide what needs to be done if you are to achieve your objectives. Clear objectives should be easy to break down into a series of tasks that need to be carried out if the objectives are to be achieved. Think about the sequence these tasks may need to be done in and the decisions that may need to be made along the way.

You can find out more about **flowcharts** on page 14

  Once you have a clear idea of what will be involved, consider sketching it all out as a flowchart to show the sequence of tasks and where the key decision points are. Having a clear and complete picture of all the tasks that must be done, will make it easier to identify the resources needed and the time it will all take.

- Resources
  You need to work out what equipment, materials, tools, books or help you need to meet your objectives. The resources you need depend on the objectives and tasks you have to do. If you need to use tools and equipment you also need to consider how to get access and appropriate supervision. Include where you will be working as one of the resource issues you need to consider.

Resources can include:
Materials
Tools
Equipment
Money
People who can give advice
People who can offer support

  You also need to consider the training or practice you may need in order to use tools or equipment properly. If you need to practise using tools or equipment or need to learn how to handle materials correctly, you need to build this into your plans and make sure you allow time for it to take place.

- Time

  The group must set the tasks in some sort of time frame. This means looking at deadlines for the overall work and working back, allocating time frames to individual tasks to help you meet your deadline.

  Consider holding a 'brainstorming' session to get everyone participating as you work out what is involved in meeting the objectives. Remember to keep the brainstorming notes and copy them for everyone's portfolio.

Who is going to do what?

Once you have a clear idea about what is going to be involved in meeting the objectives, you can discuss and exchange views and information on how the work will be divided up. The group will need to decide what roles and responsibilities are needed and allocate them to individual group members. Don't just make arbitrary decisions about who is to carry out the different aspects of the work. Try to make good use of the different group members' talents to ensure the best people for particular jobs or responsibilities are actually doing these tasks.

You need to work out how you personally can help achieve the objectives. How are you going to play your part? Is there anything you are particularly good at or are keen to do? Rather than wait to be asked, make sure you play an active part in helping to meet the objectives. Volunteer to take on some of the tasks that need to be done.

Arbitrary: not following any rules or having particular reasons for doing something

The Bottom Line

Encourage others to say what they would like to do by asking questions, or by inviting them to give their opinion.

Once you have allocated the tasks as a group, try to build in a little time to allow individual members to think about their roles and responsibilities. During this time, everyone should make sure that they are clear about what they have to do and what others are doing. Then meet again to review, confirm or amend any decisions that have been made. The goal is to make sure that everyone is happy about what they have to do (their role in the team) and that they know what will be involved and what will be expected of them.

Working arrangements

You need to be clear about who does what and ensure all the tasks that need to be done are allocated. Everyone needs to know how you will work together, where you will work and when you need to work. This means discussing if you will all work in the same place at the same time, or if you will work another way.

Regardless of how you will work, you need to make sure that everyone:

- Understands the working arrangements
- Knows what decisions need to be made, and how they will be made
- Is clear about how to keep in touch with the rest of the group
- Is clear about what is expected of them and by when
- Knows who to speak to if they need help

You also need to consider how and when you communicate with the other group members and how and when they need to communicate with you. Keeping each other informed of progress will be vital if the group is to meet its objectives.

Other issues to consider as a group include:

- How the group will actually take decisions
- How to respond to change or unforeseen circumstances
- How to deal with and resolve conflict

Decision taking is an important part of any group work and you need to consider how you can involve the whole group in key decisions. This will help to keep people motivated and encourage them to feel a sense of responsibility and commitment to the process. Establish the different levels of decision taking and how you will make them. For example, be clear about what the whole group should decide and what decisions individual members can take.

By the end of the planning phase everyone should:

- Feel they played a part in setting the objectives
- Contributed to deciding the working arrangements
- Be clear and comfortable with their own roles and responsibilities
- Be clear about the roles and responsibilities of others
- Be familiar with the deadlines

- Be committed to the success of the group and see their success as the group's success

Collecting evidence

The evidence requirements ask you to provide at least two examples of meeting the key skill standards, with one example showing you can work in one-to-one situations and one example showing you can work in group situations.

Evidence requirements in a nutshell

This is where you get the group work or one-to-one work started by establishing what it is you will do (your objectives). You then need to decide on what tasks need to be done to achieve these objectives.

Then you need to decide who does what and make sure everyone understands what they are doing (clarify responsibilities). Then make sure everyone is clear what the working arrangements are to be.

HINTS FOR PLANNING WORK

- Have a group meeting to help you agree objectives and sort out who will do what. Make sure someone takes notes
- Have a brainstorming session to explore what might be involved in meeting the objectives
- Get all group members to fill out individual action plans
- Create a master action plan that involves everyone in the group and make a copy for everyone to keep
- Use a flowchart for your own work and get the group to create a flowchart for the whole process

See the sections on **action plans** (page 8), **brainstorming**, (page 10), and **flowcharts** (page 14)

What might be in your portfolio at this point

1. An index and dividers showing where your one-to-one evidence and where your group work evidence will be
2. A copy of the agreed objectives
3. A record of any questions you had about the objectives and a copy of the answers you received

4. A record of your own responsibilities (and perhaps copies of other people's responsibilities as well)
5. Action plans showing the tasks you need to do and the time frames you need to comply with
6. Notes on how and why the tasks were allocated to certain people
7. Flowcharts, notes from brainstorming sessions, etc.

A 'working with others' journal or diary

A diary is a good way to keep a record of what is happening in your group work and can be used as evidence in your portfolio. You can record your work and also keep notes about how you think the work is going, noting down what works well and what doesn't. This will be a useful reminder when it comes to meeting the last part of the 'working with others' evidence requirements about 'identifying progress'.

You don't have to buy a diary or journal. Just use a note-pad and remember to always enter the date before you write anything else down.

KEEPING A LEARNING JOURNAL OR DIARY

As you confirm what needs to be done and who should do it, your diary or journal should have records of:

- The people you are working with
- The objectives you have been set
- The different tasks that need to be done
- The tasks you will do and the resources you need
- Deadlines for the objectives
- Deadlines for your tasks
- A note on how you thought the decision taking went when you broke down the objectives into tasks and when you allocated the tasks
- 'To-do lists' and reminders to help keep you on track

Working towards identified objectives

This section of the evidence is concerned with the group or one-to-one work in action, and going about the business of achieving the agreed objectives.

Getting organised

You must learn how to organise your tasks so you can carry out the work effectively and meet your particular responsibilities successfully. This will mean obtaining the resources you need to get your work done and making sure you complete your work on time.

You could draw up your own flowcharts for the different tasks that you have to do or create an action plan to help you do this. Show that you are capable of reviewing your work and making any slight adjustments or changes to make sure you get your work done on time.

Carrying out your work

You must aim to produce good quality work. This means making sure you follow safe working practices and appropriate working methods.

- **Safe working practices**

  Not only will you be expected to conduct yourself in an appropriate manner showing care and consideration for those working around you, you must also work safely. This means ensuring the safety of yourself and those around you by using the correct ways to work with tools, equipment and materials.

  Spend a little time finding out about the hazards and risks involved in using tools, equipment and materials and then establish what the appropriate safety requirements are. You can ask appropriate teaching staff, consult the manufacturers' instructions or speak to others involved with health and safety issues. Tools and equipment should be clean and stored in a safe way after use.

  Notes you take about health and safety issues relating to your work will help you to understand how to behave appropriately and use the resources correctly. These notes can be put in your portfolio as evidence.

- **Appropriate working methods**

  When deciding what are appropriate working methods, you need to consider:
  1. Any instructions you have been given
  2. Manufacturer's instructions (for tools and equipment)
  3. Workplace safety instructions
  4. Health and safety instructions (for example, in case of fire or accidents)
  5. Codes of practice or expectations that people have in terms of behaviour (for example, with customers, visitors)

You need to try to show that you are conscientious when you work and are responsible and considerate to others as you work.

You may be working to specific instructions or following manufacturer's instructions about how to use tools and equipment. If so, you must show you are responsible enough to follow these accurately. The instructions may be in the form of a code of conduct or expected behaviour when dealing with customers. Again you must show you can comply with these types of expectations.

If you run into serious problems make sure you know who to inform and who to ask for advice. Who to ask for advice or feedback will depend on what you need help with. For example, you may need permission from a relevant teacher or supervisor to access equipment.

> **Conscientious**: careful, mindful of others, diligent, and able to follow rules exactly

Working co-operatively

You need to show you can take part in co-operative relationships with the people you need to work with or come into contact with. The key skill emphasis is on working relationships, which means knowing when and how to offer support, share resources and help others to ensure success.

To be an effective team player you need to:

- Be conscientious in carrying out your own work and responsibilities
- Be able to offer constructive comments and help
- Show a willingness to communicate and keep others informed of your progress
- Be receptive to the views of others in the groups
- Help to sort out problems in the group fairly
- Help to create an environment where everyone pulls their weight and no one is exploited, by having to take on more work or responsibilities than others
- Help to create an open and supportive environment for people to work in

Try to bring the best out of your other group members. This means playing your part in creating a positive group environment making sure that there is no tolerance of intimidation, harassment or discrimination. Make sure you are not responsible for these types of behaviour yourself and show no tolerance of them in others.

Peer reviews: friends, or the people you are working with, comment on your performance

You must set appropriate standards for your own behaviour and not encourage inappropriate behaviour in others. You can make good use of the successful working relationships you establish by asking these people for peer reviews. These can serve as evidence for your portfolio.

Seeking advice

There are two key features in asking for help or advice. These are:

- Knowing who to ask
- Knowing when to ask

- **Who to ask**
  Who you ask for advice or feedback should depend upon what you need help with. For example, a guidance teacher may help you with problems within your group (for example, people 'falling out' with each other), while a health and safety officer or design and technology teacher can help with advice on how to use equipment. Basically, you need to show you can seek help and support from appropriate people.
- **When to ask**
  This is linked to acting responsibly. You need to show you can seek advice, help or support when you need it. This means acting in a timely way and not leaving things until they are too late. When you think you need help, you should get help.

Collecting evidence

The evidence requirements asks you to provide at least two examples of meeting the key skill standards, with one example showing you can work in one-to-one situations and one example showing you can work in group situations.

WHAT YOU NEED TO DO

Sort out what you have to do so that you can successfully carry out the work you are responsible for. When you carry out your work make sure you follow the appropriate working methods and take the necessary safety precautions. Show that you can work co-operatively and seek advice from the right people when you need to.

Evidence requirements in a nutshell

This is where you need to show you can organise the work you are responsible for and then carry it out safely and in a responsible way, following the working methods and arrangements appropriate to the tasks. You also need to prove that you can be a good team player by showing you can work co-operatively.

Make sure you ask the right people for advice when you need it.

HINTS FOR WORKING TOWARDS AGREED OBJECTIVES

- List who you need to work with directly and explain how they fit into your meeting your responsibilities
- Identify good times to share information with others
- Create a set of contingency plans that can be given to your team to explain what could be done if things go wrong
- Make sure all the people you work with are clear about your individual responsibilities. If you communicate these in writing, keep a copy for your portfolio

What might be in your portfolio at this point

1. A list of the resources that you need for your specific tasks
2. Flowcharts, action plans or gantt charts that relate to your own particular tasks and responsibilities
3. A set of the working methods or instructions you have been given
4. Any questions you had relating to the working methods or instructions and a copy of the corresponding answers
5. Notes about any special safety requirements for equipment or tools you are using or materials you are handling
6. A list identifying the health and safety risks or hazards you must avoid and an explanation of how to avoid them

EVIDENCE FOR LEVEL 2 (WWO) | **81**

The Bottom Line

Sharing information on progress

This whole section is about your questioning how you are working both as an individual group member with your own set of responsibilities, timescales and commitments and as a group. Once you are clear how well you have done in relation to your task, the key skill gives you the opportunity to explain how you would do things differently based on what you now know.

Consider the group's performance as a whole. The group could hold a 'debriefing session' to evaluate and discuss their performance once everything has been completed. If you decide to do this, make sure people know about it well in advance and have time to prepare notes and organise their thoughts.

Journals and diaries are useful ways to record your thoughts on your own personal performance and the group's performance.

What went well and what went less well

Begin by looking at how well you did in terms of meeting your objectives. Reflect on your own performance in meeting your responsibilities and also record your personal observations on the group's performance.

Consider all the stages of the work including planning, working towards your objectives and the working relationships. You could even look in more detail and consider things like resources, decision making and communication. Were there circumstances beyond your control that affected how you worked?

The factors that affect your work can be positive and negative influences. The important thing is to be honest, and where mistakes have been made acknowledge them and show how you would avoid making the same mistakes in future. Show how you have learned from your mistakes. Where there have been positive influences try to reflect on how you can improve on them further.

The table opposite shows areas that may have gone well or badly and that you can address when you reflect on your performance.

Areas to consider	Types of question
Your targets	Were the objectives realistic and easy to measure or too ambitious?
Resources	What influence did they have on your success?
Planning	Were your plans or approach flexible enough to adapt to changes or were they too rigid and difficult to adapt to changes in circumstances? Were the time frames appropriate or too tight?
Changes in circumstances	Were you prepared for changes? How well did you cope?
Quality of your work	Was it up to your expectations? Was it up to other people's expectations?
Role of others	How useful is the feedback you are getting?

Listening and responding to progress reports

As a group, you need to communicate how well you are all doing in terms of meeting your objectives. Consider using the following list of issues when you communicate your progress; the more details and reasons you are able to give the better those listening will understand:

- Time and deadlines (are you on schedule?)
- Quality
- Resources
- Successes and failures

Make sure you are approachable and receptive to progress reports and comments from others. You should try to be friendly, supportive and attentive when others are updating or discussing issues or concerns.

- **Listening to others**
  You need to show that you are an active listener, paying attention to what others say and show you are receptive to their contributions. There are a number of ways to show you are listening but the most obvious way is to ask questions informed by the contributions made by others or that acknowledge what others have said. The body language you use can also let others know you are paying attention to what is being said. Your goal is to be *attentive* when others are talking, and receptive to what they have to say.
- **Responding appropriately**
  There are a number of ways you can show you are able to respond appropriately. Firstly, politeness is always appropriate. Other ways include answering questions or points made by making sure that you address the issues properly and don't ignore them or answer a different question (for example, the one you hoped the person would ask). You can ask follow-up questions, politely ask for clarification if you don't understand something or refer to what

Receptive: willing to receive new ideas and suggestions, open-minded, approachable, welcoming

Attentive: alert, paying attention

EVIDENCE FOR LEVEL 2 (WWO) | **83**

others have said in your contributions. All are ways of responding appropriately. An important skill that you need to develop is the ability to be *tactful*.

Responding appropriately can also mean making the necessary changes to your work or plans as a result of the information you have just received.

Other issues you need to consider include how, where and when you will give progress reports to each other.

- **How and where**
  Will you update others as part of a discussion? Are you going to having meetings to discuss progress? Do you prefer to do it verbally or will you put it in writing as well?
- **When**
  Don't just leave it until the end to report that you have finished or have missed your deadlines. Find suitable times during the work to keep people updated of your progress. This gives them time to make any adjustments they may need to make to their own work. It also gives you time to ask for advice, help or support if you think you will struggle to meet your objectives and deadlines.

Progress reports need to be part of the work you do as you do it. If you reach a significant point in your work, this may be a good time to report your progress. There may also be people depending on your work for their own. So think carefully about who you need to update as well as how, where and when.

Could do better?

Now you have had a chance to consider the successes and failures of your group work and have reported progress to others and received information from them, you should be able to use all this information to agree ways to improve. Consider how you could improve working relationships and your working methods based on your experiences.

Start by asking yourself:

- Should I (we) have done things differently?
- If I had to do it all again what changes would I make and why?

You have the benefit of hindsight and you need to try to show how you would learn from your mistakes. You should address these questions to both your own performance and the group's performance. Consider how you made decisions, how you organised yourself as a group, how you communicated, as well as your individual performance. Consider how much attention you paid to others' feelings, ideas or work and judge if you could make any improvements in this area.

Ask yourself: 'If I knew then what I know now, what would I have done differently?' Remember to explain your answers, saying why you would make the changes you identified.

MAKE IMPROVEMENTS AS YOU GO ALONG

The key skill also expects you to take a proactive approach to looking at ways to improve working relationships and working arrangements. Don't just wait until the end to review what went on and to agree how things could be improved.

Make sure you discuss how things are working out with the others as you go along, and if you can agree a better way of doing something then make the necessary changes.

Once everyone has had a chance to get used to the working methods and arrangements have a meeting with the others to discuss if any changes are necessary or whether improvements could be made.

Collecting evidence

The evidence requirements asks you to provide at least two examples of meeting the key skill standards, with one example showing you can work in one-to-one situations and one example showing you can work in group situations.

WHAT YOU NEED TO DO

You need to demonstrate that you are capable of assessing what went well and what was not as successful when working with others. Make sure you include the quality of your work in your assessment of how everything went.

You need to show that you can take an active part in communicating progress and respond appropriately to progress reports from others.

You also need to show you can agree ways to improve working relationships and working arrangements to help achieve your objectives.

Evidence requirements in a nutshell

This is really where you show you can work effectively as part of a team. You need to provide information on the successful and less successful aspects of working with others. This will also involve commenting on the quality of your work.

Listen and respond to progress reports from others in an appropriate way.

Discuss and agree how you could improve work with others to help make sure you meet your objectives.

HINTS FOR REVIEWING

- Keep a log so you can note down thoughts as you go
- Spend time on your own role as well as how the group performed
- Statements from other team members can be used as evidence of how well you performed as team member
- If asked to give feedback on other team members' performance, be fair, tactful and considerate

What might be in your portfolio at this point

1. Peer reviews from others in your group
2. Copies of progress reports sent by you to others
3. Copies of progress reports you received
4. Comments that you have on other people's progress and how it may influence your work

KEEPING A LEARNING JOURNAL OR DIARY

If you have a diary or journal, remember to enter:

- Who helped you in your work (explain how they helped)
- Who you were able to help (explain how you helped as well)
- When you updated others on your progress
- When others updated you on their progress
- Records of what went well and what went badly as they happen

Improving own learning and performance

What is 'Improving own learning and performance' all about?

Although the key skill talks a lot about learning, it is really about setting targets; turning targets into an action plan; implementing plans and then reviewing progress and achievement. It is really about getting you to consider what you learn and how you learn. This key skill will help you develop and improve techniques to help your learning and performance become more effective.

The key skill can help you improve on any aspect of your life. It is trying to help you to learn effectively and purposefully and have this reflected in improved performance. You can choose to focus on improving:

- Part of your academic or vocational studies
- Part of your training
- Something related to your job or career
- A leisure pursuit
- An aspect of your personal life

You should be able to identify and try to meet new demands in any aspect of your school, college, work or home life. However, before you go too far in choosing your focus for the key skill, look at the type of learning and evidence requirements that you need to show. This will give you a better understanding of what might be a feasible focus for your efforts. You can see the different learning styles that you need to show in the 'Using your plan' section of the evidence requirements.

Deciding which level to do

What's the difference between level 1 and level 2?

You need to be clear about what level of key skill you intend to collect evidence for. This is because each level has its own particular set of evidence requirements. The crucial differences between the level 1 and level 2 'Improving own learning and performance' key skill requirements involves the amount of control and responsibility you are expected to take over your work.

What is level 1 all about?

At level 1 you will need to work closely with someone to show that you are able to:

- Understand the short-term targets you have been given, and plan how these will be met
- Follow your plan to meet targets and improve your performance
- Review your progress and the achievements you have made

You will need to provide at least two examples that show you can work towards meeting short-term targets by following a plan, and then review your progress and work out how well you did in meeting your targets.

Evidence that shows you can work with others can be collected from your GCSE work, Vocational GCSE work, or another qualification. You could use work experience or a hobby as well.

How is level 2 different?

At level 2 you are expected to take more responsibility and control over your work. You are expected to show you can:

- Get involved in setting your own targets
- Sometimes work without close supervision
- Take more responsibility for some decisions that relate to your learning
- Use your experience and learning to meet the demands of a new task

At level 2, the evidence requirements are more demanding and expect more of you in terms of how much responsibility and ownership you can take over your own learning. In other courses most of the learning is organised for you. Someone else (normally your teacher) has decided what you will learn, and when and how you will learn it. This particular key skill tries to get you to take more control over your own learning and to get involved with some of the decisions related to your learning that would normally be taken by other people.

Frequently asked questions

What are targets?

For the purposes of this particular key skill, targets are learning goals that are set to help you improve your performance. They then become something you aim for, plan how to reach and work towards to improve. The targets could relate to your personal, school or college or working life.

How long is a short-term target?

Keep in mind that the targets are about improving your performance or ability in an important area of your school, college, work or personal life. In order to try to make this improvement significant and really noticeable, give your self enough time to learn and develop the knowledge, skills and understanding you will need to make a significant improvement. You also need to give yourself enough time to devise a realistic plan and be able to implement it.

Look for natural periods of time within your school, college, work or personal calendar where you can start and finish the key skill work. For example, at school or college you have term calendars, including half-term breaks, that you could use as possible time limits. If you use work experience then you have the length of time that you are on a work experience programme to try to make the improvements, though target setting and planning should take place beforehand.

The most important factor in setting short-term targets is that the person you work with is satisfied that you will have sufficient time to develop and improve to meet the targets and that the targets are of a suitable standard. So make sure you work closely to negotiate suitable targets.

Appropriate people with whom to set targets and review work

Because the key skill is about improving learning and performance, the people you would be most likely to work with would be:

- A teacher
- Tutor
- Trainer
- Line manager
- Supervisor
- Careers adviser

If you were planning to use work experience you may want to consider using a guidance teacher and/or the person responsible for you in the workplace. Targets that relate to your personal life and outside interests may mean working with someone who supervises your outside interest or someone who is more experienced in your area of interest who can lend support and advice. If you intend to use a personal hobby or some other aspect of your personal life as the focus for your key skill activity, make sure you check with the person assessing your key skill portfolio of evidence. They should be able to tell you if the person you would like to use to help set targets and review your progress is suitable.

How should I organise my evidence?

The key skill asks (at both levels 1 and 2) that you provide at least two examples to show you meet the standards. You are also asked to improve your performance by:

- Studying a straightforward subject
- Learning through a straightforward practical activity

It doesn't really matter which type of activity (studying or activity-based work) gets done first. This might depend on where the best chances are to generate evidence. For example, there may be an opportunity coming up in a course to generate evidence for the practical activity before you get an opportunity to create the study-based evidence.

You can do both at the same time. This will take more effort to organise and you need to make sure you are meeting all the evidence requirements for both. Remember, you will also have to meet your other commitments as well, so don't be tempted to take on too much at once.

Evidence for level 1 (LP)

What is level 1 all about?

At level 1 you are expected to work closely with someone, for example your teacher, tutor, trainer, line manager, supervisor or careers adviser, to show that you are able to:

- Understand the short-term targets set and plan how these will be met
- Follow your plan, using help from others to help you meet the targets
- Review your progress and achievements.

You are going to have to show that you can improve your performance by studying a straightforward subject and by learning through doing a practical activity. The guidance in this section assumes that you are going to carry out a learning exercise large enough to produce evidence for all three sections of the key skill. This means that you will plan for and carry out, a way to improve your performance and meet targets and then review how well you did.

Confirming your targets

What the unit expects

During this section of the key skill requirements you will need to work with an appropriate person who can help you with your targets and deadlines. They will also help you make sure your plans and the tasks that you need to carry out are suitable.

You will find it makes sense to try to create a plan for meeting your targets that you can follow. This way you can work out what needs to be done to meet your targets, the order it needs to be done in and how you will use the time you have available on each task.

Setting targets

You need to establish what it is you are going to try to achieve. Then look at how this can be turned into targets for you to try to meet. Good targets will be clear, simple and easy to read and understand. They will show what you want to achieve and they will be realistic and not too ambitious. Think about what it is in your school, college, work or personal life that you want to improve. Concentrate on identifying something that is within

your power to change and improve. Then break down what you would like to achieve into a set of smaller achievable targets. This is what making your targets feasible means.

As you agree your targets try to think of what the outcome will look like if you meet each target. Think about how you will know you have met the targets. What proof will you have? Will you be able to pass a test? Will you have made something? Will you have new or better skills?

Turning your targets into action

You really need to consider three things as you decide on the action points for each target: tasks, time and resources.

Action points: the tasks and activities that need to be done if you are to meet your targets

You can find out more about **flowcharts** on page 14

You can find out more about **action plans** on page 8

Resources can include:
People who can give advice
People who can offer support
Tools
Equipment
Materials

- **Tasks**
  What work will you have to do in order to achieve your targets? You need to think about the types of tasks you need to do and the sequence that you should do them in. Flowcharts can be a useful way of helping you to plan out the sequence of tasks that you need to do. They are also useful when explaining to others how you will try to meet your tasks, helping them understand the different tasks involved.

- **Time**
  You also need to think about how everything that needs to get done can get done within your deadlines. This can be done by looking at your overall deadline and then assigning smaller deadlines and time limits to each of the different tasks you need to do. Think about creating action plans with timelines for your work. Careful planning means making sure you use the time available wisely. Make sure each task has enough time given to it to allow you to do it properly.

- **Resources**
  You need to work out what equipment, materials, tools, books or help you need from other people to meet your targets. The resources you need depend on the targets and tasks you have to do. The main resource you need to think about is the help and support you will need from others (for example, your tutor or trainer). Don't just think about who you will need help from, think about when you need their help as well.

You also need to consider any training or practice you will need to be able to learn to use the resources properly. If you need to practise using tools or equipment or need to learn how to handle materials correctly, you need to build this into your plans.

Planning for the end

You should have a clear idea about how you will know when you have met your targets. You also need to identify the person who will help you review your progress and help you establish how well you have done in relation to your targets. Look at your deadlines and identify when you need to do this review and where it should take place. If you know who is the best person to help you review your work, then agree a time and place with them early on so you both have time to prepare.

PEOPLE WHO MIGHT PROVIDE USEFUL SUPPORT OR FEEDBACK

- Subject teacher
- Tutor
- Supervisor
- Health and safety officer
- First aid officer
- Guidance teacher
- Trade union representative
- Audio-visual technicians
- Caretaker staff (e.g. janitor)
- School or college management
- Local businesspeople

By the end of 'confirming targets' stage of the key skill you should:

- Have a set of clear short-term targets which you and the person you are working with can agree
- Know exactly what you have to do to meet your targets
- Be clear about your deadlines
- Know where and when to find help and support
- Know who will help you review your work

Try to finish this section by having an action plan drawn up that clearly shows your targets, the tasks that you have to do and the time limits or deadlines you need to take into account. You will find that having some sort of actual plan to follow that shows your work and deadlines will be useful when you get to other sections of this key skill. Your plan can also be used in your portfolio of evidence.

Collecting evidence

Remember you have to provide at least two examples of meeting the evidence requirements (one must be for a study-based activity, the other for a practical activity).

Look at the section on action planning on page 7

WHAT YOU NEED TO DO

You need to work with the person responsible for setting your targets to make sure you understand them and they clearly show what you want to achieve.

You then have to work out what you will need to do in order to meet each target. You also need to identify the deadlines for each target.

Once you have your targets, tasks and deadlines sorted out you need to work out how to get the support you need and make arrangements for reviewing your progress.

Evidence requirements in a nutshell

You are going to set some short-term targets and you need to work with the person who set the targets to:

1. Make sure targets clearly show what you want to achieve
2. Identify clear action points and deadlines for each target

EVIDENCE FOR LEVEL 1 (LP) | **93**

3. Work out how you can get the support or help you need
4. Make arrangements to review your progress

HINTS WHEN CONFIRMING YOUR TARGETS

- Organise your portfolio to show where your study-based and practical activity evidence can be found
- Identify early on who will be a useful source of advice and help if you need it
- Keep written records of the original short-term targets you agreed on
- Keep a diary, journal or log so you can note down thoughts as you do the work

What might be in your portfolio at this point

1. An index and dividers showing where your study-based evidence and your practical activity evidence will be
2. A copy of your short-term targets
3. A record of any questions you had about the targets and a copy of the answers you received
4. Copies of any action plans you create or diagrams that show the sequence of tasks (flowcharts) that you will do

A learning journal or diary

You will find that writing down your thoughts about what you are doing and whether it is working will help you when it comes to reviewing your progress and achievements. You could record what is going well and what is not going so well in the different tasks you do as well as useful information like deadlines and the tasks that you have to do on certain days.

If you do decide to keep a diary or work journal then try to keep it up to date and get into the habit of writing in it as you try to meet your targets. A well-kept diary or journal could contain some important evidence and could eventually become part of your portfolio of evidence for the key skill.

You don't have to buy a diary or journal. Just use a note-pad and remember to always enter the date before you write anything else down.

KEEPING A LEARNING JOURNAL OR DIARY

At this stage your diary or journal should have records of:

- The people you are working with
- The targets you have been set
- Why the targets are important to you.
- The tasks you will do and the resources you need
- Deadlines for the targets
- Deadlines for your individual tasks
- 'To-do lists' and reminders to help keep you on track
- A date for your review with the name of the person and the place where the review will take place

Using your plan

You need to work through your action points or action plans to complete tasks on time.

Make good use of the support you receive

You need to use the advice and support provided by other people to help meet your targets. The support could involve helping you get information you need, learning new skills or assistance with something you find difficult. The point is to show that you know how to get the right sort of help from the right sort of people, when you need it.

Different ways to learn

The key skill is trying to get you to improve your performance by using different ways of learning. You need to show you can improve your learning and performance by studying a straightforward subject and by learning through a straightforward practical activity. You need to identify early on the types of learning you will use so you can set appropriate targets and make suitable plans.

- **Studying a straightforward subject**
  This would involve learning about something through class lessons, in training sessions or through your own private study. You could be reading up about something in books, or on the Internet, for example.
- **Learning through a straightforward practical activity**
  This type of learning is about taking a 'learning by doing' approach and could involve learning by watching a demonstration then trying something for yourself, or getting involved in developing skills or doing experiments.

The table shows a few examples of the sorts of learning you could consider for each type.

Study-based learning	Practical activity-based work
Learning about a particular topic in class	Learning new hand skills in a workshop
Researching a hobby or interest on the Internet	Doing some basic research, e.g. carrying out a survey
	Carrying out experiments in a laboratory
	Learning through work experience
	First aid courses

You must use methods that suit each of these different learning styles. For example, in study-based learning you need to pay attention in class and ask questions on anything you are not clear about. If you are taking a 'private-study' approach then you need to keep a record of the words, phrases

or concepts you come across that you don't understand and ask an appropriate person what they mean.

In practical activities always pay close attention to demonstrations, and ask if you are unsure about anything before you start.

LEARNING METHODS AND STYLES

If you are involved in a practical activity you need to use suitable learning methods to help you make the most of this opportunity to learn. For example, you need to listen carefully to instructions, watch any demonstrations closely and ask questions about anything you don't understand or are unsure about. You must make sure you are clear about how to use tools and operate any equipment you need to use safely.

If you are involved in studying a straightforward activity you need to make sure that:

- If you are learning in class, you are listening carefully to what is being said, completing exercises and tasks carefully and make sure that you fully understand what you are learning about. This means asking questions about anything you are not clear about, making sure your notes are clear and correct and finding ways to check that you understand what is being taught
- If you are doing some personal studying (perhaps you are learning about something that interests you but not connected with any school or college work), you need to check that you understand what you are reading or learning. This means finding someone you can discuss your learning with. Try to find someone who knows a lot about what you are learning and use them as a source of advice and support and ask them questions when you don't understand something

---

Making changes

If your tutor or supervisor suggests changes to help you improve, make sure you act on them. Incorporate their suggestions into your plans or your approach to your learning. If you are unsure about why the changes are necessary, then ask. This will help you to understand what might have been going wrong or what needed to be improved. Changes could relate to how you work, how you could improve the quality of your work or how you might present your work.

Collecting evidence

Remember you have to provide at least two examples of meeting the evidence requirements (one must be for a study-based activity, the other for a practical activity).

You are going to have to show you can improve your performance by studying a straightforward subject and by learning through a straightforward practical activity. For each of these you must show you can:

- Get on with the tasks and action points you have identified, making sure you complete each task on time. Make good use of the support you get from others to help you meet your targets
- Make changes to help improve your performance when you need to
- Pay attention to the different ways of learning or the advice given to you by your supervisor and make good use of it to improve your performance

Evidence requirements in a nutshell

As you study a straightforward subject and learn through doing a straight-forward practical activity, you must do the following:

1. Work through your action points for each target to complete the tasks on time
2. Make good use of the support available to you to help you meet your targets
3. Use the different ways of learning suggested by your teacher, tutor or supervisor
4. Make any changes that will help improve your performance. Your teacher, tutor or supervisor may suggest these changes

HINTS WHEN FOLLOWING YOUR PLAN

- Identify a point about half way through your work, when you can take a 'time out' and review your progress
- Keep making changes to action plans or flowcharts if circumstances change
- Find some way to keep monitoring how your work is going in relation to the time you have available
- Make sure you understand why changes are suggested to you

What might be in your portfolio at this point

1. Copies of revised action plans
2. Notes explaining why you had to make changes
3. Different drafts of any writing or drawing work you had to do
4. Notes from classes or training sessions to do with your key skill work
5. Notes of any health and safety requirements you have been told about
6. Copies of any questions you asked to clarify something and records of the answers you got

Reviewing your progress and achievements

You need to work with someone familiar with what you were trying to do and how you were trying to improve to discuss how you got on. You will be looking at how well you did in relation to your original targets and will be looking for ways to improve further. This section is about looking at how you review your work and assess your actual performance.

It makes most sense to review your progress with the person who set your targets. They will probably be in the best position to help you work out how much you have improved.

Reviewing

You will be expected to give your own opinion on three key areas. These are:

- What you have learned
- How you have learned
- What went well and what went less well

What you have learned

You need to consider things like what you learned about the subject you focused your learning on or the skills you were improving. Whatever the focus for your key skills work was, you need to explain a little about how much you have learned, proving what you know about your chosen area. You could do this by briefly explaining what you knew or did not know or what you could or could not do in your chosen topic before you started. Then you could describe what you now know or can do in your chosen area as a result of your key skill work. This is a good way of showing how far you have come or how much you have learned.

How you have learned

You also need to be able to comment on how you learned. This means looking at the actual process of learning and the methods you used and sharing your thoughts on them. This may seem a little strange because you are probably not used to talking about or commenting on the learning process itself. Most of the time you would have focused on the subject content rather than how you learn. However, one of the main points of doing this particular key skill is to try to get you to think about how you learn and to encourage you to take a little more responsibility for your learning. Think about the following list of suggestions and see if any apply to your own situation and try to answer them thinking about your own experiences.

- What were the learning methods you used?
- Which learning methods worked particularly well for you and explain why?
- Which learning methods did you think didn't work well for you and explain why?
- Were there any particular ways of learning that you enjoyed more than others?

What went well and what went less well?

Look back on your work and try to identify what has gone well. You could comment on:

- How you were able to support others
- How others supported you
- Successful ways you carried out tasks
- Targets, objectives and timelines you were able to meet

You also need to consider what didn't go as well as you wanted. Explain any difficulties you faced as you tried to meet your work responsibilities. Once you have identified these problem areas, spend time describing what you did about them. Things to consider include:

- Problems you faced when carrying out your tasks
- How you managed to overcome disagreements within the group
- Problems with any of your resources

Targets hit and achievements made

Starting with targets, you need to assess which of your original targets were met. You do this by looking carefully at what you set out to do and then judge whether you have done it or not. Hopefully, you will have a clear record of your original targets or an action plan that you can look at. What proof do you have that you have done what you set out to do? Do you have something to show others? Is there class work that shows you have met your targets? Can other people show that you have met your targets?

You need to work out how you are going to show that you have met

your targets and prove that you have made improvements to your learning and performance meeting the original targets you were given. Hopefully the person who set the targets has a clear idea of how they can work out if you have met them or not, so discuss with them what kind of proof they are looking for.

You must also identify the achievements you have made. Don't think about your targets this time, instead think of all the other success you may have had. Think about the following types of question:

- Were you able to stick to your deadlines?
- Could you sort out any difficulties you faced without a lot of help?
- Is there anything you did or produced that you are proud of?
- Were you able to help someone else with his or her targets?
- Were you able to answer some of your own questions by finding out the answers yourself?

How can you improve?

You need to ask advice about what you need to do to improve your performance. Hopefully, by looking at how you did in relation to your targets, and looking at what went well and worked for you and what didn't work as well, you will be able to come up with ideas about how to improve. Discussing this with a tutor or supervisor helps as well. Focus your attention on improving the quality of your work as well as on how you work.

You can ask yourself the following questions to get you started:

- Should I (we) have done things differently?
- If I had to do it all again what changes would I make and why?

Hindsight: the ability to understand after something has happened

You have the benefit of hindsight and you need to try to show how you would learn from your mistakes and build on your successes.

Collecting evidence

Remember you have to provide at least two examples of meeting the evidence requirements (one must be for a study-based activity, the other for a practical activity).

WHAT YOU NEED TO DO

Sit down with an appropriate person who can help you review your progress and achievements and discuss:

- What you have learned
- How you learned it
- What went well and what went less well
- Targets you have met
- Achievements you have made

As a final exercise check that you understand what you need to do to improve your performance.

Evidence requirements in a nutshell

You need to work with an appropriate person to review your progress and achievements. This will mean:

1. Saying what you learned as well as talking about how you learned it.
2. Discussing what went well and what has not gone as well.
3. Identifying the targets you met successfully and the achievements you had
4. Checking that you know what to do to improve your performance

---

HINTS FOR REVIEWING YOUR PROGRESS AND ACHIEVEMENTS

- Prepare for your review work by making notes about what you want to talk about
- Organise your portfolio showing what type of work you are doing, for example your study work or practical activity
- Discuss with your tutor what evidence requirements you have still to meet and how you will meet them. This will help you organise your portfolio

---

What might be in your portfolio at this point

1. Clearly indexed evidence for your study work and your practical activity
2. Your diary or journal
3. The notes you made to prepare for your review
4. Any statements from people who can say you did what you were supposed to
5. Notes explaining what you think went well and what went less well
6. Statements showing you understand what you need to do to improve

---

KEEPING A LEARNING JOURNAL OR DIARY

At this stage your diary or journal should have records of:

- Your thoughts on what you are learning about your study subject or practical activity.
- Details of when you will meet to discuss your review and who you will meet with
- Thoughts on what you did that your are proud of
- Your thoughts on how you learned something, say what you enjoyed learning and why you think you enjoyed it

Evidence for level 2 (LP)

What is level 2 all about?

There are three stages involved in 'Improving own learning and performance'; these are:

- Helping to set short-term targets and plan how these will be met
- Use your plan to meet your targets
- Reviewing your progress and achievements

Basically, this is a good method of working regardless of what you are doing, so think of it as continuous process that provides a useful framework to help you organise your efforts.

Helping to set targets

What the unit expects

This part of the key skill is asking you to work with an appropriate person to create a coherent and sensible way to achieve what you want in terms of improving your own learning and performance. It will make sense to work with someone who will be close to you and familiar with your work as you create your plan and carry it out. This means looking to people like your tutor, trainer, line manager or careers adviser for help. You will find it helpful to use the same person you work with when you set your targets for reviewing your progress and achievements as well.

What you need to know

You need to begin by doing a little groundwork coming up with accurate information that will help you set realistic targets. Before you discuss what your targets might be you need to consider the three following questions:

- **What do you want to do?**
  Think about what you actually want to achieve. What is it you want to improve? Be prepared to explain what you have done or learned in the area you are thinking about focusing on or what you have already achieved. Then make sure you clearly explain how you want to build on your previous achievements.

- **What might affect your chances?**
  You should also be able to discuss the factors that may help you achieve your targets or that may block your way. You need to ensure you meet your targets successfully and early identification of factors that might affect your success makes sense. This way you can prepare strategies to help you cope with change or even exploit opportunities that may arise. The main factors to consider that could affect your work are:
  - Cost
  - Resources
  - Health and safety
  - Other work or learning commitments
  - Conflicting deadlines
  - Changes in your own motivation
- **How will you know you've met your targets?**
  You also need to spend a little time thinking about what the end result will be should you meet the targets. A lot of this will depend on what it is you intend to do. However, you should be able to come up with ideas about how you will know when the targets have been met.

  Will you be producing something, performing a task or taking a test? If you are learning how to perform a task or improve your ability to perform a task then there may be people who have seen you do the task who can write a statement for you. Either way there will be some sort of outcome that could be used to help you show you met your targets.

Once you have thought about these three questions and perhaps made some notes, you will be able to discuss the sorts of targets that would best show what you want to achieve. Try to draw up a list of preliminary targets based on this information. You could use this as the basis of discussions with your tutor or supervisor.

When it comes to creating targets make sure they are clear, measurable and achievable.

- **Clear targets**
  While it is acceptable to have your goal written as a general statement of intent, your targets must be clear, precise and easy to understand. Targets can either break down your overall goal into a series of small, incremental steps (each becoming a target) or they can 'unpack' the goal by breaking it down into all the smaller separate targets. Make sure you spell things out in your targets. This way, planning how to meet each target becomes easier, as does assessing whether you have achieved it or not.
- **Measurable**
  At some point you are going to have to show whether you have met your targets or not. You will find that this process is easier if you have short, focused and simply written targets. When you write your targets try to make them quantifiable. This means writing them in a way that allows you to tell if you have actually met them or not or that allows you to see how much of the target has been met.

The Bottom Line

Measurable:
something you can assess, quantify or demonstrate

- **Achievable**

  Your targets must also be realistic. This means you must try not to be too ambitious. Ensure you are able to achieve your targets given the time you have available and the resources you have at your disposal. Basically, keep the challenges you set yourself within your reach.

Planning for action

You will need to show you can turn your well-thought-out targets into a plan. Start by asking yourself 'What will I have to do to meet each target?' By identifying the action points for each target and putting them in order of priority you will get a clear idea of the tasks that need to be done. By breaking the targets down into smaller action points you will find it easier to work out time frames and deadlines for your work. Consider using an action plan like the one on page 8 for each of your tasks.

Build 'time-outs' into your plans. Just as some sports coaches call 'time-out' to rethink their strategy and adjust their plan, you should do the same. Build in stages where you can review your progress, review what is going well and what is going less well and make adjustments to your plan. This reviewing process is crucial if you are to learn from mistakes and keep your work on track.

Consider everything that could possibly make conflicting demands on your time or could cause change. You need to think ahead and consider how you would minimise negative changes and maximise positive ones. Contingency planning can be one way of preparing for anticipated problems.

Contingency plan: is a backup plan in case something goes wrong (see page 9)

Identifying support

You need to identify what kind of support you will need and how you will get it. Support could be teaching, career guidance, special coaching, guidance from key people, special classes you need to attend, questions that you need to ask or skills training. The support you will need really depends on what types of task you will be doing and how well prepared you are to do them.

One aspect of support you need to think about, and perhaps even make some preliminary arrangements for, concerns the process of reviewing your progress. You need to think about when you will review your progress, who will help you and where you will carry out the review.

Collecting evidence

Remember you have to provide at least two examples of meeting the evidence requirements (one must be for a study-based activity, the other for a practical activity).

You need to work with an appropriate person to set short-term targets, then identify clear action points for each target.

Before target setting you must show you can provide the information needed to help to set realistic targets for what you want to achieve.

After target setting you must show that you can plan how you will use your time effectively to meet your targets. This includes making good use of any support available and making arrangements for reviewing your progress.

Evidence requirements in a nutshell

You are going to have to work with an appropriate person to set short-term targets for yourself and then plan how these will be met.

In order to help to set realistic targets for what you want to achieve you will need to provide some accurate information beforehand.

Once you have set your targets identify clear action points for each. You then need to plan how you will use your time well to meet your targets. As you plan you must consider how you can make good use of the support available to you.

You also need to make arrangements for reviewing your progress.

HINTS FOR SETTING TARGETS

- Base your key skills work on something you are interested in. This will help you keep motivated
- If you focus on a personal interest or hobby choose a 'quiet' time in your other work
- Discuss your action plans with the person who helped you set your targets. They will be able to comment on whether they think your targets are appropriate or not
- Give a copy of your action plans to your tutor or supervisor
- Whoever eventually reviews your performance with you could be given a copy of your targets and action plans

What might be in your portfolio at this point
1. Notes about what you want to achieve
2. Lists identifying factors that could affect your chances of success
3. Draft targets
4. A set of your actual targets
5. Action plans that correspond to your targets
6. Details of deadlines
7. Lists of health and safety issues

A learning journal or diary
You can keep a diary or journal for the duration of your key skills work. Make sure you update it regularly with your thoughts on how everything is

EVIDENCE FOR LEVEL 2 (LP) | **105**

KEEPING AN LP DIARY OR JOURNAL

Try to keep a diary or journal separate from the actual work and tasks and use it to comment on what you are finding out about the learning process itself. Use it to write down your thoughts on your own performance, your successes and failures. Because it is private, be honest. Write in it as you would a normal diary. Try not to use it to write drafts of targets or plans or any work related directly to working towards your targets, rather write your thoughts, fears and own personal observations about your progress.

Try to do it as you go, so you can look back at the end and remind yourself of the thoughts you had at the time. Don't be tempted to leave it for a while and go back and try to remember what you thought. One of the most important things to try to do is to keep it ongoing. To make this more feasible, get into the habit of making brief entries that summarise your thoughts. That way it will be less of a chore.

Try to write about:

- How you feel about the targets you set and how you expect them to go
- What worries you about the tasks you have set yourself
- What surprised you (good or bad)
- Comments about the usefulness of resources (not specific resources like books or webpages but more general comments about the school or college library, specific search engines and useful websites)

As you come into contact with different Internet search engines you may find some easier to use than others or some that suit you better. Keep a record of these search engines and their Internet addresses, as well as a reminder of why you thought they were useful. Keep records of useful Internet addresses.

If you don't think you are going to be conscientious enough to enter information into a diary regularly then find some other way of recording your thoughts as you go along. Perhaps, you could take a copy of your evidence as you generate it and annotate your thoughts about it on each of the copies.

KEEPING A LEARNING JOURNAL OR DIARY

At this stage your diary or journal should have records of:

- Your thoughts on your final targets
- Contact names and details of the people you may need to support you
- Dates for key deadlines like when you need to have your work completed and when you will start the review process.
- Thoughts on what your final evidence might look like

going, discussing what is going well or badly and describe any unexpected circumstances that come up.

Using your plan

Background information

This section is about implementing your plan, turning it into action. As you implement your plan you will also need to monitor how well it is going and make any necessary changes along the way.

What you need to know

Managing your time

Part of the key skill involves showing you can manage your time effectively. This means making the most of the time you have available to help you make sure you meet your targets. To help ensure success look at the tasks and the action points you have made and begin to sort out a sensible sequence to do them in.

Start by prioritising your work. You may have lots of different tasks to do so you must work out what should be done first or what is the most urgent. You also need to establish whether some tasks are dependent upon the completion of others first. This gives you two criteria to start prioritising your work. There could be others, for example, you may not need certain information immediately but may need to deal with the task of getting it sooner rather than later. For example, you need to send a letter requesting information and although you don't need the information right away, the reply may take time to be sent back.

Work out a list of everything you need to do and sort it in terms of what is most urgent and what is dependent on other tasks. This will help you work out the best order to do the tasks in, then try to create a timetable to help meet your priorities. Keeping notes explaining why you prioritised in the way you did will also be useful.

Always try to think ahead and prepare for the work that is coming up. This means having all the resources you need ready and available when you need them.

Keep your plans effective

You need to make sure your plans remain useful and relevant. This means revising them if you need to. As the circumstances change, so should your plans. One way to check that your plans are still suitable for the work ahead is to build in stages to review your progress. If something has changed – for example, you have completed a task more quickly than you first anticipated or you have to deal with an unexpected problem – you can adjust your plans as necessary. Build in review stages at strategic points, for example at the end of a task and before you start another task. Then use this time to evaluate your progress so far in relation to your plans and prepare for and think about the new tasks ahead, checking to see if your plans are still valid. This way your plans can be flexible and responsive to changing circumstances. What you are really doing now is monitoring your work.

Responsive: being awake or aware or quick to react to something

EVIDENCE FOR LEVEL 2 (LP) | **107**

You should also spend some time thinking about what might go wrong and making contingency plans in the event that it does. (See the section on contingency planning on page 9.)

Getting support from others

You need to be clear about who to ask for support and when to ask. The goal here is to find the right people to ask for support, advice or guidance and to make sure you ask for support in a timely way. Don't leave it too long or too late before you ask for help. Show that you can use the people around you effectively.

Feedback can be an important way of evaluating your work and getting advice from other people, so build in ways of getting feedback. You need to ensure that feedback comes from appropriate people and that it comes in a form you can use. Appropriate people will be able to speak from experience giving useful feedback as either advice or comment on your progress. Identify at an early stage people who will be able to help you with feedback and how you will work them into the process.

Learning approaches and styles

You need to make sure that you use appropriate learning styles and approaches for the tasks that you do. Show you can improve your performance by studying a straightforward subject, learning by doing a straightforward practical activity and can carry out some study or practical work without the need for close supervision.

- Studying a straightforward subject could be done in class or in training sessions and could involve activities like reading, note taking and asking pertinent questions. It could also involve self-directed study in which you follow a learning programme you negotiated with your tutor or supervisor.
- Practical activity is more about your applying knowledge, skills and understanding through activities like problem solving, experimentation, simulation, role play, field work or making something.

Both these examples tend to take place in a controlled environment of some sort where someone else sets the pace and is responsible for creating the learning environment. For example, a teacher decides on the equipment to use, the experiment that takes place or the content that should be taught. However, you need to show you can also take some responsibility and control over the learning process and work at times without supervision. The table opposite shows a few examples of the sorts of learning you could consider.

You must use methods that suit each of these different learning styles. For example, in study-based learning you need to pay attention in class and ask questions on anything you are not clear about. If you are taking a more 'private-study' approach then you need to keep a record of the words, phrases or concepts you come across that you don't understand and ask an appropriate person what they mean.

Study-based learning	Practical activity-based work
Learning about a particular topic in class	Learning new hand skills in a workshop
Researching a hobby or interest on the Internet	Doing some basic research, e.g. carrying out a survey
	Carrying out experiments in a laboratory
	Learning through work experience
	First aid courses

In practical activities always pay close attention to demonstrations, and ask if you are unsure about anything before you start.

LEARNING METHODS AND STYLES

If you are involved in a practical activity you need to use suitable learning methods to help you make the most of this opportunity to learn. For example, you need to listen carefully to instructions, watch any demonstrations closely and ask questions about anything you don't understand or are unsure about. You must make sure you are clear about how to use tools and operate any equipment you need to use safely.

If you are involved in studying a straightforward activity you need to make sure that:

- If you are learning in class, you are listening carefully to what is being said, completing exercises and tasks carefully and make sure that you fully understand what you are learning about. This means asking questions about anything you are not clear about, making sure your notes are clear and correct and finding ways to check that you understand what is being taught

- If you are doing some personal studying (perhaps you are learning about something that interests you but not connected with any school or college work), you need to check that you understand what you are reading or learning. This means finding someone you can discuss your learning with. Try to find someone who knows a lot about what you are learning and use them as a source of advice and support and ask them questions when you don't understand something

---

When studying a straightforward subject, you could do some of your own research using textbooks, local library facilities or even the Internet to help you. This might be one way of showing you can add to class work or training sessions by working without close supervision. For your practical activity work you may be able to collect primary research information by doing a survey, or practise and develop certain skills without need of close supervision. However, make sure you work safely at all times.

Collecting evidence

Remember you have to provide at least two examples of meeting the evidence requirements (one must be for a study-based activity, the other for a practical activity).

WHAT YOU NEED TO DO

You are expected to show you can improve your performance by studying a straightforward subject and learning through a straightforward practical activity. As you do each of these, you need to show you are able to take responsibility for some decisions about your learning.

As you try to improve your performance you must show you can use your action points to help manage your time and finish your tasks. If you need to revise your plan, you should.

You must also show that you know where to find support and use it effectively to help you meet your targets.

Finally, you must select and use different ways of learning to improve your performance showing you can work for short periods without close supervision.

Evidence requirements in a nutshell

As you go about trying to improve your performance by studying a straightforward subject or learning through a straightforward practical activity, you will need to show you can take responsibility for some of the decisions about your learning.

As you go about your work you must have evidence to show you:

1. Can manage your tasks and time so work gets completed
2. Can revise plans if necessary
3. Know when you need support and use it effectively to help meet your targets
4. Can chose and use different ways of learning to help improve performance
5. Are able to work without need of supervision at times

HINTS FOR PLANNING

- Change and redraft your action plans if there are changes in circumstances
- Drawing a flowchart of what needs to be done can help you sort out your tasks and see the relationship between each
- Create contingency plans to use if something goes wrong. Think of alternative resources that could be used or other ways to do things

What might be in your portfolio at this point

1. Old action plans with annotations showing where changes need to be made
2. Copies of any new action plans

3. Copies of any notes made while studying or at least a record of where to find your notes
4. Notes on any health and safety issues relating to your practical activity
5. Any flowcharts charts you created
6. Copies of any contingency plans
7. A record of anyone who helped you. You could also include a note explaining why they were suitable people to ask for help

---

KEEPING A LEARNING JOURNAL OR DIARY

At this stage your diary or journal should have records of:

- Thoughts on how your work is going and how you think it can be improved
- A record of what happened and when it happened if something changes or goes wrong. Include a note explaining what you did about it
- Contact details of people who can give you help, support or advice
- Records of when you sent letters and to whom, as well as records of any telephone calls you made connected with your key skills work

---

Reviewing your progress and achievements

Background information

This section is about evaluating your own performance and showing that you can learn from it. The aim is to show you know how to build on your strengths and are improving your weaknesses. So a key factor is honesty. The key skill isn't looking for you to try to prove that you were great at everything and met all your targets easily. It is looking for you to show that you can assess what went well and worked for you and why this was the case. You also need to show you are aware of what didn't go as well and why. You then need to show you know how to work on these weaknesses and have ideas about how to put them right.

What you must learn to do

You will need to work with an appropriate person to review your progress and achievements. This person can be a teacher, tutor, line manger, supervisor, careers adviser or someone else who is familiar with your work. It makes more sense to work with the person who helped you set your targets because they will be the most familiar with what you are trying to achieve.

What did you learn?

You need to do a 'before and after' type assessment of what you have learned. Don't worry so much about your actual targets at this stage, just look more generally at everything you have learned since you started the

whole key skill process. Don't only consider the actual knowledge, skills and understanding related to the topic or subject you focused on. Also consider the following:

- Did you discover anything about how you learn best?
- Were you comfortable taking more responsibility for your own learning?
- What did you find out about yourself as a learner?
- Which learning styles bring the best out of you?
- Did you discover any new ways of working?

How have you learned?

This may seem like a strange question and could be one that you have never even considered before. Remember that this particular key skill is trying to make you more conscious as a learner. It tries to get you thinking about your own learning and aims to make you more aware of how you learn. You are encouraged to take more responsibility for your own learning by getting more involved in the target-setting and planning process and you have to show you are able to work without close supervision occasionally. It is all about getting you to take some ownership of the learning process. So with all this in mind, you are asked to consider how you learned. Do this by asking yourself questions like:

- Where did you learn best?
- How well did you cope without supervision?
- Where there any particular learning styles that suited you best?

What factors affected your progress?

You also need to discuss factors that affect your work. These can be positive and negative influences. The important thing is to be honest and where mistakes have been made acknowledge them and show how you would avoid making the same mistakes in future. Show how you have learned from your mistakes. Where there have been positive influences try to reflect on how you can improve on them still further and how you can make the most of these successful factors in other aspects of your learning. Show that you have ideas about how to build on your successes.

The table opposite shows areas that may have gone well or badly and what you should address when you review your work. Remember to explain why you think things worked or didn't work and give examples to help illustrate your points.

You will probably find that some things are not clear cut and there will be aspects of planning that went well and aspects that went less well. Concentrate on showing you know what worked and can be built on and are also aware of what needs to be improved.

Bullseye!

What targets did you actually meet? Look through your action plans and try to establish the targets that were actually met. Think about how you can prove these targets were met successfully. Do you have any proof such

Areas to consider	Types of question
Your targets	Were the targets realistic and easy to measure or too ambitious?
Resources	What influence did they have on your success?
Planning	Was your plan flexible enough to adapt to changes or was it too rigid and difficult to adapt to changes in circumstances? Were the deadlines appropriate or too tight? How well did your monitoring go? Did you prioritise your tasks correctly?
Changes in circumstances	Were you prepared for changes? How well did you cope?
Role of others	How useful was the support and feedback you got?

as test results that show you met the targets successfully? Are there others who can say they saw you meet your targets?

Showing your achievements?

In the target-setting section, the importance of identifying ways to measure your success was discussed. You need to be able to collect evidence to show your achievements.

Start by dealing with the targets you met successfully. How can you prove that you achieved these? Then focus on the targets that you did not meet and explain why these were not achieved. Did you meet these targets in part? Were there circumstances that prevented you from meeting them? Did something go wrong?

Failing to meet targets is not necessarily a bad thing nor will it count against you in collecting evidence for this key skill. As long as you can explain clearly why targets were missed, and are able to show you have learned from the experience, this is still useful evidence.

Evidence showing your achievements could come from tutors, work colleagues, managers or anyone else who can comment on your progress. There may also be physical proof or evidence in the form of examples of your work that show you are now performing at a more competent or higher level.

The evidence you collect must help prove that you have met your targets fully or have met some partially. When you fail to meet a target, provide an explanation of why you think you didn't meet it.

In this section of the key skill there is a slightly peculiar request that you also include examples of how you have used your learning to meet new demands. This also appears in the evidence requirements. In the evidence for this section you will need to show how you have used learning from one task to meet the demands of a new task.

One way to look at this is to consider your 'Improving own learning

> **TYPES OF EVIDENCE THAT COULD SHOW ACHIEVEMENT**
>
> - Examples of your work
> - Statements or testimonials from relevant people familiar with your work
> - Records
> - Reports
> - Certificates or awards gained
> - Observation of your performance by your assessor

and performance' work as having given you experience. You have gained experience in target setting and planning, in implementing and monitoring and reviewing your plans and progress and in evaluating how well you did. So how can you use this experience to help you carry out a new task? Consider the following questions:

- Can you make use of a learning style that worked well for you?
- Is there a technique that you found useful that you could use again?
- Is there even an Internet search engine that you found useful that you could use again to help you in a new task?

You need to discuss this aspect of the key skill with your teacher, tutor or line manager (whoever is working with you on the key skill) to make sure you agree on how best to meet this particular requirement.

How can you improve?

This last section is about rounding the whole process off by presenting a strategy that can help you continue to improve your performance. After reflecting on how you did during the 'Improving own learning and performance' process and reviewing the outcome, i.e. the targets you did and didn't meet, you need to pull all this together and show how you can build on this and improve.

As well as collecting your own thoughts on how to improve. Consider asking for feedback from others. Get feedback from people who are able to comment on your learning and performance and have had a chance to look at and comment on your evidence. The more familiar they are with what you have been doing, the more insightful the feedback should be. At this stage, the most appropriate person may be your tutor, teacher or assessor. Discuss with them how you can improve in relation to the specific targets and tasks connected with the key skill but also in relation to learning generally.

You should try to use your own experience and their expertise in this area to develop a clear view about ways to improve your performance.

Collecting evidence

Remember you have to provide at least two examples of meeting the evidence requirements (one must be for a study-based activity, the other for a practical activity).

Evidence requirements in a nutshell

You need to be able to work with an appropriate person to review your progress. This reviewing stage will show that you are able to identify:

1. What you learned and how you learned it
2. What went well and what went less well
3. Targets you met successfully
4. Evidence of your achievements
5. Ways to keep on improving your performance

At some point, you should also discuss how you have used learning from one task to meet the demands of a new task.

HINTS FOR REVIEWING

- Be prepared to discuss your successes and failures honestly
- Think ahead about the kinds of evidence you will need to have and make appropriate plans
- Try not to have any surprises for the person you are going to do the review with; for example, suddenly miss targets or achieve different targets from those agreed
- Prepare a list of notes covering everything you want to discuss so you don't forget anything
- Think about ways to improve as you go. Don't just leave it until the end

What might be in your portfolio at this point

1. The notes you made to prepare for your review
2. Two sets of evidence: one relating to your studying a straightforward subject, the other relating to a practical activity
3. Your diary or journal
4. Actual proof of meeting your targets; for example, improved test scores of something you made or evidence of something you did

The Bottom Line

5. Testimonies from people who saw you perform a task or meet a target (if the target was based on performing a task)
6. Notes explaining what went well and what went less well
7. A list of the most appropriate ways for you to improve your performance further

KEEPING A LEARNING JOURNAL OR DIARY

At this stage your diary or journal should have records of:

1. Dates, times and place for your review meetings
2. Some thoughts on what you need to prepare
3. Records of what went well and badly as they happened
4. Comments about how work could be improved as you carried out the tasks

Problem solving

Deciding which level to do

What's the difference between level 1 and level 2?

You need to be clear about what level of key skill you intend to collect evidence for. This is because each level has its own particular set of evidence requirements. At level 1 you will be working closely with someone, for example, a teacher, tutor, trainer or supervisor, and you will be checking that you understand what the problem is and helping to identify ways to solve it. At level 2 the emphasis is more on your identifying your own problem, finding out what you can about it and coming up with possible solutions without as much help from someone else. Though at level 2 you still need to get permission at certain points, you are expected to take greater responsibility for identifying and solving problems.

At both levels the problem need have only a small number of ways to solve it and you will have to work within clear guidelines or instructions for deciding which option to try to solve your problem.

Evidence of your problem solving can come from your GCSE work, Vocational GCSE work, another qualification or your job. You could even use work experience or a hobby or personal interest as well.

What is level 1 all about?

At level 1, problem solving involves working closely with someone (for example, a teacher, tutor, trainer or supervisor) to show you can understand the problem you have been given and identify suitable options for solving it. You will be expected to try out options using the support and advice of people around you. You will be expected to follow step-by-step methods that you have been given to check if the problem has been solved and then will be expected to describe the results.

The problems you will be given will have only a limited number of ways that they could be solved.

How is level 2 different?

At level 2 you will be expected to identify problems and be able to describe the main features. You will be expected to show you can identify ways to solve the problems and be able to plan and try out options to find the

solution. This will mean obtaining support from other people and showing that you can adjust plans and make changes if necessary. You will be expected to come up with ways to show that the problem has been solved and to explain your approach to problem solving.

Evidence for level 1 (PS)

At level 1 there are basically three types of activities you need to do that relate to problem solving. You will need to show you can:

- Confirm problems and identify options to solve them
- Plan and try out options
- Check to see if problems have been solved

You will be expected to provide at least two examples of meeting the standard for the three areas of the problem-solving key skill listed above.

Confirming problems and identifying your options

What the unit expects

During this section of the key skill requirements you will need to work with an appropriate person who will give you a problem to work on or will help you to understand what is involved. They will also help you to make sure your plans and the tasks that you need to carry out are suitable.

Working with someone appropriate

The most appropriate person to work with when doing the key skill will depend upon how and where you do the key skill. Normally one of the following people would be suitable:

- Teacher
- Tutor
- Trainer
- Line manager
- Supervisor
- Careers adviser

If you wanted to tackle a problem relating to your work experience you could use a guidance teacher and/or the person responsible for you in the workplace during your work placement. Problems that relate to a hobby or outside interests may mean working with someone who supervises your outside interest or someone who is more experienced in your area of interest. They can give you support and advice and set a suitable problem

for you. If you intend to use a personal hobby or some other aspect of your personal life as the focus for your problem solving, make sure you check with the person assessing your key skill portfolio of evidence. They should be able to tell you if the person you would like to use to help you is suitable.

Once you have been given a problem to work on you have to show that you are able to work with an appropriate person to:

- Check you are clear about the problem
- Work out how to show success in solving the problem
- Identify ways to solve the problem

These activities don't all have to be done at once or have to take place in one conversation. Take time to think about each in turn, then discuss them with the person you are working with. This way you can take time to think things through and prepare questions to ask.

Let's look in turn at the three areas shown above to get a clearer idea of what might be involved in each.

Checking you are clear about the problem

Once you have been given a problem to work on you need to make sure you completely understand what is involved. Take some time after you have been given the problem to think about it. You may want to consider asking questions like:

- What caused the problem?
- What does the person giving you the problem already know about it?
- Who else is involved or affected by the problem?
- Are there any time limits for solving the problem?
- What help or support will be available?
- What resources might need to be used?

The type and amount of questions you ask will really depend on the nature of the problem and how much you know about it.

How to show success in solving the problem

Think about what the answer might be to the following types of question:

- How will you know if you have successfully solved the problem?
- What signs or evidence will there be to show your solution has worked and the problem has been fixed?
- What do you expect to happen when you have solved the problem?

These are the questions you need to think about when you are given your problem to solve. You might get a few ideas about how to solve the problem by thinking a little bit about the end result (the solved problem).

Identifying ways to solve the problem

Spend a little time thinking about how you could solve the problem. You need to identify different ideas for tackling the problem. You could do this in a number of different ways. You could:

- Ask someone with experience of solving similar problems for advice

- Have a brainstorming session with friends to come up with ideas, or
- Break the problem down into smaller parts (use the sunshine method or draw spider diagram of the problem to break it down)

Once you have identified some ideas you can begin to sort them out, identifying what is your best way to tackle the problem.

You can find out more about the **sunshine method** on page 6 and **spider diagrams** on page 13

Using help from others

It will be important to show that you can make good use of the help and support of the people around you. You need to show you are able to use help from people like your teacher, supervisor, and classmates or work colleagues to:

- Identify the limits to what you can do
- Decide which options are likely to be the best to use in solving the problem

Let's look in turn at the two areas shown above to get a clearer idea of what might be involved in each.

Finding out what the limits are

You need to explore the problem a little further to see what you are up against, what you have to work with and how you need to work. As far as seeing what you are up against you need to look at how you will avoid making the problem worse or how you can limit the problem's effects as you try to solve it. When you consider what you have to work with you need to look at the resources you may need to use.

Think about what resources you think you will need and then see if they are available. When it comes to looking at how you will work you must consider any health and safety issues that relate to any tools, equipment or material you may want to use. You also might want to consider how your work might affect others.

Time might be another limitation because you need to solve the problem by a certain date. You need to find out more about the time that you have been given to work on your problem.

Think about the following factors as possibly creating limitations to what you can do:

- Resources
- Time
- Training
- Health and safety
- Cost
- The effect or disturbance caused to others

Try to spend a little time thinking about these things yourself before you discuss them with others. This way you can prepare notes of issues you want to talk about and ask advice on, and you can identify questions that you want to ask.

Resources can include:
Materials
Tools
Equipment
Money
People who can give advice
People who can offer support

The Bottom Line

Which options might be the best to use

You may not have appropriate training or experience to carry out some of the options or ways to solve the problem that you identify. You may not be able to get access to the equipment, tools or materials that you want to use. Some options may take too long to try out or you may not be able to get the right level of support. So you need to think in terms of which options are the most feasible for you to try out.

Feasible: achievable or possible, because you have everything that you might need available to you

You need to narrow down all your ideas about how to solve your problem to your most feasible options. You can select your most feasible options for solving your problem by concentrating on options that you:

- Have enough time to try out
- Have the right tools, equipment or material for
- Can get support and advice on
- Have experience of doing or can get the right training to do
- Can do safely
- Will give you a suitable solution to the problem

Some of the factors may not be appropriate because of the type of problem that you have been given. However, you should always aim to narrow your list of options down to the most feasible ones that can deliver a satisfactory solution to the problem.

Collecting evidence

You will be expected to provide at least two examples of meeting these standards.

WHAT YOU NEED TO DO

You need to look at the problem you have been given and make sure you are clear about what is involved. You also need to be clear about how to show you solved it successfully.

You need to come up with different ways of tackling the problem.

Then decide, with help, which are your two best options for solving the problem.

Evidence requirements in a nutshell

The first part of the evidence is where you check you understand the problem you've been given to solve. You must also have a clear idea about how you could prove you have solved the problem successfully.

Once you are clear about what the problem is, you need to show you can come up with different ways of tackling the problem.

Get some assistance to help you decide which of your options are most likely to be successful. Try to get your options narrowed down to your best two.

HINTS FOR CONFIRMING PROBLEMS

- Don't be afraid to ask questions. This is a good way to check your understanding
- Take time once you have been given a problem to think about it before you do anything else
- Find a friend, classmate or colleague to 'bounce' ideas off of. Return the favour by doing the same for them

What might be in your portfolio at this point

1. Descriptions of your problems
2. Copies of questions you asked about each problem
3. Copies of the answers you got to your questions
4. Descriptions of all the ways to solve the problem you identified
5. Any notes from brainstorming sessions you had
6. Any spider diagrams you have drawn
7. A description of the limitations you have to work with. For example, time limits, equipment that must be used or resources that you can't use
8. Notes about why the option you chose was the most appropriate given your circumstances

Planning and trying out options

Getting the go-ahead

You need to sort out which option you are actually going to use to try to solve the problem. Then you need to get the agreement you need or permission to proceed with your option.

If you have other options that weren't quite as good as the one you chose to use, these can be used as a backup plan should something go wrong with your original choice. There may be a set way to solve the problem that could be followed and this might be the best option to use. For example, if you are trying to find a fault in something, there may be a set way of doing it following the manufacturer's instructions.

Plan what you will do

You need to plan what you need to do in order to carry out your chosen option. This will mean identifying all the tasks that you need to do, sorting out the order that you need to do them in and even working out how long each might take.

You should consider using an action plan like the one on page 8 to help you organise your tasks. Alternatively, you could create a simple flowchart to show the sequence of the tasks that you need to do and perhaps even show some of the big decisions that you may need to take along the way. You will find that by drawing a flowchart you have to start to think about which tasks need to be done first to let you get on with other work later.

You can find out more about **flowcharts** on page 14

At this point you also need to be clear about the resources you will need to use and the help that you will need along the way.

Using your plan and the people around you

Having got everything ready and taken time to plan all your work, you now need to get on with it. This means following your plans and making good use of the advice and support you are given by people around you.

Hopefully, you will have identified at an early stage who the useful people to ask for advice or help are. If not, you need to take a close look at your plans and identify where you will need help or support then identify who will be the best person to ask. You may just want someone to 'bounce' ideas off.

PEOPLE WHO MIGHT GIVE USEFUL ADVICE OR SUPPORT

- Subject teacher
- Tutor
- Supervisor
- Health and safety officer
- First aid officer
- Guidance teacher

- Trade union representative
- Audio-visual technicians
- Caretaker staff (e.g. janitor)
- School or college management
- Local businesspeople

When it comes to asking for advice or help there are two key features to keep in mind. These are:

- Knowing who to ask
- Knowing when to ask

- **Who to ask**
  Who to ask for advice or feedback will depend on what you need help with. For example, a guidance teacher may help you with problems within your group (for example, people 'falling out' with each other), while a health and safety officer or design and technology teacher can help with advice on how to use equipment. Basically, you need to show you can seek help and support from appropriate people.
- **When to ask**
  This is linked to acting responsibly. You need to show you can seek advice, help or support when you need it. This means acting in a timely way and not leaving things until it is too late. When you think you need help, you should get help.

Think ahead a little and try to identify when you might need help and identify who would be an appropriate person to ask. You could even let them know when you will need to talk to them and what you will need to talk about. This gives them time to prepare.

Collecting evidence

You will be expected to provide at least two examples of meeting these standards.

Evidence requirements in a nutshell

You are going to have to try out one of your options for solving the problem. This will mean confirming with someone appropriate which option to use to try to solve the problem. Then you can plan how you will carry it out. You need to implement your plan, getting to work on your option to solve the problem, making sure you make good use of the advice and support given by others.

HINTS FOR PLANNING AND TRYING OUT OPTIONS

- Try to plan or find some way of sketching out all the work you need to do first
- Identify all the resources you will need and be clear about when you will need them and how you will get hold of them
- Create backup plans
- Think about alternative equipment and resources that could be used in case of unforeseen circumstances

What might be in your portfolio at this point

1. A copy of your action plan
2. Copies of any flowcharts you draw
3. A list of the resources you will need
4. Notes on any backup plans you have or alternative actions and resources you could use in case something goes wrong
5. A list of the people who can help you and explanations of when you will use their help and why they are appropriate people to ask for help
6. A note about any help you needed saying who gave you the support, why they were good people to use and an explanation of the type of support you got

Checking that problems have been solved

Once you have tried out your chosen option you need to check how well you have done. This means assessing how well you have solved the problem.

How are you going to check you actually solved the problem?

You need to make sure you understand the methods you will use to check that the problem has been solved. At the start of the problem-solving process you should have spent time discussing how you would know if the problem has been solved or not. Now you need to ensure that you understand the methods you are going to use to check that the problem has been solved. This means looking at the methods you are going to use and making sure you are clear about what is involved. Ask questions about anything you are not sure about or don't understand. Make sure you know exactly how to use your methods to check to see if the problem has been solved.

Check that you have solved the problem

Whatever your methods are for checking to see if you have solved the problem, you now need to use them. The methods you use will depend on the type of problem you were faced with. There may be some sort of test, measurements or observation you can do to see if the problem has been solved. If you were fixing something then maybe checking to see if it now works properly, with your supervisor watching, is how you will tell if you have been successful or not.

Whatever your methods are, you need to follow them step by step and check to see if the problem has been solved. You are really checking to see how effective your chosen option was in solving the problem.

Describing your results

You need to describe the results of your checks. The types of questions you need to answer include:

- What happened when you did your check to see if the problem had been solved?
- Was the problem actually solved?
- How could you tell?
- Is the problem likely to come back or recur? If not, then why not?

Sometimes you can't give a definite answer to the question about whether a problem has actually been solved. However, you can give your opinions and back these up with any proof that you have or reasons why you think progress has been made and the problem has been solved.

Improving your approach to problem solving

You need to spend a little time thinking about how you can improve your approach to problem solving. You need to show what you have learned from your experience. Think of what went well and what went less well and ask yourself 'If I knew then what I know now, what would I do differently?'. Alternatively, try to answer the question 'If I had to do it all over again, what would I do differently and why?'.

Think carefully about each aspect of your problem-solving process. Include:

- What you first thought about the problem
- How you came up with different ways to solve it
- Your planning
- How you carried out the work
- Your methods for checking if the problem had been solved

All you are trying to do is to show that you have learned from your experience.

Collecting evidence

You will be expected to provide at least two examples of meeting these standards.

WHAT YOU NEED TO DO

You will be given ways to check that your problem has been solved. You need to follow these methods accurately.

You must describe the results of tackling the problem in a clear way.

Finally, you need to identify ways of improving your approach to problem solving.

Evidence requirements in a nutshell

Once you have tried out your chosen option for solving the problem, you need to check if the problem actually has been solved. You are going to check how effective your option was in solving the problem. This will mean following the methods you have been given for checking if the problem has been dealt with accurately and describing the results clearly.

Finally, you need to identify how you could improve your approach to problem solving.

HINTS FOR CHECKING IF YOUR PROBLEMS HAVE BEEN SOLVED

- If you don't understand the methods you have been given to check your problem has been solved, then ask questions
- Take time to think through what you will do once you have been given your methods for checking the problem. Don't just rush into it
- Remember to look for evidence that the problem has been solved

---

What might be in your portfolio at this point

1. Records of the methods you were given and how you used them. Include records of any questions you had and the answers you received
2. Descriptions of the results of tackling the problems
3. Statements from people who can say that the problem has been solved
4. Notes explaining how you think you could improve your approach to problem solving

Evidence for level 2 (PS)

What is level 2 all about?

The unit is about applying problem-solving skills to find a suitable solution. You will be expected to show that you can identify problems and come up with ways of solving them. You must then show you can plan and try out options and apply methods you have been given to check if problems have been solved.

Part of the problem-solving process will involve identifying the main features of each problem. At this level the problem will have a limited number of possible ways to solve it and you will be working with clear guidelines and advice about which option to implement.

Plans will be expected to be straightforward, but may involve changes as you work through the problem and perhaps encounter unforeseen circumstances. You may also have to work with resources you may not have used before.

You will be expected to provide at least two examples of meeting the standard for the three areas of the problem-solving key skill. These are:

- Identifying problems and options
- Planning and trying out options
- Checking if problems have been solved

What is a problem?

When you want to bridge the gap between your current situation (where you are now) and a desired situation (where you want to be) with no apparent way of doing it, then you have a problem. In other words, how to get to where you would prefer to be is the problem.

Here are a few examples to illustrate the range of possibilities:

- Diagnosing faults and repairing equipment
- Improving the performance of a system
- Working out something using a particular software package
- Organising an event, performance or fundraiser
- Designing or making something to specification
- Findings ways to reduce waste or cost

Any learning situation where you don't understand something, or any

practical challenge that you might face, could be seen as a problem. Note that in the examples given each problem could be broken down into more precise statements.

Identifying problems and options

What the unit expects

Identifying the problem and describing its main features

First of all you need to identify that there is a problem, then you need to find out what you can about the problem. As you look to identify the main features of the problem, try to break it down into smaller issues or mini-problems. Breaking it down into smaller problems also gives you a clearer idea of how to find suitable solutions and how different events and activities might need to be ordered in your plans. This will also help you become more familiar with the *extent* of the problem.

At this stage you can consider techniques like brainstorming to help you get down all your thoughts about the problem on paper. Also consider conducting a 'skills audit' or SWOT analysis to determine how prepared you are to tackle the problem and what you will need in terms of help and support. This is also a useful stage to use techniques like spider diagrams or mind maps to help you think through the extent of the problem and what might be involved. The more detail you get on the problem and the more you think about what is involved, then the more information you will have to help you come up with ways of solving it. It will also help you with your planning when you decide which option to implement.

How will you know the problem has been solved?

Having thought about the problem, you now need to think about the possible solution. You need to consider what the solution would look like, for example, what will it feel like or what will have changed if the problem has been solved. Ask yourself, 'How will I tell if the problem has been solved?' You may be able to run tests to show everything is working well, if the problem involved fixing something, or you may be able to ask others if the problem has been solved because it affected them. There may be standards that you have to meet when solving the problem.

You need to think about how you will know the problem has been solved or how well it has been solved. You can get a better idea of criteria or assessment standards for measuring your problems by asking others involved what they expect from you, by looking at relevant sources of information or by talking to people who have dealt with similar problems.

The type of criteria you use really depends on the nature of the problem you are trying to solve. Make sure the criteria are clear, appropriate and can be used to measure or gauge whether you have been successful or not.

You must check with your tutor, teacher or assessor that the criteria you will use are appropriate and that the criteria are comfortable with

---

Extent: the range or scope of something

For more information see **brainstorming** (page 10), **spider diagrams** (page 13), **mapping** (page 16) and **skills audits** and **SWOT analysis** (page 44)

Criteria: standards used to make judgements about something

them. Consult your teacher as you draw up your draft criteria or standards for assessing your problem. Look at their suggestions and then finalise your criteria, making sure you have taken account of their suggestions.

You are going to come back to this work when you evaluate the success of your problem solving.

Find ways to tackle the problem

Having found out all you can about the problem, attention turns to deciding the best ways to identify the various options available to you for solving the problem. You need to establish which method is best suited or most likely to generate options for tackling the problem.

You could consider any of the following methods as options for solving your problem:

- Discussions or consultation with others (e.g. brainstorming sessions)
- Looking at solutions to similar problems
- Learning from other people's relevant experience
- Using your own initiative and imagination
- Simulating the problem in some way to find out more about it (e.g. role play, 3D modelling or drawing, depending on the nature of the problem)

The key skill will ask for *two* possible options that could be used to tackle the problem.

Weighing up your options

Once you have a range of ways to solve the problem, decide which is the most suitable. Consider what the end result of taking each option might be. How close will each particular option get you to where you want to be? Having thought about each option in terms of the outcome it could deliver, you need to weigh up each in terms of what might be involved in carrying them out.

You may not have appropriate training or experience to carry out some of the options that you identify. You may not be able to get access to the equipment, tools or materials that you want to use. Some options may take too long to try out or you may not be able to get the right level of support for some options. So you need to think in terms of which options are the most feasible to use.

You need to narrow down all your ideas about how to solve your problem until you reach your most feasible options. You can select your most feasible options by concentrating on options that you:

- Have enough time to try out
- Have the right tools, equipment or material for
- Can get support and advice on
- Have experience of doing or can get the right training to do
- Can do safely
- Will deliver a suitable solution to the problem

Some of the factors may not be appropriate because of the type of problem that you have been given. However, you should always aim to narrow your list of options down to the most feasible ones that can deliver a satisfactory solution to the problem.

You can scrutinise each option by thinking about each in terms of the resources, risks and rewards it will involve.

- **Resources**
  Determine what support from other people will be needed. This includes their expertise and the time you think both you and they will need to make available. Other resources may include time or money, e.g. for expenses if you need to buy anything or travel, and the equipment, tools or materials you will need. Time is another factor to consider. How long will each option take?
- **Risks**
  These include any health and safety issues that may relate to any practical work, visits or any other aspect of what you propose to do. This part is worth discussing with other people to make sure that all the necessary precautions are taken and requirements met.
- **Rewards**
  Think of how each option might compare in terms of time, cost and the final outcome. Which outcome is closest to your desired outcome?

Once you have all the information collected about each option, select the one that is the most appropriate to use. Remember this may not be the most effective one but should be the most feasible. This means it will be the best response you can make to the problem-solving challenge given the available time, money, expertise or experience, resources or ability. The option likely to give the best result may be too expensive or take too long. This is why you need to consider the most feasible that will deliver an acceptable solution to the problem. Try to match your own personal strengths with your options and avoid ones that involve areas of personal weakness. This is where having a SWOT analysis and using it to help compare your options would help.

Before you proceed, you also need to identify how you will get the information and advice from others. You need to consider issues like:

- How the problems affect other people
- How to get information and advice from people with experience of handling similar problems
- An opinion from others on what is possible, given your time limits and other constraints that you face, e.g. on equipment or tools

Collecting evidence

You will be expected to provide at least two examples of meeting these standards.

You must identify a problem then accurately describe its main features. You must also describe how you could show that the problem has been successfully solved.

Then you must come up with a range of different ways to tackle the problem.

Finally, you need to narrow your options down to the two most realistic ways to solve the problem successfully. You can use help from others when appropriate.

Evidence requirements in a nutshell

To start the whole problem-solving process you need to identify a problem. Once you have a suitable problem to work on you need to:

1. Accurately describe the problem's main features, e.g. what issues are involved, can it be broken down into smaller problems and so on
2. Describe how you could show you succeeded in solving the problem

Once you know a little more about the problem, come up with different ways to solve it.

Decide which two options have the most realistic chances of success, using help from others at appropriate times.

HINTS FOR IDENTIFYING PROBLEMS

- Keep clear records of what the problem is
- Have a clear explanation of the scope and nature of the problem
- Get feedback from your teacher or assessor on your criteria for telling whether the problem has been solved or not
- Put your different solutions to the problem in a table to help compare one against the other more clearly
- Explain why the methods you used to help you identify ways to tackle the problem were useful
- Keep records of any brainstorming, notes of discussions or interviews, etc.

What might be in your portfolio at this point

1. Copies of any brainstorming notes
2. Copies of spider diagrams and/or mind maps
3. The results of your skills audits or SWOT analysis
4. Any tables used to compare options
5. Details of all your options and the processes you used to narrow them down
6. Lists of the resources, risks and rewards associated with each of your options.
7. An explanation of what turned out to be your most feasible option

The Bottom Line

Planning and trying out options

Getting the go-ahead

You need to sort out which option you are actually going to use to try to solve the problem. Then you need to get the agreement you need or permission to proceed with your option.

Keep your other options open. These could be useful backup plans should something go wrong with your original choice. There may be a set way to solve the problem that could be followed and this might be the best option to use. For example, if you are trying to find a fault in something, there may be a set way of doing it, following the manufacturer's instructions.

Planning

You need to draw up plans to help you solve the problem. Include in your planning, stages to review your progress. These can be put in after interim targets or when small tasks or objectives are due to be completed. Plans should give details of the expected timelines and sequence the events that must take place, showing key decision points. This is where you could use flowcharts or other techniques to help you plan. Consider putting together an action plan like the one on page 8 once you have established the sequence of tasks and activities you need to do.

You should also consider drawing up alternative arrangements (contingency plans) just in case something unexpected happens. Good plans will have backup suggestions for resources and tasks as standby arrangements, just in case.

Think through what could go wrong and try to create scenarios for how you will deal with these difficulties if they occur. This will help you begin to construct a contingency plan and alternative strategies for keeping the work moving forward regardless of whether you hit difficulties.

You will find out that time spent on thorough planning will make the implementation and review stages a lot easier to carry out.

Implementing

Now you can get to work implementing your plan. Get hold of the resources you need to make everything happen and then get on with it. Make sure other people involved are kept up to date with your progress, make use of appropriate people for feedback and advice and make the most of their expertise and experience to help you find a workable solution. Make sure you use the time that you have available effectively.

Monitoring and reviewing

The plan itself should be a dynamic set of arrangements that can be changed and adapted as circumstances change. Allow time in your planning to stop and review your progress and check on how your plan is performing. As you learn from your own experience of using your plan, make changes where necessary to help it run more effectively. By monitoring how you are doing and building stages to review your progress you can learn from what you have done and spend a little time thinking about what is coming up. You can then check to see if your plans are still appropriate. This way you can respond to any unforeseen circumstances or can invite others to comment on your progress and make adjustments based on their feedback.

Try to be honest and objective about your progress and the effectiveness of your plans and when changes are necessary make them. You need to avoid stubbornly sticking to your plan when you can adapt it to help you deal with changes more effectively.

Using the people around you

You need to make good use of the advice and support of people around you. Hopefully, you will have identified at an early stage which people will be able to give you useful advice and guidance when you need it. If not, you need take a close look at your plans and identify where you will need help or support, then identify who will be the best person to ask. You may just want someone to 'bounce' ideas off. Anything that you are not sure about must be discussed with an appropriate person before you go any further.

PEOPLE WHO MIGHT GIVE USEFUL ADVICE OR SUPPORT

- People affected by the problem
- Subject teacher
- Tutor
- Supervisor
- Health and safety officer
- First aid officer
- Guidance teacher
- Trade union representative
- Audio-visual technicians
- Caretaker staff (e.g. janitor)
- School or college management
- Local businesspeople

When it comes to asking for advice or help there are two key features to keep in mind. These are:

- Knowing who to ask
- Knowing when to ask

- **Who to ask**
  Who to ask for advice or feedback will depend on what you need help with. For example, a guidance teacher may help you with problems within your group (for example, people 'falling out' with each other), while a health and safety officer or design and technology teacher can offer advice on how to use equipment. Basically, you need to show you can seek help and support from appropriate people.
- **When to ask**
  This is linked to acting responsibly. You need to show you can seek advice, help or support when you need it. This means acting in a

timely way and not leaving things until it is too late. When you think you need help, you should get help.

Think ahead a little and try to identify when you might need help and identify who would be an appropriate person to ask. You could even let them know when you will need to talk to them and what you will need to talk about. This gives them time to prepare.

Collecting evidence

You will be expected to provide at least two examples of meeting these standards.

WHAT YOU NEED TO DO

Get permission from an appropriate person to try out a particular option, then plan how to carry it out.

Use your plan and show you can organise the relevant tasks when carrying out your option. You also need to show you can make changes to your plan if necessary.

Show you can get and make effective use of support when you need it.

Evidence requirements in a nutshell

Now you have to take one of your options forward. Agree with an appropriate person which option should be used to try to solve the problem, then plan how to carry out this option.

Put your plans into action, showing you can organise the relevant tasks. If you need to make changes to your plans, make them.

Show you can get hold of and make good use of the support you need.

HINTS FOR PLANNING AND TRYING OUT OPTIONS

- Find ways to monitor and check your progress
- Find time to review your work and to plan for the next stages
- Establish early on who and where your different sources of advice and help are
- Flowcharts can be useful as a way to check on your progress and can be used as evidence
- Have some way of tracking and recording the changes you need to make, including explanations of why the changes where necessary

---

What might be in your portfolio at this point

1. An explanation of how you chose which option to use
2. Copies of any flowcharts or action plans you created to help you carry out your idea for solving the problem
3. A list of the resources you will need
4. A list of the people who can help you, with an explanation of when you will use their help and why they are appropriate people to ask

Checking that problems have been solved

Understanding how to check your problem has been solved

You must ensure you understand the methods you have been given for checking if your problem has been solved. You could make sure you understand by asking questions to clarify something. You could watch someone else demonstrate how to do it or you could do some practice runs of your methods yourself. How you make sure you understand really depends on the methods you are using but your ultimate goal is to be completely clear what it is you have to do before you start doing it.

Checking you've solved the problem

This part of the evidence requirements is about identifying possible ways to check if the problem has been solved. This is where you could use the assessment criteria or standards you should have identified when you explored the nature of the problem early on. If you have these criteria, check that they are still relevant and use them to assess how well you have done in solving the problem.

Describe your results

Once you have applied your methods for measuring your success you need to describe the results and draw conclusions from them. Your conclusions need to address how successfully the problem was solved and how each aspect of the problem was dealt with.

Why did you do that?

An important aspect of this part of the key skill is explaining your decisions and actions during your problem-solving process. At this stage you need to be explaining your choice of option. If you had to make changes or adjustments to your plans or ended up using different resources then you should explain the reasons for this too.

The aim here is to show that you were in control of what was happening, that you were able to execute your plans successfully and, if you were faced with problems, that you were able to take appropriate decisions to deal with these issues.

Strengths and weaknesses

You need to look back over your whole approach and produce an honest account of how you think you did. You will need to identify the strengths and weaknesses of your approach to problem solving, taking care to comment on each stage of the process. Look at each stage in turn from exploring the problem through to your final solution. You should consider factors like:

Methods for checking problems could involve:
Doing tests
Observing
Measuring
Sampling
Inspecting
Asking others for comments
Watching someone test your solution

The Bottom Line

Exploring your problem	Planning	Resources
• How well you understood the problem's nature and extent • How effective the methods you used to find out more about the problem were • Selection methods for choosing best option • Ways of coming up with ideas about tackling the problem	• How successful the plan was • How useful contingency plans were • How well you responded to changes in circumstances • Did you stick to the time limits? • The expected or unexpected consequences of your work	• Availability of resources • Suitability of resources • The role of other people • How effectively you used the key resources

Try to assess how well you did in each area of the work and comment on the factors that helped or hindered your progress.

Would you do anything differently if you faced a similar problem?

This is the question that you really need to ask yourself. You have had the chance to consider the successes and failures of your problem solving and have gained some valuable experience along the way. Now you need to use all this experience to describe what you would do differently if you were faced with a similar problem.

Start by asking yourself:

- Should I have done things differently?
- If I had to do it all again what changes would I make and why?

You have the benefit of hindsight and you need to try to show how you would learn from your successes and mistakes. Consider how you made decisions, how you came up with ideas and options and how you planned. Ask yourself 'If I knew then what I know now, what would I have done differently?' Remember to explain your answers saying why you would make the changes you identified.

Collecting evidence

You will be expected to provide at least two examples of meeting these standards.

WHAT YOU NEED TO DO

You will be given methods to use to check if the problem has been solved and you need to show you can apply these methods accurately.

You then need to clearly describe your results and explain the key decisions you took at each stage of tackling the problem.

Finally, you need to identify the strengths and weaknesses of the approach you took to problem solving. This will also involve describing what you would do differently if you were faced with a similar problem.

Evidence requirements in a nutshell

Once you have tried out one of your options you need to check if the problem has been solved. This means accurately applying the methods that you have been given to gauge your success.

You must then show you can describe the results of applying your methods.

To help others understand how you set about solving the problem, explain the decisions you took at each stage of the process. For example, how you chose which option to implement, your planning decisions, how you handled difficulties, etc.

You must show you can identify the strengths and weaknesses of your approach to problem solving. You must also describe what you would do differently if you met a similar problem. This is a way of showing what you have learned.

HINTS FOR CHECKING IF PROBLEMS WERE SOLVED

- Identify early on useful evaluation criteria or methods to identify if your problem has been solved. Start thinking about the problem and what the solution might look like
- Don't be afraid to change how you intend to evaluate your solution to the problem
- Make sure the eventual methods you use are appropriate
- Keeping diaries of journals can be a useful to remind you of how things went

What might be in your portfolio at this point

1. Records of the methods you used to check how effective your options were in solving the problems
2. Descriptions of the strengths and weaknesses of your approach to problem solving (have notes for each problem solved)
3. An explanation of what you learned solving each problem and how you could use this experience or make changes when solving a similar problem
4. Statements from others affected by the problem that could say you dealt with it successfully
5. Statements from others who witnessed your dealing with the problem successfully

Part 3: Opportunities

This part contains suggestions to help get you thinking about how and where you can generate key skill evidence.

At the beginning of any new course, module or unit, take some time to look at the subjects and activities involved and think about how one of the key skills could help you achieve your subject goals. Be on the look-out for particular parts of your course that overlap the key skill requirements allowing you to generate evidence for both without too much extra work. When you find a relationship between a course topic or activity and the key skill evidence requirements, sketch out a few ideas and notes and discuss them with your course teacher and/or key skills assessor.

This part is split into two sections:

- **Course-related opportunities**
  The section aims to get you thinking about how to generate evidence in a wide range of courses. But don't just look at the courses you are taking! Look at the related courses for more ideas; for instance Business students should also look for ideas in Leisure and Tourism and Retail for ideas. It may even be worth looking at other courses just out of interest. This will give you more ideas about how you could generate evidence.

- **Evidence from other activities**
  This section deals with general opportunities to gather evidence that are not related to any course in particular: Creating a webpage (WWO); Cooking (WWO); Gardening (WWO); Working on a school, college or workplace publication (WWO); Taking part in a club or event (WWO); Study groups (WWO); Homework and course work strategies (LP); Outward bound courses and extra-curricular activities (LP); Taking your driving test (LP); Hobbies and interests (LP); What do you want to do next? (PS); Fault finding (PS)

Though the activities in the second section are aimed at a particular key skill, some could be used for more than one key skill. For example, creating a webpage could be viewed as an opportunity for problem solving or working with others.

Course-related opportunities

You need to work closely with your subject teacher if you intend to use the subject to help you generate evidence for 'Working with others', 'Improving own learning and performance' or 'Problem solving'. They will be able to help you set objectives (WWO), set short-term targets (LP) and identify problems (PS). Your teachers will be useful sources of advice and guidance and can help you review your work. They will also advise you about where best to find opportunities within your courses and help you make sure the key skill work supports and doesn't interfere with your subject work.

Art and Design

Context

The following ideas look at opportunities to generate 'Working with others' (WWO), 'Improving own learning and performance' (LP) and 'Problem solving' (PS) in both Art and Design GCSEs and Vocational GCSEs.

Working with others

Exploring other people's work

In both types of qualifications there will be opportunities to look at a variety of approaches and methods used in Art and Design and the contributions made by contemporary practitioners and others from different times and cultures to art, craft and design. This could give you a chance to generate WWO evidence. For example, if you are asked to explore the art, craft or design work of a professional, this could be an opportunity to work in a small group. Alternatively, you may be asked to find out about a given style or different individuals in a particular movement or period. You could plan with the group what needs to be done and who should do what. Make sure you confirm your understanding of who is doing what in the group by going over everyone's individual responsibilities and the group's working arrangements.

You could be working with others to collect relevant information and visual evidence. As you work together to collect the information you need, make sure you keep checking with the WWO key skills specification to make sure you are covering all the evidence requirements.

Working in art

When you are producing a portfolio of artwork that includes developmental ideas as well as your finished artwork there could be a chance to do some of the work in a small group. For example, you could carry out an investigation into using or working with 2D media as a group. Get your teacher to either set or help you set clear objectives for the group and check that everyone understands what needs to be done and by when.

Plan with the group what needs to be done to help you explore the media, materials and techniques fully. Then confirm that everyone is clear about their responsibilities and the group working arrangements. Work with the group to produce a range of developmental ideas making sure that these are recorded in sketchbooks, studies, design sheets or models. Make sure you carry out the tasks necessary to meet your responsibilities and work co-operatively to help others meet their objectives and responsibilities.

Work together to identify and review your progress by discussing and sharing your visual records and results. Though you will be expected to work individually on your finished art pieces, check to see if you are allowed to work in groups as you experiment with media and develop relevant skills.

Working in 3D crafts

When you are producing a portfolio of 3D craft work that includes developmental ideas as well as your finished art work there could be a chance to do some of the work in a small group. For example, you could carry out an investigation into using or working with 3D media in a group situation. Get your teacher to either set or help you set clear objectives for the group and check that everyone understands what needs to be done and by when.

Follow the same steps given above in the 2D idea. You could use the same type of approach when working with graphic design and surface design.

Preparing for employment

If you have to produce an employment folder this might be a good opportunity to generate evidence for working in a one-to-one situation. The other person could be your tutor or careers counsellor as long as they are not assessing you as well. Agree with them what needs to be done to find relevant employment information. Once you have agreed what your objectives are, and you are clear about your responsibilities and the other working arrangements, you can work out what tasks need to be done to meet these objectives.

Make sure you keep any records of the information you find. These could be job applications, list of telephone contacts made, personal CV and questions to ask at interview.

Health and safety in art and design

As you are investigating health and safety issues for an Art and Design workspace, consider working in pairs. This will help you fulfil the WWO

requirements for providing an example of working on a straightforward activity in a one-to-one situation. Once you have been given your objectives, spend time discussing them with your work partner then ask any questions that you have about your objectives. If you are doing this as a level 2 WWO activity, work with your partner to identify suitable objectives.

Improving own learning and performance

Visual language

You may be asked to explore the application of visual language and allied techniques. As you learn to develop visual language skills should be able to generate evidence for all aspects of the LP key skill. At level 1 you could:

- Check understanding of which techniques to use, the formal elements to be explored and the time available. Then plan how to combine formal elements and techniques to achieve different effects
- Follow the plan, discussing with others what is being done and what can be done to improve the work
- Review achievements and progress in developing skills in 2D and 3D visual language and discuss these with peers and others

At level 2 you could be looking at the following:

- Target the practical activity part of improving your performance
- You could focus on developing visual language skills like mark-making techniques and object-making techniques
- Work out and agree targets with the tutor and plan how to combine formal elements and techniques to achieve different effects
- Create and use a plan showing you can make decisions about combination of formal elements and techniques
- Review achievements and the progress you made in developing 2D and/or 3D visual language making sure you use the correct technical terminology

Materials and techniques

There could be an opportunity to generate LP evidence by exploring the use of 2D techniques and media or 3D techniques in a range of resistant and non-resistant materials. You would follow a similar process to the one mentioned in the visual language suggestions above.

Understanding social, historical and cultural contexts

There will be an opportunity to do some personal study as you investigate how images and artefacts relate to their social, historical and cultural contexts. This may mean establishing short-term targets with your key skills tutor, Art and Design teacher and even perhaps someone in your History department. These people are all possible sources of help and advice. Try to focus on something that you are particularly interested in. That way you will find it more enjoyable and easier to stay motivated.

Problem solving

Working to a project brief

There may be an opportunity to look at tasks involving working to a set brief as an exercise in problem solving. You could treat the brief as the problem-solving challenge and investigate the best ways to solve it.

Confirm your understanding of the brief (problem) with the teacher and collect visual information to create a range of early ideas. These ideas will become your range of problem-solving options. You need at least two possible options for meeting the brief.

Follow your plans using advice and support from others to help you cope with any difficulties you encounter and work within your constraints and the deadlines of your brief. Check whether the brief has been met by presenting your final piece of work. Back it up with an explanation of how it meets the requirements of the brief. Make sure you include an explanation of how you would improve your approach to meeting the brief (problem solving) if you had to do it again.

2D and 3D visual language

When you are developing your understanding of 2D and 3D visual language there may be an opportunity to follow through a particular theme or brief for one area of specialism in art, craft or design.

You could identify a particular specialism and come up with at least two options for exploring the formal elements and techniques used to develop visual language. You could then plan to try out at least one option for combining elements and techniques. Make sure you take time to discuss what you are trying out with your peers and seek advice and guidance at appropriate times.

Use the theme, topic or brief and visual records to demonstrate that the area of specialism has been fully explored and discuss the skills that you have developed. Make sure you use the correct technical terms when you discuss what you have found out and how you have resolved your original problem. Using the correct terminology is another way of demonstrating what you have learned.

Working in 3D crafts, graphic design or surface design

You could set the question 'How do I find out about a professional craftsperson, graphic designer or surface designer?' as your problem to be solved. This will allow you to begin to generate evidence for your problem-solving key skill.

The following example uses finding out about a 3D professional craftsperson as the problem-solving challenge. You could use similar steps for investigating graphic or surface designers.

Confirm your understanding of the focus of the investigation with your tutor and identify the most appropriate solutions (for example, organising a visit or through work experience). Then you can work out which option is the best to take forward. Plan how to carry out your chosen option, making sure you make good use of the advice and support available.

One way to check how effective your option has been is to see how well you are able to meet your vocational evidence requirements in the Art and Design unit. For example, if you have found out a lot of information about the professional craftsperson you were investigating then your chosen option must have been quite effective. If you have gathered sufficient information to help you understand the work of the craftsperson then you will have solved your problem.

Materials, techniques and technology

You may be asked to investigate media materials and associated tools, equipment and technology. This may be an opportunity for you to generate PS evidence. Work with your Art and Design teacher or key skill tutor to frame a PS issue or question for you to answer.

You could look to identify a topic or theme and come up with at least two ways to investigate the combinations of 2D media, 3D materials and mark-making techniques. You would then look to try out at least one option for combining materials, techniques and technology. Plan what needs to be carried out and make sure that you make good use of the help and support around you.

Make sure you keep visual records to check and show that the investigation has been well organised and that creative work is skilful and controlled.

Business

See also: **Leisure and Tourism**, page 179, and **Retail and Distributive Services**, page 196

Context

The following ideas look at opportunities to generate 'Working with others' (WWO), 'Improving own learning and performance' (LP) and 'Problem solving' (PS) in both Business Studies GCSEs and Business Vocational GCSEs.

Working with others

Marketing

If you have the chance to learn about marketing or to carry out a market research project, this provides you with the opportunity to generate WWO evidence. The focus could be on identifying and satisfying customer needs in a competitive business environment. You may even be using market research as a way to help find out more about customer needs or markets.

You should be able to agree WWO objectives based on your intended course aims and will have a range of issues to discuss and plan as well as different responsibilities and working arrangements to sort out. You will need to:

● Agree the market research techniques you will use (for example, surveys or questionnaires)

- Organise your primary research methods and co-ordinate the activity allocating different roles and responsibilities
- Agree which secondary sources to use
- Agree how to analyse and discuss findings, draw conclusions and present your results

You could even go on to work out a marketing strategy based on your results. This will mean applying the results of your market research to develop a suitable marketing strategy based on your findings.

If you think that doing the market research and then working on a marketing strategy is too ambitious a task, concentrate on one or the other as the focus of your WWO work. Alternatively, one could be the focus of one-to-one work, the other the focus of group work. This way this single topic could help you meet most of the WWO key skill requirements.

School activities

Very often Business Studies departments are at the centre of wider school or college student business activities. Initiatives like Young Enterprise or other business activities could be used as a way to generate WWO evidence.

Exam preparation for finance or accounting units or modules

There could be an opportunity to use WWO to organise a study group to revise a challenging subject area like finance or accounting. You may be able to practise and support each other as a group, generating WWO evidence while you study. The group could set targets and use homework, class tests and mock exams as a way to evaluate your performance. Meetings could be used to discuss case study work or topics that are proving to be particularly difficult. Try to focus on a particular aspect of finance or accounts rather than dealing with the whole course.

Internal assessment projects

Business Studies courses like the GCSE may have a significant amount of the final grade given to internal assessment – for example, a project. You might be able to set up a support group of people working on similar project ideas to:

- Discuss work
- Share ideas
- Seek feedback and advice
- Find support

This could be a useful way of helping to improve the quality of your Business work and collect evidence for the WWO key skill. Keep time set apart to plan and set objectives, individual responsibilities and arrangements and to discuss how the group is performing. By setting some time aside at each meeting to discuss the group set-up and look at the type of WWO requirements and evidence you need to create you will be able to meet the key skill needs.

Remember that you will be expected to submit your own individual work for internal assessment. So make sure your WWO group is about discussing ideas and finding support. It should not be seen as a way to share work. This may result in being penalised in your Business assessment so be careful and make sure your Business teacher is aware of what you are doing and ask them for advice.

Producing a case study of a business

You could use this type of work as an opportunity to generate evidence of a straightforward activity carried out in a one-to-one situation or in a group. You could:

- Identify objectives for the work
- Sort out who will do what and identify working arrangements
- Plan the activity with your work partner or other members of your group
- Consider using action plans for all group members and share the information around
- Work out the tasks you need to do and the timelines
- Make sure you support others in the group and know when, where and how to get help and support
- Make sure you exchange information on your progress
- Agree ways of improving your work with others

Improving own learning and performance

Becoming more confident in a particular topic

Take time to look at the range and type of learning and content in your Business course and try to identify an area that may cause you difficulty. You could use this as the focus of your LP activity. Consider taking topics like Accounting, Economics or Finance and using one of these as the basis for LP work. These types of areas generally tend to give students the most problems and the key skill can provide a useful way to help support your course work and perhaps help you cope better with the course assessment demands.

Start to work on the target-setting process, working out timelines and identifying who could be useful sources of support and guidance. You also need to assess what self-help guides are available. Are there any 'teach yourself' books, revision guides, specialist CD-ROMs and/or specimen exam papers that can be used.

The aim is for you to devise a learning programme that supports your course work, allowing you to spend more time on a specific topic within the course content. Get your teacher to work with you to set appropriate targets and help you work out how best to support your class work.

Problem solving

Marketing

You could frame a marketing challenge as a problem-solving activity. You will certainly be able to come up with two alternative strategies to choose from and then implement. Market research could help you decide which strategy to choose. Make sure you clear this approach with your key skill assessor. Try to look at straightforward marketing problems and strategies, perhaps in markets where there are only one or two competitors.

Personal finance

This type of topic may be an opportunity to gather evidence for problem solving. If you are asked to produce a guide on personal finance suitable for a friend, your problem would be based around finding out which savings scheme is the most appropriate and best suited to your friend. You may have a couple of ideas about how to work out the best personal finance plan. Focus on ways to find out about the personal circumstances of the person involved and how to find out more about the savings schemes. You need to test one of these options out, choose what you think is the best scheme and then assess how suitable your chosen savings scheme is based on your friend's personal circumstances and needs.

Construction and the Built Environment

See also: **Design and Technology**, page 151, and **Engineering**, page 154, for further ideas

Context

Both the core units and the optional units within the Vocational GCSE will provide you with a range of opportunities to generate evidence. Here are a few suggestions for how to use the compulsory units in the Vocational GCSE to create key skill evidence. This information is designed to help you start planning and collecting the evidence you need.

Working with others

Construction technology and design

Units or topics that involve producing a design portfolio from a given customer brief could be used to generate evidence for the WWO group or one-to-one evidence requirements. When working individually, your relationship with the customer could be the basis for the one-to-one work. If you are working in a group you could look to include a group investigation of the space and produce exploratory sketches, drawings and associated notes as part of the WWO group objectives and responsibilities.

Area or building case studies

Consider working in small groups or even with a partner to investigate and collect information on an area or building you have to produce a case study for. This gives you an opportunity to meet the group or one-to-one WWO evidence requirements.

Development of the built environment

You could work with others to investigate your local area and search for and discuss the information you need to complete your vocational work. Collecting the appropriate information, planning visits and exploring the local area could all be turned into objectives for your group.

Construction materials and processes

You could work in pairs to investigate a particular material or craft process. This will help you share the vocational work relating to collecting appropriate information with a work partner and give you someone to discuss your findings with. While you do this you could also be generating evidence for the WWO key skill requirements to show you can work in a one-to-one situation.

You could use the same idea for investigating construction crafts, looking at the skills, tools and equipment involved.

Improving own learning and performance

Developing a skill

You may want to add to the skill elements of the Vocational GCSE course by developing a specific skill. You could use the LP key skill as a way to oganise your approach and to develop a learning programme to help you achieve your goal. The skills could be in any area of construction craft skills. It really depends on what your interest is. You would be generating evidence for that part of the LP key skill that asks you to show you can improve your performance by carrying out a straightforward practical activity.

You could develop craft or hand skills by looking to take an NVQ unit. The LP key skill can help you devise a learning programme with suitable targets to help you take the NVQ unit. The NVQ unit will help encourage you to develop competence in an area of skills that you may have touched on in your Construction course. It will allow you to develop your skills further while also encouraging you to take a more independent approach to your own learning. You don't even need to do the actual NVQ, just look at the appropriate standards and design a learning and skills development programme around them with your tutor.

You might be particularly interested in drawing so why not make it the focus of your LP activity. You could use it as a way to generate evidence for improving your performance by learning through a straightforward practical activity.

Construction materials and processes

Consider investigating a particular craft process. If you are particularly interested in a craft process, perhaps because you are thinking about working in this area, use this as the focus for your LP work. As you learn more about the area you could be creating evidence for the part of the key skill that asks you to show you can improve your performance by studying a straightforward subject. The added advantage may be that as you follow up your interest you help to improve your chances of better grades in your Construction course.

Work carefully with your Construction tutor to set appropriate short-term targets based around the particular craft process that interests you.

Problem solving

Construction technology and design

There may be an opportunity to generate PS evidence as you produce a report about construction technology and design. You will need your teacher's help to frame part of the vocational work as a problem to be solved. Then you can start to identify options to solve the problem. You can then put one option into action and then judge the results.

Construction materials and processes

Carrying out investigations into craft processes can be a useful way to generate PS key skills. You could either focus the investigation on the craft processes themselves or alternatively look at investigating the health and safety issues involved. Work with your tutor to try to identify a possible problem to work on, then start thinking about options that you could put into practice to try to come up with the solution.

There may be another opportunity to start generating PS evidence by carrying out some work on particular materials. You could be investigating raw materials looking at ways to come up with alternative materials or exploring ways to reduce costs. Perhaps you could focus on the characteristics of materials, getting your teacher to set a problem for you to solve that relates to materials properties and characteristics.

Design and Technology

See also: **Engineering**, page 154; **Manufacturing**, page 183; and **Hospitality and Catering**, page 168, for further ideas

Context

Your GCSE will require you to design and make good quality products. You will have an opportunity to generate evidence for all three key skills during your course work or as you prepare for different assessments. The guidance provided focuses on types of activity common in most Design and Technology (D&T) courses.

Working with others

Design work

You may need to conduct some research to find out how best to solve a design problem or to come up with a better design solution. You could approach this task as part of a small group.

The group activity could focus on collecting information, selecting and

Opportunities

using research techniques and then implementing them. Once the information has been collected, the group could discuss it as well as any ideas group members have relating to what needs to go into the final design brief or specification.

This means that WWO objectives would need to focus on two group activities (collecting evidence and discussing ideas). You would need to sort out who does what, agreeing individual responsibilities and working arrangements. For the second part of the group work, objectives and responsibilities are more about active participation and involvement in the group discussion sessions. This means not only bringing ideas and issues to discuss but also encouraging others to take part.

When you have fully discussed the information collected and everyone has ideas about what the design brief or specification needs to address you can review the work with others and agree ways of improving group work in future. You may be able to act on these suggestions for improving the collaborative work if you work in the same group for another activity, for example making a product.

Making products

Whether you are involved in making a single prototype or batch producing there will be an opportunity to build your WWO portfolio of evidence. It really depends on the size of the task you do and the type of product you intend to make. Larger, more complex tasks will give you a better opportunity to meet more of the WWO requirements. It will be easier to get everyone fully involved in carrying out individual as well as group responsibilities.

In this type of activity the WWO objectives focus on making part of the product. You will also need to establish how to take a decision as a group. You also need to build in some time to review your WWO work and agree ways of improving group work in future. This will involve:

- Agreeing how successful your work with others has been and whether the objectives have been met
- Identifying factors that influenced the outcome
- Agreeing ways of improving future group work

Large-scale projects

Many schools and colleges have a large project at some point during your course. This is either done in class time or as an extra-curricular activity. This type of activity could be a useful way to generate WWO evidence. The key skill may be a useful way to help you organise the whole project or could be used to help sort out just one particular part of it.

Improving own learning and performance

You could look to extend or develop a particular skill in an area you have covered in your D&T course. Perhaps, you were interested in something you have covered and want to take further. The LP key skill would give you an opportunity to work out targets with your teacher and get you to sort out how best to measure your progress.

For example, if you were interested in skill development you could look at some of the occupational standards or NVQ standards that relate to your area of interest. You don't need to do the actual NVQ, just look at the appropriate standards and expectations and design your own learning and skills development programme with help from your teacher. The standards will give you and your teacher an idea of how to assess the progress you make. You could choose a particular hand skill, production process or even drawing skills to focus on.

The aim is to support your class learning and to focus on an area that interests you, learning more about it than may be necessary for your GCSE D&T. You are not trying to achieve the standards in NVQs. Instead you are using these as a way to find out more about the skills and to start to develop some abilities in the chosen area.

There may be a skill that is a hobby or personal interest you want to take further. You can still use it as a focus for your LP work and it will still be important to find some way of measuring your progress. This is where NVQs, British Standards or some other courses could help. They can give you ideas about how to set targets and how to judge your performance.

Alternatively, you may want to focus on an area of the course that causes you some difficulty and devise a learning programme to use in your LP work that supports your class work and helps you to improve. You need to discuss this approach with your D&T teacher because they can help you set targets to support what happens in the classroom. A similar idea might be to follow up on what you learned about CAD or CAM or some other aspect of new technology that interests you.

Problem solving

Designing

The whole process of design is really a problem-solving exercise. Basically you are taking the problem of how to design a quality product that meets the design brief or the customer requirements. How to fulfil the design brief to the satisfaction of the customer or the person setting the brief becomes the problem. Your problem-solving options are your design ideas, and the one option you choose to take forward will lead to your design solution. You can discuss how well your design specification and final design solution meet the brief with the person who sets it.

Hopefully your course requirements will have a clear relationship with the PS key skill requirements and you should be able to work on both at the same time without adding too much extra work. The same evidence you generate for the design work will also be useful for your PS key skill portfolio. Make sure you are clear about what is needed in the D&T work and the PS requirements before you start work. This way you can look at where there is overlap between the two activities and where the PS and D&T may have different evidence requirements.

Occupational standards set the quality of work and skill that people expect of you when you work in a specific industry like engineering

NVQ is short for National Vocational Qualification

Opportunities

Making products

The whole process of making something can also be seen as a problem-solving exercise. You may have to produce something to specifications you have been given and working within constraints that have been set. This helps to set up your problem which is 'How to produce the best product you can within the constraints and restrictions you have been given'. As well as design constraints there may also be time, cost and equipment constraints that you have to deal with. These can also be worked into your problem solving.

Engineering

See also: **Design and Technology**, page 151, and **Manufacturing**, page 183, and **Fault finding**, page 226, for further ideas

Context

Engineering courses combine a range of studies, both practical and theory, and will provide you with a range of opportunities to generate evidence for all three of the keys skills.

Working with others

Projects

Many courses contain projects or project units where you work in groups to design and build an engineering product of some sort. It could be something that is done as part of your course work or it might be done for enjoyment at the end of your course. This is a good chance to generate WWO evidence.

You need to make sure that you are working with a group of like-minded people, motivated to do the engineering project work and meet the WWO requirements. A key part of the work will be making sure you have appropriate permission and supervision and will be working safely at all times.

Design and graphical communication

You could consider generating one-to-one WWO evidence when you are designing a product as part of a customer brief. Your one-to-one would be between you as designer and the customer (the person setting the brief). See the main guidance on using design as a way for generating WWO in the Design and Technology guidance on page 151.

Application of new technology

You may be asked to produce a case study looking at particular types of new technology products. This might be a good opportunity to work either with a partner or in a small group to investigate particular aspects of new technology. Your final vocational work will have to be the result of your own interpretation of the information you collect. You will not be allowed to work with others to produce this work. However, you could generate evidence for WWO by doing some investigation work into an area of interest, collecting information, looking at specifications and materials involved in the product. You could discuss what you find out in your group.

Making an engineered product

This could be a way to generate evidence for either the one-to-one or group work requirements of the WWO key skill. The one-to-one could be you either working with a partner or working to fulfil design specifications given to you by your teacher (the other one). Alternatively, depending on the type of product you are making, you may be able to work in a small group to generate evidence for the other part of the WWO key skill.

Remember, in one-to-one work you cannot work with the person who will assess you

At level 1 you might be given a production plan. Work with your teacher to turn these into objectives for your group. Then you can plan with the others how you can achieve your objectives and check that you understand your responsibilities and the working arrangements.

Other level 1 opportunities to work with others can be found in units involved with:

- Producing mathematics and science information about engineered products or services
- Investigating automation applications in particular industries
- Investigating health and safety issues
- Exploring different employment opportunities
- Exploring the use of computers and computer applications in engineering
- Investigating service and maintenance engineering

At level 2, you will find a range other possibilities to generate evidence in the optional unit choices and pathways.

Improving own learning and performance

Developing an area of skill

You may want to add to the skill elements of the Vocational GCSE course by developing a specific skill area. You could use the LP key skill as a way to organise your approach and to develop a learning programme to help you achieve your goal. You would be generating evidence for the part of the LP key skill that asks you to show you can improve your performance by carrying out a straightforward practical activity.

Occupational standards set the quality of work and skill that people expect of you when you work in a specific industry like engineering

You could be trying to develop hand skills by looking to take an NVQ unit, using, with your teacher's help, the LP key skill to help you create a learning programme with suitable targets. The NVQ unit will help encourage you to develop competence in an area of skills that you may have covered in your Engineering course briefly. It will allow you to develop your skills further while also encouraging you to take a more independent approach to your own learning. You don't need to do the actual NVQ,

NVQ is short for National Vocational Qualification

just look at the appropriate standards and expectations then use this to and design a learning and skills development programme with your tutor.

There may be a skill, hobby or personal interest that you want to learn more about. This could be the focus for your LP work. It will still be important to find some way of measuring your progress. This is where NVQs, British Standards or some other course standards could help, by giving you ideas on how to set targets and to judge your performance.

Alternatively, (at level 2) you may want to focus on an area of the course that causes you some difficulty and devise a learning programme to use in your LP work that supports your class work and helps you strengthen your performance. Mathematics and Science are areas that students find difficult. Perhaps you could focus on a specific topic in one of these subjects. You need to discuss this approach with your Engineering teacher because they can help you set targets and devise a programme that supports what happens in the classroom. You could also look at incorporating some independent learning based around self-help guides, the Internet, specialist CD-ROMs, work experience and/or advice and help from others.

You will find other opportunities to generate evidence for LP when doing the following types of exercise:

- Investigating opportunities for employment
- Developing computer skills like CAD/CAM
- Investigating the use of computers in engineering
- Developing electronic, electrical or mechanical skills
- Learning about motor vehicle engineering

Problem solving

There are a number of different areas in Engineering that provide opportunities for PS. Look for opportunities in subjects like:

- Designing to meet a customer brief
- Designing and making an object to meet a specification
- Mathematical engineering problems
- Scientific engineering problems
- Finding appropriate materials or alternative materials to make products
- Fault diagnosis and rectification
- Equipment or product repair

The basic design and making process involved in meeting a brief or specification, selecting appropriate materials and testing the end product should cover all aspects of the PS evidence requirements.

The design process itself is a type of problem solving. Producing a design specification and design solution for an engineered product or service from a given customer brief should take you through all the stages of the PS key skill. Remember to keep checking your PS key skill requirements to ensure that you are generating the right types of evidence. Keep the design ideas that you dismissed, as well as records of the design option, that you decided to take forward. Explain why you preferred this option saying why it is more suitable. Plan what you need to do to turn your favoured idea into a final design solution and make sure you make good use of the support and advice around you.

If you don't want to focus on design you could look at making an engineering product as a way to generate PS evidence. The problem could be based around making the product itself or identifying suitable materials or processes to use. Discuss with your teacher how you could use this type of approach to help you meet the PS requirements. They will be able to get you started by helping you come up with an appropriate problem.

English

Context
There should be chances to generate evidence for each of the three key skills during the course of your GCSE. The opportunities could occur when you do your class work, when you are preparing for exams or important course work, or when you follow up your own interests.

Working with others

Book clubs
Think about joining a discussion group if one exists or setting up a group to discuss a book that you have read as part of your English course. This will give you a chance to learn more about the book and share what you thought with others as well as creating evidence to use in your WWO portfolio.

If there isn't a club in your school or college then set up a group that will meet to discuss just one book. If the group is successful you can use it to discuss other books, but start small. Concentrate on one chapter at a time and set targets and objectives that are based on reading each chapter and taking notes so you can discuss them at your next meeting.

You could meet at lunch times, after school or college or some other time to discus what you are reading. Your teacher will give you ideas about what you should be discussing. Remember that while your English targets might involve reading and discussing the book, your WWO is more concerned with how you work together and co-operate in organising and running the club. You don't have to use books (i.e. narratives) as the focus, you could use a play instead.

Organise special events for the group. For example, if there has been a television or film adaptation of the book (or play), then try to sit and watch it as a group and use this as the focus of discussion. There may be a cassette recording of someone reading the book. Perhaps you could also listen to this as a group as well as reading the book individually.

Improving own learning and performance

Finding out more about what you are reading
If you are particularly interested in what you are reading, why not find out

more about the context of the book or play. You may have to read a book written before 1914 as part of your GCSE course. You could find out a little more about society at the time the book was written and this could help you not only to understand a little more about the book but also to generate evidence for your LP portfolio as well.

This activity is aimed at the key skill evidence requirements that ask you to show you can improve your performance by studying a straight-forward subject. You don't need to get too involved in learning a lot about what was happening at the time the book or play was written. You are just trying to get an idea of what was going on. There may be films set in that period or history textbooks you can look at to help you get a better idea of what society was like. You might want to study what theatre might have been like if you are looking at a Shakespeare play. Think about what the original audience for the play would have been like and how and where the plays were acted out.

Your English teacher and even a History teacher can help you to identify suitable targets and can provide useful guidance.

If you are particularly interested in what you are reading then consider looking at another piece of work by the author. Your English teacher will help you set some appropriate targets. This could be an alternative way to generate LP evidence.

Problem solving

Part of the assessment requirements for your GCSE will involve learning how to distinguish between fact and opinion and how to evaluate information. You will also be expected to follow arguments and identify the implications of the argument and be able to recognise inconsistencies. Both of these features are part of the GCSE reading requirements. Another reading requirement is to show that you can understand and evaluate how writers use different techniques and devices to achieve what they want to convey to the reader.

This type of learning is a little like detective work as you try to deduce meanings in the text and learn to appreciate the writer's intentions. This might be a useful way to approach generating PS evidence using your English course. Ask your teacher about helping you frame one of the English course objectives mentioned above in a problem-solving context to allow you to generate appropriate evidence.

Geography

See also: **Leisure and Tourism**, page 179, for further ideas

Context
As you build knowledge and understanding of a range of places, environments and geographical patterns at a range of scales from local to global there should be opportunities to generate evidence for 'Working with

others', 'Improving own learning and performance' and 'Problem solving'. As you work on the internal assessment that counts towards your final Geography grade, or practise the skills you will need to complete the internal assessment successfully, you will have opportunities to generate evidence for the key skills as well.

Working with others

Fieldwork and research

Most Geography courses involve some sort of investigative fieldwork, based on evidence collected from primary and secondary sources. The Geography course will encourage you to identify and collect evidence from primary sources (for example, fieldwork) and secondary sources (for example, maps, photographs, satellite images and statistical data, and census data). Carrying out fieldwork and researching secondary sources will give you a chance to generate WWO evidence.

When you use fieldwork as the focus of your key skill work you need to agree clear objectives. Your WWO responsibilities need to cover things like obtaining the necessary equipment, knowing how to use it properly, recording results accurately, sharing appropriate information and meeting deadlines.

The interpretation and analysis of the fieldwork results may have to be done individually, especially if the fieldwork is part of a formal assessment process. However, you could work in small groups to organise and carry out the fieldwork and to discuss your data.

WWO objectives and decision taking will need to address:

- Where to collect evidence
- When to collect evidence
- What evidence to collect (e.g. primary, secondary; quantitative and qualitative)
- How to collect evidence (i.e. what techniques to use)
- Who does what
- How to report and discuss findings

Consider working in pairs if you are working only with secondary sources; this makes sense if you work in a group when doing your fieldwork. This could help you cover both aspects of the WWO key skill. The key skill asks you to provide evidence of working effectively in a one-to-one situation and a group situation.

Working in pairs

You could work in pairs to investigate any part of the Geography course, perhaps presenting your results on your findings. For example:

- When looking at the physical environment you could investigate the impact of coastal processes like erosion, the characteristics of valleys, or river processes and their impact on the environment
- When looking at the human world you could investigate a local urban area or even local demography

The NFU website is found at **www.nfu.org.uk**

- Economic geography might mean investigating farm systems, perhaps exploring the Internet as a source of information (for example, the NFU has its own website)
- Studying the natural world may mean working in pairs to take weather measurements or again investigating the many weather and meteorology websites

Improving own learning and performance

Course work and internal assessment challenges

Each time you are given a piece of course work or are set an assessment challenge you have an opportunity to generate LP evidence also. The LP key skill can help organise your efforts and keep you focused and on track. You can make your LP targets the same as your assessment targets and then plan how you can meet them. The plan for your LP work is also the plan that will help you do the course work. Consider creating an action plan to help you organise your tasks and work out suitable timelines. Your action plan could cover:

- Data collection
- Getting hold of the resources you need
- Writing up your results and findings
- Writing your final version
- How and where you could find help and support

The only extra work that you will have to do is for the last part of the LP key skill where you need to review your progress with an appropriate person. Your final piece of course work will be the evidence you need to show your achievements. However, you also need to review how well you did identifying what and how you have learned. Provide information on what has gone well and what went less well. You can then discuss what action you could take to improve your performance.

Course work tasks are also a good way to show you can use learning from one task or activity to meet the demands of a new task. You could treat the course work as the new task and you could show how you can meet some of the demands in this task by using what you have learned in your Geography course or other class work.

Problem solving

Validity: the soundness of your argument or the power it has to convince others

An important part of any Geography GCSE is learning how to analyse and interpret evidence and justify conclusions you make. You also need to work out the validity and limitations of the evidence you collect and the conclusions you draw. This means recognising the strengths and weaknesses of your data and conclusions.

This type of work will create opportunities for problem solving. You will need your teacher to help to frame a geography problem for you, then you can think about ways to find the solution. It could be anything from working out how to manage a problem in the physical environment like a flood, or coming up with a solution for disposing of rubbish, redeveloping a brownfield site, cutting down on car emissions by coming up with an idea for an integrated transport policy, etc.

There are a number of different scenarios that you could use for problem solving. One other alternative could be to use computers and specialist software to deal with geography-related problems.

Another good opportunity to generate problem-solving evidence is when you do fieldwork. Perhaps you could set your fieldwork task as a problem to solve. The different options that you come up with could be related to the equipment or methods or the data-collecting techniques you could use. Once you have decided on the most appropriate way to conduct the fieldwork (your chosen option for solving the fieldwork problem) you could plan how to put it into effect. You could explain the accuracy of your results or methods, this will help to describe how well you solved the problem.

Health and Social Care

Context
Although there are a number of opportunities to generate evidence for these key skills in the compulsory units, remember to look at the possibility of using the more specialist, optional units as well. If you start early enough and look at the range of topics to be covered during your entire course, you will be able to identify the best opportunities for generating evidence for both the key skill and health and social care work at the same time. Your course will be long enough to allow you to address more than one key skill. Try to plan how to sequence each key skill and complete one before you start another. However, try to avoid having too many conflicting and competing demands at the same time.

Working with others

There will be a number of opportunities to address both the group and one-to-one aspects of the WWO evidence requirements in health and social care. Topics where you may find the best opportunities include:

Health, social care and early years provision (investigating health and social care)
You could work in a group to carry out your research or fact-finding. Whether you are doing a report based on different health or social care settings or trying to get a better understanding of your local services and work roles, you could gather the information you need in groups. Alternatively, you could work in pairs to gather the information you need using this as a chance to show you can work in a one-to-one situation.

Focus your WWO objectives on getting the information you need, perhaps meeting as a group from time to time to discuss your findings and

share your progress. Once you have the information you need, and have discussed it with your group, you could work on your own individual reports.

Health and well-being

If asked to produce a plan for promoting health and well-being for a particular individual (perhaps your teacher is role playing as someone at risk), you could use this as an opportunity to generate WWO evidence showing you can work in a one-to-one situation.

Personal development

Look for opportunities to work in small groups or in pairs to collect and discuss case study materials. Your WWO objectives could be based on identifying the information and support you would need and then dividing up the tasks and responsibilities accordingly. You should also have one or two objectives focused on preparing for and taking part in group discussions. Try to target the WWO work on fact-finding, looking for the factors that affect growth and development. Focus on searching for ideas using secondary sources like the Internet, textbooks and other resources, then discuss your findings. You can then look to apply what you have learned by discussing appropriate case studies in groups.

This type of WWO opportunity will need to be organised by your teacher.

Common hazards and health emergencies

Look to work in pairs or closely with appropriate personnel (for example, supervisors or health and safety officers) as you carry out a workplace survey. This will help you to generate evidence for the WWO evidence requirements about working in a one-to-one situation. You will need to work with your teacher or another appropriate person to set objectives. Target some of your objectives on your preparation work. Plan carefully for your visit to the workplace, prepare for what you will do, the questions you need to ask and the types of precautions you need to look for. Look to create an action plan to cover the tasks that you need to do to meet your objectives and show that you can organise them.

Exploring recreational activities

Whether by working in pairs or in a small group, you will have a chance to generate evidence for WWO. You should target your WWO activity on the collection of information and discussing your findings. This is because you will be expected to produce your own individual report about the locally available recreational activities and facilities.

Improving own learning and performance

You could focus on improving a specific skill as a way to help you meet the LP requirements. This might be one way of showing you can improve your performance by learning through a straightforward practical activity.

One way to improve your skills and give your Vocational GCSE a more practical focus is to look at learning a little about the occupational standards for care work (or some other area) at your level. You could look at the particular skill you are interested in and investigate what the occupational standards are for this skill at your level.

Look at what the industry expects and, working with your teacher, you could devise a way to try to improve your performance in a particular skill to try to get you to meet part of the standard. Get your teacher to help you set some appropriate short-term targets and make these the focus of your LP work.

Alternatively, you could choose to take a more study-based approach. Again focusing on something you are interested in and want to find out more about. Then work out some appropriate short-term targets and plan how you could meet them.

The LP key skill shows you a useful way to prepare for any type of learning and gives you the type of guidance you need to take more control over your learning. Use your teacher as a useful source of support and guidance and explore a range of different ways to find out more about your chosen topic, for example the Internet.

If you want to concentrate on work within your Health and Social Care course, you could focus on any topic that could involve taking some responsibility for decisions about your learning. Don't be too ambitious and try to take on too much. Don't try to do a whole unit, just concentrate on a small, self-contained part of the unit that you can work on independently sometimes.

Problem solving

Health and well-being

If you can, get your teacher to frame producing a plan for promoting health and well-being for a person at risk as a problem-solving challenge. Your solution would be a plan for promoting health and well-being suitable for the person studied. The suitability of your plan could then be discussed with your teacher. You can check your health plan's suitability by looking at how you think it could improve the physical, social and emotional effects on the person's health. This would involve checking to see if the problem has been solved. Then you could assess what influence your plan is likely to have and use this as a way of judging how successful you were.

Work with your Health and Social Care teacher to set up this type of exercise as a way to generate problem solving.

There may be further opportunities to generate problem-solving evidence in units to do with:

- Investigating hazards and health emergencies. The 'problem' could be how to work out whether a workplace is safe from a health and safety point of view or how to correctly recognise what first aid procedures to take in certain types of emergencies

Occupational standards set the quality of work and skill that people expect of you when you work in a specific industry like care

NVQ is short for National Vocational Qualification

Opportunities

- Producing a balanced diet capable of meeting the nutritional needs of a person could be set in a problem-solving way
- Exploring physical care. Trying to work out the physical care needs and appropriate care support for a client could be set in a problem-solving context

In each case, you will need to work with your Health and Social Care teacher to try to set up an exercise suitable for problem solving. Each of the units mentioned above has some limited opportunities for problem solving; however, your teacher may be able to adapt your work to make problem solving a more comfortable fit with what you are doing.

History

Context
The History GCSE will help you learn how to:

- Gain knowledge and understanding of particular periods in history as you look at significant historical events, people, changes and issues
- Use historical sources and record key information as you form conclusions about events
- Develop an understanding of how the past has been represented and understood

As you learn to develop these types of skills and abilities in class and practise them in preparation for exams or projects you will also have an opportunity to generate evidence to allow you to gain all three of the key skills.

You must work closely with your History teacher. This is because you are trying to identify the best opportunities to do history work and generate evidence for your key skills at the same time. Your History teacher will know what is covered in your course and should be able to help you find the best fit for your particular key skill.

Working with others

Collecting and analysing historical information
You will probably be required to investigate specific historical questions, problems or issues. Depending on the topic and the amount of information you need to gather and interpret, you may be able to generate WWO evidence as you go. Ideally, you would work with a partner in a one-to-one context or with a small group.

Make your WWO objectives the same as the course objectives focusing them on the collection and analysis of information. Then add in some objectives relating to your group aspirations (how you should work together).

Read all about it!
Why not reinforce what you are learning in class by working with others

to produce a mock newspaper covering a historical event or period you are covering. You could produce articles written from different perspectives, create graphics and use images to help support the stories, and even carry adverts that might be typical of the time.

Your WWO group needs to:

- Decide on a period or issue to cover
- Set objectives for the group
- Decide who does what and by when
- Make sure everyone is clear about individual responsibilities and working arrangements
- Work to get the text and images together
- Decide how you are to lay out the newspaper and edit the text
- Exchange information on progress and agree how to improve your work with others

You may be able to find ideas or images on the Internet. Consider producing the newspaper on computer.

Other WWO ideas

Other possible ways to generate WWO evidence include:

- Joining a history club or historical society
- Carrying out an group investigation into your local history
- Helping to organise a history field trip

Helping to organise a history field trip could be quite a good way to generate WWO evidence without having to do any History course or class work as part of the key skill. The key skill work will be more about the organisation of the trip than the history experiences you will have. Objectives could be based around:

- Raising money for the trip
- Sorting out an itinerary for the trip
- Booking museums or events to see

Alternatively, you could focus the WWO activity on producing a pamphlet for people going on the trip. The brochure could explain what to bring, what people will do and how they can be contacted. It could also contain information on the travel arrangements with the arrival and departure times included.

Improving own learning and performance

The bigger picture

There may be a specific country, part of the world or people that you are particularly interested in that doesn't feature in, or is not addressed by, your History course. If so, then consider devising your own learning programme to allow you to investigate your area of interest. Looking at what was happening in your chosen country or area during the period covered by your History syllabus will give you an interesting comparison.

Alternatively, you could work with your teacher to set targets for finding out more about the historical context surrounding a particular issue. Your teacher could help you to set your targets and help to monitor and review your progress. You could present your work as a piece of homework helping to explain how it relates to the historical issue you learned about in class or you could present it to your class.

Learning more about a particular historical perspective

Your History course will encourage you to learn history from at least two perspectives, for example, political, economic, social, technological, scientific or cultural. Why not work with your teacher to set some short-term targets for whichever perspectives you find the most interesting. Because this type of approach is designed to support your class work you really need to work with your History teacher to set targets and plan how to meet them. This way you can keep on track and use the key skill to support your class work. You should be able to use the same type of learning that you would cover anyway as part of your History course. However, you will need to show that you are able to take some responsibility for your own learning and can take some of the decisions involved with it yourself. You can use your History teacher as a source of help and advice.

There may be a specific part of the History course that your teacher can set up as a challenge for you to learn about and use as the basis of your LP work. For example, there may be a chance to use Information and Communication Technology as a way of finding out more about certain events. You could be given a topic with some short-term targets set for it and try to use the Internet or specialist CD-ROMs to find out more about it. Alternatively, you could use local resources like museums or libraries as potential sources.

Useful web address: **www.bbc.co.uk/ history**

Basically, what your teacher would be doing is taking a small part of the course and setting it up as an LP key skill project for you. Hopefully the skills that you have learned during your History class work will help you meet your targets.

Course work, projects and internal assessment challenges

Each time you are given a piece of course work or are set an assessment challenge you have an opportunity to generate LP evidence. The LP key skill can help organise your efforts, keep you focused and on track. Make your LP targets the same as your assessment targets and then plan how you can meet them. Your plan for your LP work is also the plan that will help you do the course work.

Consider creating an action plan to help you organise your tasks and work out suitable timelines. Your action plan could cover:

- Data collection
- Getting hold of the resources you need
- Writing up your results and findings
- Writing your final version
- How and where you could find help and support

The only extra work that you will have to do is for the last part of the LP key skill where you need to review your progress with an appropriate person. Your final piece of course work will be the evidence you need to show your achievements; however, you also need to review how well you did, identifying what and how you have learned, and provide information on what has gone well and what went less well. You can then discuss what action you could take to improve your performance.

Course work tasks are also a good way to show that you can use learning from one task or activity to meet the demands of a new task. You could treat the course work as the new task and you could show how you can meet some of the demands in this task by using what you have learned in your History course or other class work.

Another idea to help you generate LP evidence could be to improve your grammar, punctuation and vocabulary, working out a plan with your History and/or English teacher. The quality of your written work will matter and you could use the LP key skill as a way of developing and improving your writing skills. This will have the added benefit of helping you not just in your History course but in other courses as well.

Problem solving

Course work and internal assessment

The personal study, individual assignment or historical investigation that you need to do as part of your internal assessment may be a good way to generate PS evidence. Very often internal assessment focuses on investigating specific historical questions, problems or issues.

Discuss your plans with your History teacher and key skills tutor. If you do decide to combine the two then use the history deadlines to help establish a time frame for the PS also. But remember that you can always go back to the PS work so your history work must come first.

Other problem-solving opportunities

Further opportunities to generate evidence for PS could exist in your GCSE course when you:

- Study change over a period of time and try to determine or analyse its causes and consequences
- Explore and understand the significance of particular historical events, individuals, issues and societies
- Use historical sources critically to help you draw conclusions about certain events

Look carefully at the areas of your syllabus that address these types of activities and see if any can be used as an opportunity to generate PS evidence.

COURSE-RELATED OPPORTUNITIES | **167**

Hospitality and Catering

See also: **Cooking**, page 207

Context

There will be opportunities to generate evidence for each of the key skills in the compulsory units and in the more specialist units. Spend a little time looking at all the units you will cover and try to identify where your best opportunities to generate evidence for your chosen key skill lie. Ideally, you are looking for an activity that will allow you to generate key skills evidence and evidence for your Hospitality and Catering course.

Working with others

In hospitality and catering there will be a chance to carry out large- and small-scale investigations into a range of different topics. Look for opportunities in topics about:

- Investigating hospitality and catering outlets. Perhaps you could generate one-to-one evidence for your WWO when you interview staff
- Working with food and drink, i.e. when you prepare, cook and serve different dishes or meals to customers
- Investigating accommodation and front office operations. This type of topic may mean investigating and carrying out some research into facilities, products and services provided
- Customer service. There could be opportunities to generate one-to-one evidence as you work with real or simulated customer service situations. Alternatively you could work in a group to provide a range of customer services; it really depends on how you approach the work in this unit
- Health, safety and food hygiene. This type of topic may involve investigations into hazards, controls, monitoring and review procedures as well as having to carry out risk assessments

The types of investigation listed above are probably best done in smaller groups. Keep the group focused on gathering information and discussing what you find out. Base your WWO objectives on this type of approach to the work. You may be expected to analyse and interpret the information yourself in order to meet the vocational evidence requirements, so concentrate the WWO efforts on activities that can be done in groups. Clear the approach you intend to take with your Hospitality and Catering teacher and key skills tutor before you start. They will be able to help you set your objectives and give you some guidance on what you can and can't work on in groups.

All investigation work used to generate evidence for WWO must involve:

- Confirming or identifying your objectives
- Planning how these objectives will be met
- Sorting out who will do what

- Agreeing the group working arrangements
- Working co-operatively with individuals using their plans to meet their responsibilities
- Exchanging and sharing information about your progress with others
- Identifying ways to improve working with others

You can find the exact requirements in Part 2 of this book.

Health, safety and food hygiene

You may be asked to investigate health, safety and food hygiene issues in a workplace. If so, you could work in small groups to explore the common causes and ways of preventing accidents and ill health in the workplace. This could be focused on gathering information, discussing case studies and finding out more about the possible medical consequences and the causes of ill health. Perhaps part of the group work could involve preparing for a visit to a workplace. If so, you could create a list of questions and issues you want to talk about with staff. Group work objectives could involve:

- Organising and planning a visit
- Creating questions for the visit
- Finding out information about possible risks to health and how to prevent them
- Finding out about possible accidents or hazards and how to prevent them

You could then work individually to prepare information on safe and hygienic working practices.

Make sure everyone is clear about what their own responsibilities are and what the group working arrangements will be. Consider getting everyone to make an action plan to help organise the tasks that need to be done in order to meet the objectives. You also need to work out the deadlines for each task.

Planning diets

This type of activity might be a good way to work on the one-to-one evidence requirements in the WWO key skill. The other person you work with could be the person you are preparing a balanced diet for. You will have to work closely with them to look at their lifestyle and food preferences while, at the same time, working out what a balanced diet that suits their individual needs might look like.

Improving own learning and performance

Skills development

You could focus on improving a specific skill as a way to help you meet the LP requirements. This might be one way of showing you can improve your performance by learning through a straightforward practical activity. One way to improve your skills and give your Vocational GCSE a more

Occupational standards set the quality of work and skill that people expect of you when you work in a specific industry like catering

NVQ is short for National Vocational Qualification

practical focus is to look at learning a little about the occupational standards for doing catering work at your level. You could look at the particular skill you are interested in and investigate what the occupational standards are for this skill at your level.

You don't have to actually do an NVQ unit. You could have a look at what the industry expects and, working with your teacher, you could devise a way to try to improve your performance in a particular skill to let you meet part of the standard. Get your teacher to help you set some appropriate short-term targets and make these the focus of your LP work.

You could even consider focusing your LP work on learning how to cook and prepare a specific dish.

External assessment topics

You should consider focusing on a topic for external assessment and using this as the focus of your LP work. Establish early on in your course which units are to be externally assessed, then spend time looking at the knowledge, skills and understanding that will be covered. Try to identify an aspect of the content that may be a challenge for you and use this as your focus. Try not to choose something that you are able to cope with comfortably. You are trying to take some of the pressure off your vocational external assessment by tackling an area of potential difficulty early on. Look at the content and see if there is anything that has caused you difficulty in the past. If so you can start your LP work by trying to establish what the particular problem has been. Otherwise, look for an area that might be totally new to you and that you are not sure about or identify an area that you know will cause you some difficulty.

Your goal will be to increase your confidence and ability in your chosen content area by spending some private learning time focusing on the problem area. Your teacher will be able to help you identify areas of potential difficulty.

Discuss this strategy with your Hospitality and Catering teacher and ask their advice on issues like:

- Setting appropriate short-term targets and objectives
- How to assess your progress – for example, setting interim and final targets
- How to tie in the LP work to support your hospitality and catering work
- Working out a suitable time frame

Problem solving

Investigating accommodation and front office

If you are going to be involved in a role-play or simulation exercise, or perhaps will be helping out in an actual workplace (perhaps as part of some work experience), consider putting together a folder of possible problem-solving tips for the job you do. You could do it either as a way of preparing for the job or after you have done it using your experience.

You need to identify the important tasks or frequent problems that you could or did encounter and come up with appropriate solutions. Your final report will be a brief guide to how to solve the problems you are most likely to encounter when working in accommodation and front office. You can discuss your guide with your teacher and try out the methods they give you to check to see if your solutions are suitable.

You could present your problems and solutions as a flowchart, highlighting the different decisions that take place and the consequences of the decisions. This is a technique commonly used in manuals for fault-finding, so look at how they tackle the issue and consider doing something similar for your problem-solving work.

As you work on each of your possible problems and decide how they could be tackled, do a little research or ask someone with suitable experience how they would tackle them. Plan and try out an option for solving the problem either through role-play or in discussion with someone appropriate. Once you are happy with your solution and think it is suitable, work it up as a flowchart of steps that have to be taken and put it into your guide. Then move on to the next problem. You may get a chance to put your problem-solving idea into practice during your simulated work experience or your real-life work experience.

Food production

The preparation and production of a range of balanced, nutritional meals to budgets or other constraints like time could be viewed in a PS context. The practical issues involved in working in a catering facility could also be turned into a PS challenge.

One major problem to overcome is preparing the food in a reasonably fast time without reducing the quality. If the food is pre-prepared then you also need to consider how you can keep the quality levels up. Either of these could be seen as suitable problem-solving challenges.

If time is the issue then you could investigate what meals are the best to prepare within the time constraints you have. These would be your problem-solving options. After deciding which one to choose, you could practise preparing the meal within the time constraints to make sure you have selected an appropriate meal. You would be trying out your option. Once you have completed the meal you could discuss with your tutor just how suitable it was, looking at the time it took to prepare, the quality of the meal or other important factors.

Information and Communication Technology

See also: **Creating a webpage**, page 204, and **Fault finding**, page 226

Context

Regardless of whether you are taking the GCSE or Vocational GCSE course there will be a range of different opportunities to build a portfolio

of evidence for each of the three key skills. Start the process by looking at the type of content you will cover, the activities you will perform and the type of assessment you will be required to do. Then you can establish where the best opportunities exist to generate evidence for your particular key skill.

Working with others

There are a number of different types of activity in Information and Communication Technology (ICT) courses that could be used to generate WWO evidence. Listed below are a few examples of activities to get you thinking about how you can use your own particular course to generate WWO evidence. Start the whole process by looking at the types of topics, activities and projects you will be doing during your course and identify where the best opportunities lie. Ideally, you want to find opportunities to generate your course and key skill evidence at the same time.

Hardware and software

If you need to produce specifications, configuration requirements, macros and HTML programs to meet user requirements, this may be your opportunity to generate WWO evidence. You could look to make the user setting the requirements the other person in the one-to-one WWO work. You could then work with them to find out their exact user needs. You could set appropriate objectives for this work then get on with it, organising tasks to meet your objectives. You could use this person to exchange information with as you report on your progress. They could then help you to work out ways to improve your work with others. Your teacher could be the one setting the user requirements.

Programs to meet user needs

The course may require you to create working programs to meet user needs as well as supplying user support documentation. This is another opportunity to generate one-to-one type WWO evidence. There will be opportunities to involve the user in different stages of the design and testing process ensuring that the program(s) eventually meet their needs. Each time you meet to discuss something this gives you an opportunity to develop and refine your programming and related documentation. It also represents a chance to maintain your co-operative working relationships over an extended period of time and to agree changes to achieve your agreed objectives. This is an important aspect of the WWO evidence requirements.

Keep in mind that while your course may be concerned with creating working programs, the key skill is more concerned with demonstrating that you can work effectively in a one-to-one context. Remember this when you generate your WWO evidence.

Multimedia

Look for opportunities to work in a small team to produce multimedia presentations. You could work with your teacher to set your WWO group objectives in line with your course objectives and try to use the same work for both portfolios of evidence. However, while the ICT course may be more concerned with your final Information Technology (IT) work, the WWO is more concerned with your working effectively with others. This means that while you can use your final IT work to show that you could work effectively to meet your objectives, you should also try to generate WWO evidence that shows you can:

- Plan with others what needs to be done to achieve your objectives
- Confirm what the working arrangements will be and what your responsibilities are
- Carry out your tasks working with others
- Ask for help and offer support to others

Study the WWO requirements carefully to make sure you cover the evidence requirements. Remember to identify what went well and report any difficulties that you had, saying how you coped with them.

You should sit down with the group at certain points and discuss ways of improving the work with others to help achieve the objectives.

Internal assessment and course work projects

Most Information and Communication Technology courses have a substantial amount of the weighting of the final grade based on internal assessment. Find out exactly how much of your final grade is based on internal assessment and what form this assessment is expected to take. This represents a good opportunity to generate WWO evidence. You may not want to, need to or be allowed to involve others in the actual production of your work. However, you could set up a small support group and discussion forum. This would allow you to:

- Discuss your ideas with your peers
- Discuss aspects of the course
- Give and receive feedback
- Practise presenting your work
- Work out organisational and presentational issues

If you follow this type of approach you will need a clear remit (and objectives) for the group as well as a plan showing how you will use the group during the internal assessment work or project. You will also need to establish individual responsibilities and working arrangements. The WWO work will need to focus more on the organisation and effective running of the group and not on the IT work itself.

Improving own learning and performance

Following up an interest in something IT related

As you go through your ICT course you may come across something that really interests you and that you would like to spend more time on than your course allows. This is where the LP key skill comes in. You can use

COURSE-RELATED OPPORTUNITIES | **173**

it as a way to pursue your interests further because it will help you organise your efforts. For example, you may be really interested in the Internet or webpage design or computer graphics. Your interest could be a hobby you have or it could be something you have just learned about for the first time in your course and you would like to find out more. Either way, speak to your Information and Communication Technology teacher about your interest and ask them to help you work out appropriate targets.

Try to pick something you are interested in. This way you won't find it a chore. Also, set modest targets (you can always build on them as you go), don't get too ambitious and set long, difficult targets. Keep focused and think small. The reason for this is that you are still going to have to do all your course work as well. This is why you will find it more enjoyable if you target something that interests you as well as something you can enjoy doing in your own time.

Mastering software

You could be interested in learning more about a particular software application or program. Why not consider generating evidence for the LP key skill as you follow up your interest and learn how to use the software effectively. The LP key skill can help organise your learning. Because you are interested in the software anyway, all the LP will do is help you set realistic targets for the short term (you can always build or add on to these targets as you go). Then you can plan how to meet your targets and start following up your interest. The LP is useful because it gets you to think about what it is you want to learn and tries to focus your interests more. This will make your learning more purposeful and hopefully more rewarding for you.

Create your own **electronic action plans** to help you meet your targets and organise your tasks

As you begin to create your plans think about the resources that are available to help you. For example, self-help guides, software manuals and instruction booklets and even the specialist support that may be offered on the Internet. These can be useful ways of learning. Also think of the people around you that could help, for example, IT specialists or people who are already familiar with the software. Use these people as sources or advice, support and help. Make the most of their expertise.

GCSE course work

Work that counts towards the internal assessment marks for your course could be made up of several small, focused tasks like solving specific IT problems. Though this represents a good opportunity for problem solving, each task also represents a good opportunity for generating LP evidence. You could set short-term targets based on the course work and then plan how you could carry the work out in order to meet your targets. This way the key skill can help you organise your course work efforts and as you do the course work you will also be collecting LP evidence.

Speak to your Information and Communication Technology teacher about what extra evidence you may need to include in order to meet all the LP requirements.

Problem solving

Your GCSE course will give you opportunities to choose, use and design information and communication systems to carry out a range of tasks and to solve problems. This is a central feature of all GCSEs in Information and Communication Technology. You need to establish where these opportunities are in your particular course and when they will come up. Then you need to select the opportunities that best match the PS key skill requirements. This means that you will have the best chance to generate PS evidence while you do your IT work.

Creating programs to meet user needs

During your course you could be asked to create working programs to meet user needs. This is an opportunity to generate PS evidence. Basically, programs could be seen as ways to solve problems. There should be only a small amount of additional work that you need to do for your key skill. Get your teacher to set your programming challenge in a way that will help you to generate key skill evidence also. Then set about thinking through potential options for solving the programming problem. As you think about how to solve the problem, also think about how you could prove it has been solved. You will need to do this later. In IT it may be something as simple and straightforward as running the program correctly and successfully. However, remember to discuss this aspect of the work with your teacher as well.

Hardware and software

Working to satisfy an IT user's needs by producing specifications, configuration requirements, macros and HTML programs could be viewed as a problem-solving challenge. Your teacher could be the one setting the user requirements. At the early planning stages try to identify methods that you could use to check if you have met their requirements. You can use these later.

Once you have a clear idea of what the user needs are (your problem) you can set about working out what options might best meet their needs. You can target the package of IT provisions that you need to produce – for example, the specifications, configuration requirements, macros and HTML programs – or alternatively you could focus on just one aspect of it for your PS work. For example, you could choose to make just the HTML program the focus of your PS work.

Once you have completed your IT work, you could bring in the IT user to help you judge how well you have met their requirements and thus how well you solved the problem.

Handling information

If you are asked to produce a relational database and/or spreadsheet, this could be a chance to generate PS evidence as well. You need to think about creating table structures and spreadsheets and, as you work to find properly functioning databases and spreadsheets, you will actually be working out the solution to a problem. Get your teacher to help you frame the IT challenges of producing a database and spreadsheet as a problem to help

you get started. Think about the problem and try to come up with at least two options for solving it. As you think about the problem also think about how you could test that it has been solved. It could be something as simple and straightforward as using the database and/or spreadsheet correctly and successfully. However, remember to discuss this aspect of the work with your teacher as well.

Design project

Producing an operational product as the result of your project proposal notes, design proposals and design plans will give you a chance to generate PS evidence. For example, if you get your teacher to frame the ICT course work as a problem-solving challenge then:

- Your design notes and proposal notes could be your coming up with options to solve the problem
- Your design plans could be your taking your best option forward and putting it into work
- Your product would be your solution to the problem
- The tests that you do to check the operation of the product could also be used to confirm that you have in fact solved the problem.

GCSE course work

Course work often comes in the form of problem-solving exercises. If you use actual course work opportunities to generate problem-solving evidence make sure you know what will be required to get the key skill, but give priority to your ICT course work. This is because deadlines and requirements for the course work are more important: you can always come back to the PS key skill and try again later if you miss something.

Course work problems could involve:

- Creation and manipulation of databases or spreadsheets
- Data logging and control
- Multimedia
- Programming
- Website publishing
- Desktop publishing

Land and Environment

See also: **Gardening**, page 209

Context

There will be opportunities to generate evidence for each of the key skills in both the compulsory units and in the more specialist units. Spend a little time looking at all the courses you will cover and try to identify where your best opportunities to generate evidence for your chosen key skill are. Ideally, you are looking for an activity that will allow you to generate key skills evidence and evidence for your Land and Environment course at the same time.

Working with others

Investigating the land and environment sector

Whether you are producing a report on a land and environment organisation or doing a survey of the land use in a local area, there will be an opportunity to carry out some WWO tasks. You could choose to work in pairs and look to generate evidence for the WWO evidence requirements for working in a one-to-one situation or work in a small team to show that you can meet the WWO group work requirements. Either way this type of unit and activity should be a useful way to help you meet some of the demands of the WWO key skill.

Try to focus your WWO work (and your objectives) on gathering information rather than on writing the report. You will probably be expected to work on the Land and Environment assessment requirements individually, so you must make sure you don't work on actually writing your reports jointly. Your teacher will be able to give you more advice on how best to do this. Focus on collecting information and perhaps even discussing your findings for your WWO work.

You need to identify what needs to be done; if you are going on a field trip or to visit an organisation, you need to include this in your organisation plans as well. For example, when you visit an organisation you need to prepare questions that you need to ask. If you don't get a chance to ask them, have a copy of them ready to leave with an appropriate person. Perhaps they could answer them for you and post them back to you. This means finding out the type of information you require and organising your list of questions.

You need to agree who will do what and make sure everyone understands their responsibilities. You also need to agree the working arrangements for the group. Try to get everyone to do their own individual action plans and sort out what the different deadlines are for work.

Once you have all met your individual responsibilities and gathered all the information you can start to discuss what you have found out and talk about how it could be used to help you meet your course requirements. When you meet to discuss the course work also discuss how your WWO work went and agree ways to improve on how you worked with others. Just think about how you would do the task differently if you had to do it again.

Plants and animals

There should be an opportunity to generate some sort of WWO evidence depending on the types of activities and exercises that you do as part of your course. You could look to work in pairs or small groups to either propagate plants or carry out care activities for animals.

Regardless of which one you choose to do, you still need to set objectives and share out the responsibilities between the group.

Investigating science (or the environment) in the land and environment sector

Whether you are investigating something specific like how soil and weather is managed in land and environment businesses or investigating

the effects of environmental factors on different enterprises, you can still use this as an opportunity to generate WWO evidence. You could look to gather information for this work either in pairs or in small groups. Look at the 'Investigating the land and environment sector' guidance above because the suggestions there are similar to what you would need to do if you were using this type of activity to help you meet the WWO requirements.

Taking part in an enterprise

This type of activity might be a good way to generate evidence for either the group work or the one-to-one part of the WWO key skill. You need to work out what the objectives for the enterprise are and what your own responsibilities will be. Then plan how you will carry out the tasks you need to do if you are to meet your responsibilities. Keep a log or journal of your work and record your thoughts on how you think the work with others could be improved.

Improving own learning and performance

Looking after plants

You could consider learning about the plant species you decide to propagate using the LP key skill to help organise your learning. You could work with your teacher to set some short-term targets and then plan how you could meet them. You will be trying to produce evidence to show you can improve your performance by studying a straightforward subject because the focus will be on some independent learning and investigation into your particular species of plant. You could use specialist magazines, specialist books and even the Internet as potential sources of information on your chosen plant. You could also identify people locally who have some relevant expertise and could offer advice and support.

Alternatively, you could focus on improving your performance by learning through a straightforward practical activity if you focus your LP work on targets involving the propagation of your chosen plant species.

Looking after animals

You could use the same suggestions given above but use the animal species you are working with as your learning focus rather than the plant. You still have the option to use your chosen animal and the related care activities as the focus for improving your performance through studying a straightforward subject or learning through a straightforward activity.

Investigating environmental factors

You could work with your teacher to set some short-term learning targets focusing on one environmental factor in particular. For example, you could focus on soil and try to learn about the particular soil types and their features. You could do this either through experiments and fieldwork or through some individual study. This gives you the option of focusing on the part of the LP key skill that requires you to improve your performance either by studying a straightforward subject or by learning through a straightforward practical activity.

A completely different idea

Another idea to help you generate LP evidence could be to improve your grammar, punctuation and vocabulary, working out a plan with your Land and Environment teacher and/or English teacher. The quality of your written work does matter and you could use the LP key skill as a way of developing and improving your writing skills, which has the added benefit of improving the quality of the written evidence you submit as part of your Land and Environment course.

Problem solving

Caring for plants

You could look at the whole exercise of propagating and caring for plants as a problem-solving challenge. The search for and maintenance of the best conditions for the growth of the plants you choose to propagate could be the problem that you have to solve. You could consider a number of different conditions (for example, soil types), trying to find out which is the best for the plant.

Choose the conditions you think are most suitable and try them out as your favoured option for finding the solution. You even have the opportunity to test some of the other options for growing conditions that you dismissed as unsuitable. You could then compare your results. This could be one way of showing how effective your solution was, helping you to build evidence for the last part of the PS key skill.

Taking part in an enterprise

If you want to use this type of exercise as a way of generating problem-solving evidence try to identify some area of responsibility or task that will involve problem solving. Perhaps you could carry out some market research as a way of finding some information on how to solve a problem facing the business. Coming up with an acceptable solution could be one of the contributions you make when you take part in the business enterprise.

Leisure and Tourism

See also: **Business**, page 146, and **Retail and Distributive Services**, page 196, for further ideas

Context

Leisure and Tourism courses cover a range of different core subjects and will include opportunities to specialise in different areas. Take time to get a clear picture of the range of different subjects that you cover and find out a little about each. Then you can look at which units give you the best

opportunities to generate key skill evidence. Once you have looked at the suggestions below, you should also look at the suggestions in related courses like Business and Retail and Distributive Services.

Working with others

Investigating leisure and tourism

When you investigate the leisure and tourism industry in a particular area you could consider working in a group to collect evidence. Your WWO objectives could relate to how, where and what evidence to collect, and if you are planning any visits then you could include the organisation of the trip in the objectives as well.

Start the process off with a meeting and give people plenty of notice about what will be discussed. This way they can prepare for the meeting and come with ideas to share. This will start your evidence-gathering process. Alternatively, you could start off the group with a brainstorming session to try to get down on paper what needs to be done, then you could meet to narrow down the list of ideas.

Learn more about **brainstorming** on page 10

You need to sort out everyone's responsibilities and agree the working arrangements. You will probably be expected to write your own reports or draw your own conclusions from the information collected in order to meet the Leisure and Tourism evidence requirements. However, you could work with others to gather the information and discuss your findings.

Marketing

If you are asked to produce promotional material for a tourism organisation aimed at a particular target market this could be a good opportunity to generate WWO evidence. While your Leisure and Tourism evidence focuses on producing promotional material, your WWO could focus on market research or survey work to find out more about your target audience. The results of your market research could be used to make your promotional material more effective in reaching the intended audience.

You could carry out some primary research, collecting data and then discuss the results either working in pairs (for the one-to-one WWO requirements) or working in a small group. You will have to decide what type of research you are going to do, how you are going to prepare your material and where and when you are going to do the research work. Work with your teacher to set appropriate objectives for the group, then sort out what everybody's individual responsibilities will be.

Consider having a brainstorming session to get you started. Keep thinking about how the WWO work can be used to improve the quality of your Leisure and Tourism work.

Customer service

You may need to get involved in a variety of real or simulated customer service situations. If you find that one of the activities you are involved in will take a little time to sort out, this could be a good opportunity to generate WWO evidence. For example, if you are asked to sort out a travel itinerary for someone, this would mean working with the customer to establish their needs and then checking from time to time to clarify decisions or to offer options to them as you put together their travel plans.

Learn more about **action plans** on page 8

This type of idea would provide you with an opportunity to meet the one-to-one evidence. You need to have enough contact with the customer (either in a real-life or simulated environment) to help you to meet this particular aspect of the key skills. As soon as you have agreed a task that would be suitable start identifying your objectives. Try to identify the steps you need to take of tasks that you must do and sort them out using an action plan.

Leisure and tourism in action

At some point in your Leisure and Tourism course you may get a chance to plan an event or to carry out a team project. The WWO can help provide a useful framework for holding your vocational teamwork together. This type of opportunity would probably represent your best opportunity to generate WWO evidence without having to do too much additional work. You could be helping to organise a:

- Trip or visit
- Social function like a school or college disco
- School or college event, for example an open day or sports day
- Concert or play

Improving own learning and performance

Investigating the leisure and tourism industry

You could take an aspect of the leisure and tourism industry that interests you and make it the focus of your LP work. For example, you could be interested in a specific sport or pastime and want to find out more about it or perhaps you are interested in a particular travel destination (for example, Universal Studios, Florida) or an activity like whale watching.

You could work with your teacher to set some short-term learning targets that fit in with work you are doing in the course. You would be generating evidence for the part of the key skill that talks about improving your performance by studying a straightforward activity.

Plan how to find information on your chosen interest. Remember to consider:

- Travel brochures
- Specialist magazines
- The Internet to find useful websites

Other ideas

You could use any part of your course to help you generate evidence for the LP key skill. You need to find a part of the course or a particular unit that contains a small, self-contained piece of learning (it doesn't even have to be directly tied into your Leisure and Tourism assessment) and use this as the focus of your LP work. Ideally, you are looking for something that

Opportunities

COURSE-RELATED OPPORTUNITIES | **181**

can be done relatively independently with you being allowed to take some of the decisions about the learning yourself.

You need to work closely with your teacher to identify a suitable part of the course, then to develop some appropriate targets. Another similar idea would be to focus on an area of the course that causes you difficulty. This way you can work with your teacher to devise a learning programme that will aim to help you improve your performance. You could build a programme of self-study around a range of different resources like textbooks, self-help manuals or specialist CD-ROMs. If you begin to see improvement in your course work, keep any examples that you have of this improvement as evidence.

Another idea to help you generate LP evidence could be to improve your grammar, punctuation and vocabulary, working out a plan with your Leisure and Tourism teacher and/or English teacher. The quality of your written work will matter and you could use the LP key skill as a way of developing and improving your essay-writing skills. This will have the added benefit of helping you not just in your Leisure and Tourism course but in other courses as well.

Problem solving

Marketing

You could frame the task of producing an item of promotional material as a problem-solving challenge. You could carry out a small market research activity to help you find out a little more about your target audience. This type of information can be used to help you produce a more effective promotional item correctly targeting your ideal audience.

The market research could be done before you come up with your problem-solving options. This way the results may give you some ideas about how to solve your problem. Alternatively, you could decide on an option and use the market research as a way to help you develop and refine your ideas for the preferred option. Either way you will be able to use the market research as evidence in your problem-solving portfolio.

Once you have produced your promotional material you can use the results of your research to help explain why you took certain decisions when coming up with your promotional ideas.

Travel planning

Producing an itinerary that meets the needs of a customer can be a good way to generate evidence for the PS key skill. The customer could be real life (for example, from work experience) or someone playing a part in a simulated exercise.

By looking at the customer requirements you should be able to come up with a range of options. Asking follow-up questions or finding out a little more information about the customer's wishes should help you narrow it down to a preferred option. This would be the one you take forward and develop more fully as a solution to your problem.

A good way to measure the suitability of your solution (the final travel itinerary) is to sit down with the customer, take them through it and then see if it meets their needs. Your itinerary solution is going to have to take account of issues like:

- Travel arrangements
- Accommodation needs
- Cost
- Details of any excursion possibilities or leisure interests
- Anything else asked for by the customer

An alternative way to approach this could be to set yourself the challenge of finding your own (or a friend's) ideal holiday, then set some restrictions like cost and what you would like to try to do. Your problem-solving challenge would be to come up with the best possible holiday given your restrictions. You could think about a range of possible options then narrow it down to one option you want to work up into an actual itinerary. This will eventually become the solution to your problem. If you work with a friend, setting each other challenges, then you have someone to review your intended solutions with when you present your solution to them. This will help you generate evidence for the last part of the PS evidence requirements.

Manufacturing

See also: **Design and Technology**, page 151, and **Engineering**, page 154, for further ideas

Context

The Manufacturing course covers a range of topics; the compulsory units give you a broad understanding of some fundamentals and the optional units are focused on particular aspects of manufacturing. Both can be used to generate key skill evidence. It is worth learning a little about each of the units in order to build up a picture of where your opportunities to generate key skill evidence may come from.

Here are a few suggestions for how to use the compulsory units in the Vocational GCSE to create key skill evidence. This information is designed to help you start planning and collecting the key skill evidence you need.

Working with others

Working effectively in teams is an important part of the manufacturing and production process. So there should be a number of opportunities to generate evidence for this key skill. Look especially to the 'Product design and creation' type units as well as units like 'Manufacturing products'.

The 'Manufacturing products' unit in the Vocational GCSE may well ask you to work in teams to produce a product. This will mean you have a chance to generate vocational and key skill evidence at the same time. This will be a good opportunity to generate WWO evidence without doing

too much additional work. Make sure you understand what you need to do for the vocational unit and the WWO key skill before you start. Try to keep your

- Manufacturing targets and your WWO objectives the same or similar
- Manufacturing and WWO responsibilities the same
- Manufacturing and WWO working arrangements the same

There may well be vocational evidence that could be used in your WWO portfolio of evidence as well. Check with your Manufacturing teacher and key skills tutor where they think the overlap might be and ask them for their advice.

Working with a design brief

You have two possibilities with this type of unit. You could try to generate evidence for the one-to-one situation in the WWO key skill specification or you could look at generating evidence for the group work requirements. In the first example, the one-to-one situation would be between you and the person who set the brief. You would work with them to set appropriate objectives and they could help you judge the suitability of your final design solution, looking at how well it meets their brief.

If you prefer to work in a group situation you could include market research, the creation of design specifications, proposals and final solutions as part of the WWO group objectives and responsibilities. Collecting and discussing data would be the main WWO activity. This leaves you to come up with your own individual response to the design brief, though you could discuss some of your ideas and developments with the group.

Application of new technology in manufacturing

There may be an opportunity to collect evidence for WWO if you are asked to investigate how a product is made. Working in a group, you could plan with others what needs to be done to achieve the objectives. Check that you understand what your responsibilities are and how the group will work.

At level 1 you may be given the product to investigate, while at level 2 you could be asked to look at a process for making a chosen product that involves new technology rather than the product itself. Either way, the WWO focus for your activity will be on working together to collect appropriate information and discuss your findings.

Health and safety

If you are asked to investigate health and safety issues in a particular workplace you could use this as an opportunity to generate WWO evidence. You could work in small groups to carry out a risk assessment of workplaces or work in a team to assess what the health and safety issues might be in your chosen workplace.

Most of your WWO activity should be focused on collecting information, carrying out inspections and discussing your findings and ideas about the health and safety issues. This way you can prepare for the vocational assessment. Your Manufacturing evidence requirements will probably expect you to work individually on your final manufacturing portfolio, so focus your WWO objectives on the preparation work that you may need to do. This way you can work in teams to collect and discuss information, but then answer the manufacturing evidence requirements as individuals. Work with your Manufacturing teacher to set appropriate WWO objectives for your group that will fit in with your manufacturing evidence requirements.

Improving own learning and performance

There will be lots of opportunities throughout the Manufacturing course to generate evidence for this key skill. You will be introduced to different areas of manufacturing and have to learn new skills. Each one offers a chance to generate evidence for either improving your performance by studying a straightforward subject or by learning through a straightforward practical activity. You don't need to try to create LP evidence by focusing on the whole Manufacturing unit's evidence requirements. You could concentrate your LP efforts of just a part of the Manufacturing course. For example, focus on improving a specific skill or follow up on a particular interest you might have.

You will find opportunities to generate LP evidence using either of the above ways in topics like:

- Application of new technology (improving your performance through studying a straightforward subject)
- Working with a design brief (improving your performance by learning through a straightforward practical activity)
- Manufacturing products (practical activity)
- Health and safety (practical activity or study based)
- Servicing and maintenance (practical activity)
- Application of technology (study based)

Alternatively, you could set your LP targets for improving the general quality of your written work. This would mean looking at improving your use of grammar, spelling, punctuation and vocabulary (especially the relevant technical terms). This would allow you to try to show your improvements through your Manufacturing portfolio using your manufacturing reports, investigations and other written work as examples of your progress. This may have the added benefit of improving the quality of your written work. Either work with your Manufacturing teacher, or even an English teacher to sort out what would be appropriate targets for you to try to meet in your written work.

Problem solving

Working with a design brief

Design units provide a great opportunity to address the PS key skill. How

to fulfil the customer brief to the satisfaction of the customer becomes the problem. Your options are your design ideas, and the one option you choose to take forward will lead to your design solution. You can discuss with the person setting the design brief how well your design specification and final design solution meet their brief. In other words how well does your solution solve the problem.

The vocational assessment requirements should have a clear relationship with the PS key skill requirements and you should be able to work on both at the same time without adding too much extra work. The same evidence you generate for the design unit will also be useful for your PS key skill portfolio.

Manufacturing products

In many ways the whole process of production can be seen as a problem-solving exercise. You may have to produce something to specifications working within constraints that have been set. This helps set up your problem which is 'How to produce the best product you can given the constraints and restrictions you have been given'. As well as design constraints there may also be time, cost and equipment constraints that you have to deal with. These can also be worked into your problem-solving process and the decisions that you need to take.

Mathematics

Context

There will be opportunities to develop evidence for each of the three key skills during your Mathematics course. You may have to wait until you have learned and developed certain mathematical skills and abilities before you proceed; however, this will allow you the time to look at your course content and help you plan what key skill you want to generate evidence for. It also gives you time to become more familiar with the knowledge, skills and understanding you will need to show in your key skill portfolio of evidence.

Spend time discussing with your Mathematics teacher and your key skills tutor where you think the opportunities are and ask for any thoughts they have on how best to proceed.

Working with others

Study buddies

Have a look at the suggestions given in the 'Improving own learning and performance' section. You could follow the same type of approach but work with a partner setting objectives for 'working together' to improve your maths work. This approach could help you generate evidence for the one-to-one part of the WWO evidence requirements.

Work closely with your Mathematics teacher to sort out your objectives. They will be able to offer advice about how to set work objectives which could support or build on the work you do in class.

Gathering data

You may be asked to collect data using various methods. For example, you could be observing, carrying out controlled experiments, data logging or working with questionnaires and surveys. As well as using primary research methods you could be gathering data from secondary sources like working with printed tables and working with computer databases.

Depending on the size of the project you are working on, this could be a good opportunity to generate evidence for working in a group as part of the WWO requirements. Focus your WWO work on collecting the data. You could also discuss the findings but it may be best to analyse the data and draw conclusions individually. You will be expected to work individually on any Mathematics course work so it may be best to work on this aspect yourself. So, focus your WWO objectives on working together to collect evidence using appropriate methods and techniques. You could include the design of data-collection sheets as one of your WWO group objectives.

You need to sort out what your deadlines are, what methods you will use, who will do what and what you will do with the data once you have collected it.

Improving own learning and performance

You could use any part of your Mathematics course to help generate evidence for your LP key skill. You need to identify a small section of your course that you could work on and practise on your own. Your teacher can help you identify a suitable part of the course to use as your focus and help you set targets and create a suitable plan.

Another important factor to consider is how much of the course you want to use as the focus for your LP work. Don't be too ambitious and try to focus on too much. Think small. Choose something that is self-contained with a clear starting and stopping point. It could be anything, for example solving simple percentage problems confidently, calculating moving averages, or solving linear equations. Your teacher will be able to help you set standards for your work as part of the target-setting process.

Your plan could include:

- Target dates and a timetable for studying
- Reviews and self-set tests to check on your progress
- Dates for when you could discuss progress with your teacher
- What resources you need to use

Resources could include:

- Exercise books
- Self-help guides
- Specialist CD-ROMs

You could build in any class tests, homework or course work as a way of checking your progress. It is important to find as many ways of possible to check your progress. This will help you know how well you are

doing and how effective your learning programme and plan are. The information and feedback you get from tests and homework can help you judge what parts of the work you have mastered and what still needs to be worked on.

Other LP ideas could be based on:

- Planning for and working towards your externally assessed coursework
- Planning for and carrying out statistical analysis
- Working on spreadsheets or databases

While the short-term targets may be different depending on your chosen topic, the planning and LP work requirements are the same.

Problem solving

Think about generating evidence for the 'Problem solving' key skill once you have had time to learn and develop number and/or data-handling skills. You will then be able to tackle a problem large enough to allow you to meet more of the key skill requirements. The problem that you decide to tackle will show that you can apply what you have learned in your Mathematics course and could be part of a class exercise or homework set by your teacher.

Number problems

Many GCSE courses will spend time teaching how to solve numerical problems. This will mean you have an opportunity to use your learning and your knowledge of number to solve problems involving:

- Measures like speed
- Conversion between metric and imperial
- Ratio and proportion
- Repeated proportional change
- Fractions
- Percentages and reverse percentages
- Compound measures

You should work with your teacher to set up an appropriate number problem suitable for the level of 'Problem solving' key skill that you intend to do. This means matching your maths work (for example the tier that you are doing) with the appropriate level of key skill (PS level 1 or 2). Your teacher will be able to help you identify an appropriate number problem with a suitable degree of difficulty.

In your Mathematics course you will be expected to select appropriate number operations and methods or strategies to solve your number problems. In key skill terms this means selecting a problem-solving technique/option and using it so solve a problem.

Using different procedures to check the number solution will help you generate key skill evidence for the last part of the PS requirements. For example, working out the problem backwards from your solution can be a useful way to check your results. You could also think about whether your result is of the right order of magnitude. In key skills terms this is you using methods to check your solution.

Make sure you use appropriate degrees of accuracy and show that you are aware of the limitations of your data and the conclusions you draw. Limitations could relate to accuracy in your data or the measurements taken. This might also involve being able to identify possible sources of bias and you should plan how to minimise bias in future. This will show that you understand just how suitable your solution is and what its limitations may be.

Handling and solving data problems

There may be a chance to generate evidence for problem solving when you get involved in handling data. You might be taught how to select problem-solving strategies to use in statistical work and how to monitor the effectiveness of the strategies you use. This type of work fits well with what the PS key skill asks you to do.

Problem solving using data could involve:

1. Describing a problem and working out a plan. This means deciding what data to collect (perhaps looking at sample size) and what statistical analysis will be needed. (This could be you identifying a problem and then thinking about options to help you find a solution)
2. Collecting data from a variety of suitable sources using appropriate methods. This could include primary data collection methods like surveys, or secondary data collection methods. (This could be you trying out one option to help you solve the problem)
3. Sort, process and then present your findings
4. Analyse the data using it to answer your initial question (the problem) by drawing conclusions from the data. (This could be you looking at the solution based on your conclusions and checking your findings)

You will need to work with your teacher to set up a suitable exercise capable of generating PS evidence. Your teacher can help you define your problem and help you work out how suitable your methods for finding the solution are. They can also advise you on how to check your results.

Media

Context

There will be opportunities to generate evidence for each of the key skills in the compulsory units and in the more specialist units. Spend a little time looking at all the courses you will cover and try to identify where your best opportunities to generate evidence for your chosen key skill is. Ideally, you are looking for an activity that will allow you to generate key skills evidence and evidence for your Media course.

Working with others

Investigating media industries

When you investigate media industries you could work in a group to gather the information you need for your vocational assessment. Your WWO objectives could relate to how, where and what evidence you need to collect and if you are planning any visits then you could include the organisation of the trip in the objectives as well.

Start the process off with a meeting and give people plenty of notice of what will be discussed. This way they can prepare for the meeting and come with ideas to share. This will start your evidence-gathering process. Alternatively, you could start off the group with a brainstorming session to try to get down on paper what needs to be done, then you could meet to narrow down the list of ideas.

You also need to sort out everyone's responsibilities and agree the working arrangements. You will probably be expected to write your own reports or draw your own conclusions from the information collected in order to meet the Media course evidence requirements. However, you could work with others to gather the information and discuss your findings.

Learn more about **brainstorming** on page 10

Developing media proposals

You could consider working in a group to come up with a media proposal. The main WWO work objective for the group would be the same as your Media course objectives for developing a proposal. For example, they could focus on developing a proposal for a media artefact that shows you are able to develop ideas and conduct appropriate research.

As a group, you then need to discuss:

- The type of artefact you intend to make
- The different objectives and timelines
- Your individual and collective responsibilities
- The different working arrangements
- The type of research you need to do
- How to take decisions
- Any constraints that face you

If you actually follow through and put your proposal into production, then you have the option to continue the group effort into the production stages if you want. You could use the natural break that occurs after the proposal is finished to evaluate your group performance and review how you could improve your working with others to make your group more effective.

Marketing strategies

You may have a chance to learn about marketing by trying to create a marketing strategy for a new or existing media product. This could provide you with an opportunity to work in a group and generate evidence for WWO. You could focus the group activity on carrying out research on audiences and competitors, working as a group to carry out primary and secondary research. Once you have generated the research information you could discuss it as a group and discuss how successful you were as a group. At this point, you could then work individually to produce your own marketing strategy based on the information your group collected.

Producing media artefacts

When you have to produce a media product, you will probably have to work in teams. This provides you with a natural opportunity to create evidence for WWO also. You will have to set clear objectives for your production based on careful planning and research and also establish the different team roles. You can also use this type of evidence for your WWO key skill portfolio as well as your media portfolio.

If you intend to use production units as a source of evidence for WWO, take time to look at both sets of evidence requirements (WWO and your Media course) and make sure you are clear about where they overlap and where they differ. This way you will be clear about what needs to be done for both.

Organising a film club

This might be a fun way to generate some WWO evidence and create an opportunity to apply some of your media skills at the same time. The film club could use school or college resources and show one film each time it meets with a brief discussion afterwards. The WWO objectives would focus on issues like:

- Establishing and running the club
- Organising film viewing and events
- Organising equipment and booking rooms
- Putting together a schedule of films to watch
- Raising money (to pay for the rental or purchase of videos or DVDs)

You will need to get assistance from a teacher to help you secure school or college resources like a TV, video-recorder and room. They will also help you pick suitable films that show what you will be learning about in class.

By setting up a club like this you could create an opportunity to apply some of the knowledge, skills and understanding you have learned and developed in units like 'Exploring media products'. You don't necessarily have to establish and organise a club to do this. You could work as a group to put together a 'film season' lasting for a term and showing only a few films. How you decide to organise is up to you. Try to make the club or film showings useful for your course as well as your WWO work.

Improving own learning and performance

You could use any part of your course to help generate evidence for the LP key skill. You need to find a part of the course or a particular unit that contains a small, self-contained piece of learning (it doesn't even have to

Opportunities

be directly tied into your Media assessment) and use this as the focus of your LP work. Ideally you are looking for something that will allow you to take some of the decisions about the learning.

You need to work closely with your teacher to identify a suitable part of the course, then to develop some appropriate targets. They will be able to help you decide which parts of the course would be suitable. Another similar idea would be to focus on an area of the course that causes you a little difficulty. This way you can work with your teacher to devise a learning programme that will aim to help you improve your performance. You could build a programme of self-study around a range of different resources like textbooks, self-help manuals or specialist CD-ROMs. If you begin to see improvement in your course work keep any examples that you have of this improvement as evidence.

Another idea to help you generate LP evidence could be to improve your grammar, punctuation and vocabulary working out a plan with your Media teacher and/or English teacher. The quality of your written work will matter and you could use the LP key skill as a way of developing and improving your writing skills. This will have the added benefit of helping you not just in your Media course but in other courses as well. This might be an especially important factor to consider if you want to specialise in print media.

Skills development

This may be your best opportunity to generate evidence for the part of the LP key skill that requires you to show you can improve your performance by learning through a straightforward practical activity. There should also be an overlap between the two different evidence requirements (LP and your Media unit) which will allow you to use the same work as evidence for both. As you produce a practical record of work for your particular area of interest and skills development you will need to:

- Demonstrate good working habits
- Respond positively to instructions
- Be observed demonstrating your skills

You can use this as evidence for both your LP and Media portfolio. The short-term targets that need to be set for your LP key skill can focus directly on the work that you need to do for the Media unit. Your LP targets don't need to cover the whole of the Media assessment requirements. Work with your teacher to identify a small section of the work or a particular skill you need to develop and use that instead. Try to focus on something that you can take some control of and responsibility for. You will need to show that you are capable of taking some of the decisions that relate to your learning so keep this in mind when you choose what skill you want to focus on.

Your own private film club

There is no reason why you couldn't set up your own personal film watching club to help support some of the knowledge, skills and understanding you learn and develop as you do units like 'Exploring media products'. You need to discuss what types of films might be appropriate with your Media tutor and find someone to work with to help you set targets and discuss the films. This could be your Media teacher or someone else with suitable expertise.

Problem solving

Marketing strategies

Perhaps you prefer to work on marketing by yourself. This will give you an opportunity to generate evidence for the PS key skill. You could frame the whole issue of producing a marketing strategy for a new or existing media product as a problem. You could then carry out your own research and use it to generate two possible strategies based on your findings.

Producing media artefacts

There could be an opportunity to present the production of a quality media product that meets the timelines, budget and other constraints as a problem. You should discuss this approach with your Media tutor and your key skill supervisor before getting started just to make sure both are happy for you to proceed.

Performing Arts

Context

Opportunities to generate key skill evidence for 'Working with others', 'Improving own learning and performance' and 'Problem solving' will exist throughout your Performing Arts course. There will even be occasions when some topics or units could be used to generate more than one key skill. However, try not to be too ambitious and remember the more you take on, the harder you will need to work to organise your evidence. At the same time you must ensure that your vocational course requirements don't suffer as a result of your key skill work.

Working with others

Performing work

This type of topic probably represents one of your best chances to generate course and key skill work at the same time. As you begin to organise your group, look at the course requirements and the WWO evidence requirements identifying where overlap exists and where there may be differences. You may find that the WWO requirements break down what you need to do when working with others into more detail. By meeting the WWO requirements you may be automatically generating appropriate evidence for your vocational course requirements.

Production diaries are useful as evidence for WWO as well. Make sure

you evaluate your own performance, review group work and keep track of your individual responsibilities and deadlines in your diary. All this will be useful in your WWO work.

Opportunities in performing arts

You could consider taking on the responsibility of organising a visit or trip to a venue or performance. Not only will it give you a chance to develop a better understanding of your course work, it will also give you a chance to generate some WWO key skills evidence.

The WWO objectives and work responsibilities need to address issues like:

- What type of performance and when
- Transport
- Tickets and finance
- Entertainment on the way to and from the performance

This might be a good way to see performing arts in action as well to generate evidence for the WWO key skill. You will need to work closely with your teacher to make sure the whole trip is possible. Use them as an important source of help and advice on some of the key organisational issues as well.

Performing work

This is another natural opportunity to generate WWO evidence while you carry out your vocational work. Set your WWO objectives so they fit with what you have to do as part of the vocational work. You should be able to use any performance journals or logs that you keep as a record of your collaborative work.

Rehearsals are perfect opportunities to discuss with others how the work is going and to identify ways to improve your group working. This will help you generate evidence for the last part of your WWO key skill. Make sure you are clear about your own individual responsibilities as well as how you fit into the rest of the group's work.

Promoting an event

There should be an opportunity to work in a group to come up with ways to promote an event. You have a chance to include a little research in the activity to find out the most effective way to promote an event. You can look at how others handle promotion and then decide on how you will do the promotion. You will need to organise how you will make and distribute the promotional materials. You also have the opportunity to produce an exit questionnaire to give to the audience. This will help you determine how effective your promotional materials were.

Make sure you are clear about your own individual responsibilities and how they relate to the work of others. It would be a good idea to meet regularly so everyone can report on his or her progress. This will also give you a chance to identify better ways of working and then put them into practice.

Improving own learning and performance

Skills development

This may be your best opportunity to generate evidence for the part of the LP key skill asking you to show that you can improve your performance by learning through a straightforward practical activity. There should be an overlap between the two different evidence requirements (LP and your performing arts unit) which will allow you to use the same work as evidence for both. For example, as you produce a practical record of work for your particular area of interest and skills development you will:

- Demonstrate good working habits
- Respond positively to instructions
- Be observed demonstrating your skills

You can use this as evidence for both your LP and Performing Arts portfolio. The short-term targets that you need to set for your LP key skill can focus directly on the work that you need to do for the Performing Arts unit. Your LP targets don't need to cover the whole of the Performing Arts assessment requirements. Work with your teacher to identify a section of the work or a particular skill you need to develop and use that instead. Try to focus on something that you can take some control of and responsibility for. You will need to show that you are capable of taking some of the decisions that relate to your learning on your own. Keep this in mind when you choose what skill you want to focus on for your LP work.

Performing work

This might be another good way to meet the LP evidence requirements that ask you to show you can improve your performance by learning through a straightforward practical activity. Focus on a specific skill or learning task and work with your teacher to set some appropriate short-term targets. You should be able to use the actual performance as a way of demonstrating how much you have learned and you can review your achievements and the progress made with your tutor afterwards.

Problem solving

Creating work for performance

Rather than using the whole process of creating a performance as an opportunity to generate WWO evidence, you could use it as a way of meeting the PS key skill requirements instead.

Make sure you are fully aware of all that is involved in meeting the PS requirements and spend some time mapping out where an overlap between PS and your vocational work exists. That way you will know what evidence can be used for both courses and what needs to be done in addition to your performing arts work. Your PS work needs to focus more on the difficulties faced when creating a piece for performance.

Putting on a performance

Every role involved in putting on a performance could be seen as a problem-solving challenge. This is regardless of whether you are involved in:

- The actual performance as a performer
- Working on the set design
- Lighting
- Sound
- Costumes
- Publicity and promotion

Look at the possibilities that exist within your particular role and work with your teacher to frame part of your responsibilities as a suitable problem-solving challenge.

Promoting an event

Taking part in a local event can be an excellent way to generate evidence for the PS key skill. You should be able to combine the two activities (problem solving and your vocational work) and use some of the evidence in both portfolios. Your problem could be 'How can I promote this event effectively?'

There may be several different methods of promotion you could use (these could be your problem-solving options). Consider doing a little research to try to work out what might be the most effective way of promoting your particular performance. This will be the option you take forward. It may be that you decide to use a variety of techniques. Then your problem might shift to how you divide your efforts, time or resources between each method. This would be a little more complicated and you may need to rely on help from your tutor to guide you and to ensure you still meet the evidence requirements.

You could ask the people you are working with to help you evaluate the suitability and effectiveness of the promotional method you decide to use. You could even survey the audience at the event to get their opinions.

Retail and Distributive Services

See also: **Business**, page 146, and **Leisure and Tourism**, page 179, for further ideas

Context

You will find opportunities for each of the key skills throughout your Retail and Distributive Services (RDS) course. Start early on in the course by identifying where the best opportunities exist. Ideally you want to try to generate evidence for both the key skill and your vocational course at the same time. This will help cut down on the amount of extra work you need to do to gain the key skill. Look carefully at the vocational course context and the key skill requirements and identify where there is overlap.

Working with others

Introduction to retail and distributive services (shopping and deliveries)

There are two possibilities to generate WWO evidence in this type of unit. The first involves the actual organisation of the visits to retail outlets, the second relates to carrying out surveys of the types of shops and delivery services in your local area.

1. **Organising the visits**

   This type of activity doesn't just include the organisation of the trip to various appropriate retail outlets. It could also include the preparation of appropriate materials to use when you get there. This could include materials like:

   - Questionnaires to use
   - Lists of questions to ask specific personnel

   The organisation aspects of the visits could include arranging interviews with appropriate staff. You could even set up your visit to coincide with regional managers visiting the store. This will take time to organise. This type of suggestion will not only help you generate WWO evidence, but also help you learn more about your retail course.

2. **Conducting surveys**

   An alternative suggestion would be to work in a small group or in pairs to prepare and carry out a survey of your local area. You could be looking at the different types of shops and delivery services in your area. Once you have your results you can analyse your findings and draw some conclusions.

Merchandising and display

You can use the same two ideas shown above in the 'Introduction to retail and distributive services (shopping and deliveries)' suggestions. However, this time, if you want to follow the 'organising' suggestion you should try to arrange to speak to the appropriate personnel responsible for merchandising and display. Like the suggestions above, you should focus your WWO work not just on setting up the visits but on preparing the materials you will need as well, for example lists of questions, questionnaires or surveys.

Alternatively you could carry out a survey to try to establish how effective a particular display is. This could involve observing how many people respond positively to a display and comparing that with how many others choose a similar, competitor product not involved in the display. You could stand close to the display area and take a simple tally of how the customers behave. Make sure you have the outlet's permission to carry out this type of survey. Your WWO objectives would focus on:

- Deciding on a suitable product to survey
- Designing an appropriate way to do the survey

- Collecting the data
- Analysing and presenting your findings.

You will also need to sort out who does what and make sure everyone involved is clear about their own responsibilities and how these fit with everyone else's. Everyone also needs to be clear about the working arrangements.

Improving own learning and performance

You could use any part of your course to help you generate evidence for the LP key skill. You need to find a part of the course or a particular unit that contains a small, self-contained piece of learning (it doesn't even have to be directly tied into your RDS course assessment) and use this as the focus of your LP work. Ideally you are looking for something that can be done relatively independently with your being allowed to take some of the decisions about the learning yourself.

You need to work closely with your teacher to identify a suitable part of the course, then to develop some appropriate targets. They will help you decide which parts of the course are suitable for you to do. Another similar idea would be to focus on an area of the course that causes you a little difficulty. This way you can work with your teacher to devise a learning programme that will aim to help you improve your performance. You could build a programme of self-study around a range of different resources like textbooks, self-help manuals or specialist CD-ROMs. If you begin to see improvement in your course work, keep any examples that you have of this improvement as evidence.

Another idea to help you generate LP evidence could be to improve your grammar, punctuation and vocabulary, working out a plan with your RDS tutor and/or English teacher. The quality of your written work will matter and you could use the LP key skill as a way of developing and improving your writing skills. This will have the added benefit of helping you not just in your RDS course but in other courses as well.

Sales and finance

Finance is an area that has caused students problems in the past. If you think you may find it difficult why not make part of it the focus of LP key skill activity. Your aim would be to devise a learning programme to give you more practice in certain areas and helping you to learn about the area at your own speed.

Problem solving

Merchandising and display

Merchandising could be set in a problem-solving context. How to produce a carefully thought out, well-presented and effective merchandising and display strategy or a specific product or service would be seen as the problem-solving challenge.

You could start by looking at how different retail outlets are merchandising and displaying the product or service. This might help you come up with a number of problem-solving options to consider. You can then work on how to decide which option to take forward in an attempt to solve your problem.

This type of approach encourages you to apply your vocational knowledge, skills and understanding, allowing you to use the evidence you create for the problem-solving key skill in your vocational course.

Looking after money

If you have to produce a report on the different types of banking organisation and the services they provide, think about doing a related problem-solving exercise that might help you understand some of their products and services a little better. Get your teacher to help you set up a problem-solving challenge about which bank provides the best type of savings account or some other service for a particular type of customer. You could use a real-life example of a potential customer or get your teacher to create an imaginary one. Either way, you will not only be generating suitable problem-solving evidence for your portfolio, you will also be applying some of the knowledge, skills and understanding you have gained in your RDS course.

Science

Context

The following suggestions are for courses like GCSE Science and the Vocational GCSE in Science. The suggestions focus on common types of activities that should feature in a range of different courses. You may find that particular specialist courses, for example biology or chemistry, have similar types of activities. Remember to check the suggestions in Land and Environment and Engineering for some more ideas.

Working with others

The buddy system

There might be aspects of your science investigation work or science projects that can be done with a work partner or in a small group. Working with a lab partner will help you generate evidence for the WWO requirements about working in a one-to-one situation. You need to show you can negotiate and agree roles and responsibilities and that you are capable of working together to complete your scientific work successfully.

Keep records of your lab work in a suitable journal and discuss your progress together. If you can think of ways to improve your work together then discuss them; and if you agree, put them into practice.

You could use this type of approach to collecting WWO evidence when doing topics like:

- Measuring and observing science
- Obtaining and making in science

- Applying practical skills
- Scientific enquiry

Applying scientific knowledge and skills

You may be asked to monitor the activities of an organism. If so, this could be an opportunity to work in a group generating evidence for the WWO requirements for working in a group situation. You should be able to use the Science course objectives when you work out your WWO objectives. Your first group discussion could be about working out what your objectives should be.

Look at what the course expects you to do and then look to see how you could merge these expectations with your WWO work. Your teacher should be able to help you set appropriate objectives and help you to use the WWO work to support your class work.

You could use this type of approach for collecting WWO evidence when doing topics like:

- Growing plants
- Investigating life processes and living things

Improving own learning and performance

Working on investigative skills

You will be expected to devise and plan investigations, drawing on your science knowledge and understanding to select appropriate investigative strategies. You will also be expected to show you can use appropriate investigation methods safely to obtain data. Each investigation you do could be an opportunity to generate LP evidence, especially for the section about showing you can improve your performance by learning through a practical activity.

Your short-term targets could relate to your investigation targets and you could use the same plan for both your science work and your LP work. You teacher can help you set your targets and show you how both sets of work (science and LP) can be tied in together. This could be a good way to work on both courses at the same time and use the same work for each different set of evidence requirements.

The good thing about using this type of activity to generate evidence for your LP portfolio is that you will have to take some of the decisions about the investigation yourself. This will mean taking some responsibility for how you do the work and for getting it done in time. This will suit the LP key skill requirements. The LP key skill expects you to show you are capable of taking some decisions and responsibility for planning and doing the work yourself.

You will be expected to evaluate your data and your investigation methods. You could also evaluate this type of approach (carrying out an investigation) as a way of learning. Think about whether it suited you and how you could improve your performance further. This will help you meet the last part of the LP requirements.

Preparing for examinations

Basically you would be using the LP key skill as a way of identifying what will be expected of you in some part of the exam. Then you can create some short-term targets and a plan to help you prepare for this topic.

Try to pick something that will be of real benefit to you. Perhaps you could focus on something you are not too confident about. Your LP work would be like a mini-revision course. Don't be too ambitious and pick too large a topic. Think small.

You could use any part of your Science course to help you generate evidence for the LP key skill. You need to identify a small section of your course to work on. Your teacher can help you identify a suitable part of the course. They can work with you to set targets and come up with a plan. Your teacher will also be able to help you set standards for your work as part of the target-setting process. Try to identify a part of the course where you can take some responsibility for decisions relating to your learning.

Your plan could include:

- Target dates and a timetable for studying
- Reviews and self-set tests to check on your progress
- Dates for when you could discuss progress with your teacher
- What resources you need to use

Resources could include:

- Exercise books
- Self-help guides
- Specialist CD-ROMs

You could build in any class tests, homework or course work as a way of checking your progress. It is important to find as many ways as possible to check your progress. This will help you find out how well you are doing and how effective your learning programme and plans are. The feedback you get from tests and homework can help you judge what parts of the work you have mastered and what still needs to be worked on. This means you can go back and make changes to your plans. You can also think about making changes to how you learn, trying out new ideas to see if they are more effective.

While the short-term targets may be different depending on your chosen topic, the planning and LP work requirements are the same.

Problem solving

Basically, any experimental and investigative work in science is a type of problem solving. The key will be to work with your teacher to set your science experiment or investigation as a problem-solving challenge. This way much of the work that you do will count in your science course and be useful for your problem-solving portfolio of evidence.

Investigation-type work and the problem-solving key skill involve similar activities. For example, in the science investigation work you will be expected to:

- Devise and plan your investigation (identify a problem)
- Select appropriate strategies and investigation methods (come up with at least two options for solving the problem)
- Demonstrate appropriate investigative methods and practical techniques (plan and try out at least one of the options)
- Interpret your data and draw conclusions
- Evaluate your data and methods (apply methods to check whether the problem has been solved and describe and explain the results)

When doing Science GCSE, one of the main pieces of investigative work you may have to do is your course work project. This might be a good opportunity to generate problem-solving evidence, depending on your topic. If you don't want to use something as important as your course work assessment for your PS key skill work, then use a practice exercise instead. Hopefully you will be doing investigative-type exercises to help prepare you for the course work. Consider using one of these to help you generate PS evidence.

If you decide to use the main Science course work then make sure it is your main priority. This is because the key skill deadlines may be more flexible than the Science deadlines. Make sure that you are completely aware of the PS evidence requirements so you can use the same work for your Science and your PS portfolios.

Evidence from other activities

This section looks at how you can generate evidence for each of the three key skills covered in this book: the different ideas cover both level 1 and level 2. There are some important differences in demand and in the evidence requirements at each level. Make sure you understand the particular requirements that relate to your chosen key skill.

To help with the organisation of this part of the book, each idea for generating evidence has been broken down into the three main sections that appear in the key skill it covers. Now, because the ideas can be used in level 1 and level 2 and the headings in each key skill specification can be similar but not the same, this book uses general titles that apply to both levels. Where the titles are exactly the same at each level, this book also uses the same titles.

Look at the tables below and you will see how the sections in each key skill sometimes have different headings at the different levels. Then in the last column of each table you will see how this book uses a heading that applies to both levels 1 and 2.

At level 1 the headings are:	At level 2 the headings are:	In this section the headings are:
Working with others		
Confirming what needs to be done and who should do it	Planning work	Getting started and planning
Working towards given objectives	Working towards identified objectives	Working towards your objectives
Identifying progress	Exchanging information on progress	Making progress
Improving own learning and performance		
Confirming your targets	Helping to set targets	Developing and understanding your targets
Follow your plan	Using your plan	Implementing your plan
Reviewing progress and achievements	Reviewing progress and achievements	Reviewing progress and achievements

Opportunities

At level 1 the headings are:	At level 2 the headings are:	In this section the headings are:
Problem solving		
Confirming problems and identifying options	Identifying problems and options	Problems and options
Planning and trying out options	Planning and trying out options	Planning and trying out options
Checking if problems have been solved	Checking if problems have been solved	Checking if problems have been solved

WWO = Working with others
LP = Improving own learning and performance
PS = Problem solving

MESSAGE FOR PEOPLE TAKING LEVEL 1

At level 1 a lot of the organisation for the types of ideas you see here will be done for you. For example, in WWO the objectives will be given to you; in LP you will be given short-term targets; and in PS your will be set a problem to be solved. However, you will still find much of the guidance and many of the suggestions helpful. The suggestions will help you check your understanding and confirm exactly what is expected of you.

MESSAGE FOR PEOPLE TAKING LEVEL 2

At level 2 you will be expected to identify objectives and plan straightforward work (WWO), help establish short-term targets and plan how these will be met (LP), and identify problems and come up with ways to solve them (PS). You are expected to take much more responsibility for planning, carrying out your work and reviewing how well you did.

Creating a webpage

Context

Creating a webpage could be used as an opportunity for 'Improving own learning and performance' and 'Problem solving'. Though this signpost takes you through ideas to do with WWO, many of the questions, issues and ideas will be the same if you did LP or PS instead.

Creating a webpage could be done as a task carried out for a 'client' (i.e. working to a brief) or with a partner. This would help you generate evidence for the one-to-one evidence requirements. You could also do it as a group work project.

The signpost gives some idea about what needs to be covered in your WWO activity. However, it doesn't give too much of the 'how to' detail when it comes to actually constructing your webpage. This is because there are a number of ways to do it and finding out the best one for you or your group is all part of the WWO activity and will help you generate appropriate key skill evidence. Break down the work that needs to be done as objectives and share the work out as part of each group member's individual responsibilities.

For this type of key skill activity, you don't need to create a complicated webpage, just something simple and straightforward.

Getting started and planning

You could start by looking at different web pages. Look at company ones, retail sites (e.g. Amazon) and webpages for different clubs or societies, even schools or colleges for ideas. These are all more complicated than you need to do so try to find some simple webpages using your search engines as well. Many people and families have webpages that are straightforward and tell you about their lives, pets, interests, etc. Try to find some of these to look at as well.

At level 1, you will be able to get a lot of help and advice to get you started and keep you on track. You could even be given a clear set of instructions to follow to build your webpage. You might even concentrate on designing your webpage on paper, working out what you would like it to do and how it should look. This way you don't need to worry too much about some of the technical work to get it up and running on the web.

You need to agree on the purpose, design and content of your webpage. You need to work out and understand what the main objectives are and you may need to spend a little time carrying out some research into how you will create the webpage. Gathering this information will allow you to set more precise objectives or ask better questions about how to achieve the objectives. For example, once you have agreed a purpose, you are going to have to consider:

- How to get your page on the Internet. Which Internet Service Provider will host your site? Can you do a paper-based model of your website instead?
- What software are you going to use? Consider the software not just to create your webpage but also for the graphics you might use
- What are the training or learning needs of the group? People will need to learn how to use the software properly
- What resources, support and guidance are available to you?

If you are going to try to get your webpage on the Internet there are a number of ways to do it. You need to find out which methods are the most appropriate to you.

Useful places to find guidance include:

- Your IT teachers or trainers in the computer or IT departments in your school, college or workplace
- People who have already created their own webpage
- Self-help manuals. For example, there are a number of 'How to' guides for beginners that deal with designing and creating your own webpages

EVIDENCE FROM OTHER ACTIVITIES | **205**

- Software manuals. Companies producing the software also have manuals to show you how to use the software effectively. For example, Microsoft produces a manual to support its Microsoft Word software. Microsoft Word has a facility to help you create simple webpages.

You need to divide up responsibilities based on group members' interests and sort out who does what. Try to include everyone as much as possible. Don't limit the IT learning and training to just a few people, try to keep everyone involved. Be careful not to let the more confident people take over the design and creation work leaving others just to write content.

Try to encourage everyone to develop a basic understanding of the technical language and relevant processes involved in creating a webpage. Set this as an objective for the group.

Remember to spend some time thinking about the computer equipment you will need, how to get access and permission to use it, as well as the training you might need.

Working towards your objectives

Once you have sorted out what the objectives are and agreed who should do what, you need to work with others towards achieving these objectives. Individually, you need to be clear about your role, who you need to work closely with and precisely what your deadlines are. Ask yourself:

- What are my objectives and work responsibilities?
- How do I share these with others?
- Who needs to know what I am up to?
- What training or support do I need?
- Who can help me?
- How can I contribute to group organisation and decision taking?
- Who do I need to work closely with?
- Do I have a role in other people's work?
- How do I report progress to others?

Making progress

Find a way to keep others informed of what you are up to and the progress you are making. Keep thinking about how you could improve the way you work with others. Could you be doing some private reading or study to help you improve the quality of your work? Is there anything you could change to make it easier to work with the others in your group?

You also need to be honest about difficulties you had. Was there anything that you thought was too complicated or didn't understand? How did you cope with it? Who did you ask for help and advice?

You will have a range of different issues to discuss as you look at how much progress has been made on the following:

- The purpose
- Design and layout
- Content, even the

- Name of your webpage
- Decisions about software you use

Try to focus on how you took these decisions together. Think about what went well and what went less well. For example, did everyone contribute in these group decisions? If not, why not?

You could also consider the quality of your work. Look at things like design and layout, content used.

Try to reach agreement with the people you worked with about the lessons learned and how you could improve. One way to look at the group performance is to discuss how much the group has learned about creating a webpage. For example, do individual members feel confident enough to create another webpage, perhaps without as much help this time?

Cooking

Context

This idea is based around having to work in a group to prepare food as part of an organised and planned event. It could be a full meal for particular people, you could be making bread, biscuits or cakes to sell at an event, or you could even be preparing birthday food. The most important thing to keep in mind is that the aim will be to show you can work with others effectively. Make sure your key skills assessor or tutor is comfortable with what you plan to do.

If you think that this might be a good way to create evidence for your key skills portfolio and you think you have identified an opportunity to carry out the cooking tasks, then speak to someone willing to oversee the process. Perhaps they will be willing to work with your tutor or supervisor to set objectives or be willing to help you set your own WWO objectives.

Getting started and planning

At level 1, much of the organisation work will be done by your tutor or supervisor. You will need to confirm what needs to be done to achieve the objectives you were given and make sure you understand what is involved. This will mean making sure you fully understand your responsibilities and the working arrangements.

At level 2 you will be expected to contribute to the organisation and take greater responsibility for sorting out what has to be done. This will mean planning straightforward work with others. You will be expected to identify objectives, sort out and clarify the different responsibilities and working arrangements.

The kinds of issue you may need to ask questions about and confirm (level 1) or plan and establish objectives for (level 2) could include:

- What you are going to be cooking for
- How many you will be cooking for
- What the costs involved will be

- What ingredients or food you will need
- The equipment available
- Time needed for preparation
- How and where you are going to work
- What your role is to be
- How your work relates to the work of others

Working towards your objectives

At level 1, you need to work with others towards achieving your given cooking or food preparation objectives. You need to carry out tasks to meet your responsibilities in a safe way, so take time to find out how to operate equipment safely. You also need to learn about the appropriate health and hygiene requirements that need to be followed. As these are explained to you, ask questions to make sure you fully understand what is expected in terms of health and safety. Think about the environment you will be working in and how you need to behave in order to carry out your tasks in a safe and responsible way.

At level 2 you need to work co-operatively with the others around you in the group to achieve the identified objectives. You need to organise your tasks to allow you to meet your responsibilities. As you sort out the working tasks and arrangements try to think in terms of the following areas:

- Getting hold of your resources
- Getting access to an appropriate working environment
- Getting appropriate supervision
- Preparation
- Cooking
- Presentation

HEALTH AND SAFETY FOR EVERYONE TO THINK ABOUT

- Food preparation and handling
- Safe use of tools and utensils
- Safe use of equipment
- Storage
- Cleaning and storage of tools and utensils
- Cleaning of equipment
- Cleaning of surfaces

At both levels you need to think about when you might need help and where you can find it.

Making progress

Although you could be sharing information as you go along, it may be better to leave the last part of the key skills requirements until all the work is done and everything has been cleared up. However, make sure you are aware of what is involved so you know what to expect.

Once everything has been completed you can discuss and agree:

- What went well and what went less well
- How you dealt with difficulties of unexpected circumstances
- How you kept everyone informed of your progress
- The quality of your work
- How you could improve your working with others

When it comes to thinking about the improvements that could be made, try to go over all aspects of the work and think about things like:

- How work could be managed more efficiently
- How you could improve communication
- How work could have been organised better

Focusing on how to improve the quality of the food, cut costs or work more efficiently is important but you will need to think about how you could improve on working together to generate suitable key skill evidence.

Gardening

Context
This particular idea is aimed at gardens or areas of ground that could be used to create a garden at school, college or work. However, there may be an opportunity to use a private garden, owned by either a parent or a friend or perhaps even someone you want to help. The most important issue will be making sure you have the appropriate permission to use the space. If you have a garden or space in mind, think about who you need to speak to in order to work on it and then discuss the matter with your key skills tutor.

You could be doing any one of the following, or you may have your own ideas:

- Creating a garden from waste ground
- Maintaining an existing garden
- Restoring an overgrown or neglected garden
- Creating a vegetable plot and growing vegetables
- Growing seedlings in a greenhouse

This type of work may take some time so you need to get involved with people who are dedicated and likely to see the project through. If you don't want to do the work in a group you could look to do it in a one-to-one situation with the other person being either the garden owner, someone needing seedlings or someone able to supervise your work. Alternatively, you could work with a partner.

Gardening work changes with the seasons, so you need to set objectives that will be appropriate for the season you will be working in.

Getting started and planning

Before you get started there will be a lot of preparation work to do. You need to find out about the garden and the soil types and what is likely to grow well in these particular circumstances. You will need to identify what plants need to be grown or encouraged and what needs to be discouraged.

You are either going to have to make sure you understand what is being asked of you and the objectives set for you or you are going to have to plan the work and identify the WWO objectives yourselves. This will depend which level of key skill you intend to do.

You will need to consider:

- Where you will be working and what you need to wear
- When you will be working
- How you will work together and who will do what
- The tools and equipment you will need and how you can use them safely
- Health and safety issues (this includes handling different materials, using different tools, lifting heavy objects, and other potential hazards)

Working towards objectives

Once you are clear about what you have to do and who does what, you need to work out how you will manage the time and how long it will take to meet your objectives. One of the advantages of doing this type of work is that it takes time to meet your objectives. This means you have time to discuss how your portfolio of evidence is building up as well as discussing, reviewing and monitoring how the work is going. You will also be able to share and rotate tasks. For example, people can have a chance to try a number of different tasks.

One key issue in this type of work is learning from other people's experience and making use of appropriate expertise. This may be found in books or other sources of information or could be gained by asking appropriate people. There will be people with gardening expertise within your local community and you should spend a little time discussing how to find and use this expertise.

Making progress

Make the longer time period work for you. You will have enough time to make changes if you think your working arrangements and methods could be improved. As you make changes make sure you keep records and explain why you decided to make these changes. You will have time to talk about what is going well and what is going less well with the rest of the group, so make sure you build this into your working arrangements.

Working on a school, college or workplace publication

Context

This idea is more about working with a group on an existing publication. However, you could also look at working in a group to create a 'one-off' publication like a brochure or pamphlet. The process will involve a lot of hard work and dedication so make sure you get involved with people who are as committed to the project as you are. Get involved with this type of work because it is something you want to do, then use the key skill as a way to help you organise your efforts. Don't get involved just so you can do the key skill.

Getting started and planning

Make sure you are clear about the following issues:

- Purpose and target audience
- Type of publication, for example is it a one-off publication?
- Content
- Size
- Costs involved
- Title
- Deadlines

Your objectives should address most of these issues and if you are unsure about anything your should seek advice from appropriate people. You also need to decide who does what. Start by thinking about the roles that are required. Questions you need to consider include:

- Who will gather information and generate the different text?
- How will you edit the material and design the layout?
- How are you going to reproduce the publication? Think about printing, copying and supplies of paper
- How will you deal with the distribution of the publication?

Think of the other people who need to be involved. Are there people who control access to the equipment and resources you may need? What about permission? Remember to organise your meetings and keep records.

At level 1, your teacher or tutor will take many of the decisions and give you your objectives. However, you can still use the ideas and questions above to confirm your understanding and check you are clear about what will be involved. You will probably be asked to perform tasks that link to the work of others. If so, make sure you are clear about your deadlines and how your work relates to that of other people. For example, will they be checking your work, providing photographs for you, writing some text for the same page.

At level 2, you need to be taking a little more responsibility for ident-

You could be working on:
Newsletters
Magazines
Circulars
Brochures
Pamphlets
Leaflets
Flyers
Posters

Opportunities

ifying objectives and tasks, organisation of the tasks, confirming working arrangements and planning how and when work will be carried out. You will be able to get help and advice to sort out the working arrangements and to check that your objectives are appropriate so make sure you identify who will be useful people to ask for advice.

See **brainstorming** on page 10

You don't need to rush into anything. Meet as a group and focus the first few meetings on fact-finding about what you need to do. Brainstorming can be a useful way of getting everyone to think through what might be involved and to identify questions that need to be answered. Brainstorming sessions and meetings can be useful to sort out roles and plan for the work more effectively.

You may even have to do a little market research to establish the kind of publication people would like to see available. This would introduce a set of targets and tasks before you even start producing your publication. However, it will help you find out what people would be prepared to read and may save a lot of wasted effort. You could consider doing the market research in pairs working on particular issues involved with the publication and then move on to producing your document as a group. This would help you meet the one-to-one and the group work situations that you need to produce evidence for in the WWO key skills. If you want to generate evidence this way then plan to carry it all out over the course of a term or at least several weeks. This way you can focus on the individual tasks and take time to build up your portfolio carefully, ensuring you cover all the evidence requirements.

Take time to find out what advice and help are available. Think about who might be a source of useful information in your school, college or community (for example, in a local library or even local newspaper). Also look for support on the Internet.

Very simply, you will have to deal with the following stages:

- Agreeing the type of publication and who it is aimed at
- What information you need
- What help you need
- How you will get the text and information you will use
- Who will gather the different information needed
- How you will pull it all together and present it as a publication
- How you will copy and distribute it to your target audience

Working towards your objectives

Once you are up and running, you need to synchronise your personal targets and responsibilities with those of the team and keep in mind how your deadlines relate to the overall deadlines. It will be important to keep people informed of how well you are doing.

Make sure you work safely at all times and that you have the necessary permission you need. Consider creating an action plan like the one on page 8. This will help you organise the tasks you have to do and encourage you to work out an appropriate sequence for your tasks. The action plan can then be used as evidence in your portfolio, helping you to show that you were able to organise your tasks so that you could meet your objectives.

Make sure you know where to find help if you need it and report any difficulties in a responsible way. This means letting the right people know at the right time. Your aim is to cope with difficulties you face in a way that does not negatively affect the work of others. For example, try to make sure that missing your deadlines doesn't mean that the publication comes out late. Think of ways that you could deal with potential difficulties before you start and how you could make up time if you are running late for some reason.

Making progress

One of the difficulties of doing this type of work is keeping an eye on how everything is going, making sure that when all the work is finished it will all fit together. So consider building in times when you can all meet and discuss how well you are doing. This will give you an opportunity to exchange information and discuss what is going well and what is not going so well. It also gives you an opportunity to make changes to how you organise the work and to change people's responsibilities if this is necessary.

Taking part in a club or event

Context

In most schools, colleges or workplaces there will be opportunities to work with others by helping to run a club, society or by organising an event. This could be anything from a school chess club, work social evening, picnic or college disco. Think about helping to run a club that already exists rather than setting up something new. Alternatively, you could get involved in helping to organise a one-off event with WWO covering the initial planing, organisation and running of the event.

You don't have to be working with a group of people all doing the WWO key skill. You may be able to work with people already involved in running a club, with you being the only one doing the WWO key skill. You will still be able to meet all the evidence requirements for the WWO key skill. However, you need to have suitable people to advise you. You need to speak to your key skills tutor and try to identify someone already working within the club, society or responsible for organising the event who could act as a mentor and oversee your work. They could help you identify suitable objectives and you could use them to confirm your working arrangements.

Getting started and planning

Your objectives will really depend on the type of activity you intend to use for WWO. However, most activities will involve some or most of the following issues:

- Venue
- Dates
- Health and safety
- Access to equipment or other resources
- Costs
- Scheduling
- Communication

Communication could involve advertising for one-off events, keeping up or improving the communication necessary to run a club or society. If you look at the list above you will see that responsibility for each aspect may lie with different people. Therefore you may have a range of people to liaise with in order to get what you need to do, done.

By the end of the first stage of WWO activity you need to agree:

- What it is you are using as the focus for WWO
- What you will do
- What the working arrangements are

The types of issues to consider when agreeing working arrangements include:

- How decisions will be taken
- How you will communicate with each other
- What time issues need to be kept in mind (for example, deadlines)

Note that in ongoing activities (like running a club) it will be useful to give yourself and the group an end-date or target date to work towards. This way you can review how things have gone once you have reached this point, even if the work needs to continue. Try to identify a major event, e.g. an annual general meeting or the last meeting of term, and use this as your end-date.

Working towards your objectives

This is where you get on with business, whether it is running a club or preparing for a one-off event. As you organise the work, keep evidence that shows you are co-operating with others in your group and are communicating progress where appropriate. Meetings (and the paperwork that goes with them) are useful sources of evidence for your WWO portfolio. For example, minutes can be a useful record of the decisions that have been taken, and by having someone (an assessor or teacher) sit in on the meeting you will have a written testament of your participation in the meeting.

In meetings you should not only play your part in the decision-making process but try to encourage others to do so as well. Meetings can be useful venues to discuss progress and talk about what is working well and what is not going so well. Meeting with others responsible for organising the event or running the club will allow you to talk about difficulties and to suggest ways of improving the work with others. You could make these changes and evaluate if they worked or not. Meetings are also useful ways to exchange information and report on your individual progress.

Journals or diaries are also useful records of your individual planning, thoughts and work on your contribution to the group work.

Making progress

Journals can be a useful way to record your own thoughts of how you are doing in terms of carrying out your responsibilities. Journals are also a good way to record your thoughts on the group work. This way you have a record of your thoughts on work and the progress made at the time and you won't need to try to remember what happened at the end of the process. Every time you meet with others, you will have an opportunity to review and discuss the work you have done and to exchange information on your progress. You will also have the chance to discuss what changes could be made and then make them.

Study groups

Context

One interesting way of collecting evidence for WWO is to organise a study group. If you have important examinations to study for (e.g. GCSEs) or will be doing a large piece of course work (e.g. a GCSE project or course work for a Vocational GCSE) then consider using the WWO key skill to help you organise your efforts more effectively. You will benefit in two ways:

- By potentially improving your course grades
- By generating evidence for your key skill

There are two key points to remember to help make the experience a success. Firstly, find a small number of like-minded people who are motivated and want to do well in the work you decide to use as your WWO focus. This will make it a more rewarding experience. Secondly, in this instance, though the key skill is important it should take on a supporting role to help you perform better in your examination or do well in your course work. The deadlines for your target work (for example, your GCSE work) will probably be less flexible than for your WWO so make your target work your priority.

This is a good way to generate evidence because it gets you to think about taking greater responsibility for and control over your own learning and progress.

This doesn't necessarily have to be a group activity. You could focus on the one-to-one requirements and find yourself a 'study buddy' rather

than a study group. If this is how you prefer to do it, the advice below is still the same.

Getting started and planning

As a study group you need to:

- Be clear about the group focus
- Discuss what the group will actually do, e.g. discuss particular topics, focus on discussing key questions or assignments, review and discuss your past week's learning

The study group is not about pulling together to share the work. It is about helping each other become more aware of the issues, topics and concepts involved. It is about preparing each other to meet the challenges set in your course as individuals. At the end of the day, you will all be graded either in an examination or by your teacher as individuals so use WWO to support each other while learning about the subject. Use the following steps as guidance:

- Set feasible and measurable objectives. Don't go for something like 'Do better in the exam' or 'Get a better grade'. Discuss in your group what key aspect of a course you could focus on, consider the issues that are involved and generate a more precise set of objectives for your study group
- Set small-scale targets that can be built upon. This will be possible only if you devote plenty of time to organisation. As you reach each target or milestone review your progress. Milestones could be built around homework deadlines, mock exams, mid-term or end-of-term breaks. All of these give you a chance to review your progress as a group
- Discuss how you will manage the different timelines for your primary goal (the course you are taking) and the supporting goal (WWO)
- Share with the group what each member wants out of the experience and what your own individual targets need to be
- Remember to keep a record of discussions and decision taking to use as evidence for your key skill portfolio. Discuss and record how the group's activities can support individual and team objectives
- Establish how, when and where you will meet and what you will discuss and study. Will you each prepare something and bring it to discuss? Will you take turns? How will you decide what should happen from one meeting to the next? (Keep creating evidence for your key skill but keep in mind the real focus is on your subject work so leave plenty time and space for getting on with that)
- Try to allocate some time to discussing your WWO progress and organisation focusing particularly on the study group work

Working towards your objectives

Getting started is often the easiest part. Keeping your group focus, momentum and motivation is often harder. Be prepared to make changes to help keep the group effective.

Keep reviewing how often the study group meets and the venue. Only time will tell if you are meeting too often or too infrequently. Both can have their problems. For example, meeting too often may mean that you don't have enough to discuss, attendance by everyone isn't always possible or it becomes a chore. Hardly meeting at all could mean that you forget what to do, begin to lack motivation or feel embarrassed discussing something in front of others.

Find some way of involving your teacher or tutor and make use of their expertise and advice. You may want advice on what it would be best to focus on and the types of questions you should be trying to answer. They may also have useful exercises for you to try out.

Making progress

Bring in outside help to give you an objective opinion on your progress. If you choose a school or college library to work in, see if an appropriate teacher can join one of your sessions.

Does any of your homework show signs that you are improving? Are class test results getting better? These are all things that can provide your group with important feedback on your progress. You can also discuss how well the study group is going and whether you think it is actually helping.

Work out what is going well and what is going less well. Review your progress after each major piece of subject work you do or at convenient breaks like half-term or end of term. Try to identify factors that are helping or hindering the study group and how you could overcome these. Are you meeting your original objectives? How can you improve?

Once you have decided on a strategy to improve collaborative work in future, celebrate it by putting it into effect with the launch of 'Study Group II'.

Homework and course work strategies

Context

You could use three or four different pieces of homework or focus on preparing a large piece of course work as a way to generate LP evidence. You need to come up with targets and a plan for improving your performance in the homework you are set for a particular subject you are studying (for example, English or Business) or course work that you have to do.

At level 2, you could consider trying to improving your work across two or more courses; it doesn't have to be just one course. The more courses you focus on, the more varied your targets might be, because there

will be a range of timelines and feedback from different people to take into account. There may also be different skills involved in doing well in each of your subjects so you need to identify these early on and build them into your strategy for improving your performance.

The key skill can help you organise your efforts and as you improve your homework or course work, you will also be collecting evidence along the way for your LP key skill. So not only does this type of approach benefit your course performance but, as you improve, you also generate evidence for your LP portfolio.

Developing and understanding your targets

Start by asking your teacher/tutor to comment on your homework performance up until now and ask them for ideas about how you could improve. Think of the information you need under the headings:

- Knowledge and understanding of the topic
- Presentation
- Grammar, punctuation and spelling
- Punctuality (are you putting it in on time?)

These headings can be developed into markers to help you to judge your progress and improvements in your progress and performance. The headings also give you an opportunity to create clear and realistic targets, allowing you to improve your performance.

Base your plan around actual course work deadlines or events. Make sure you also use the full range of resources at your disposal. For example, libraries, self-help guides and teaching staff. Perhaps there are exercises on CD-ROM that can help you improve on certain aspects of your work. The Internet may also offer useful support.

Implementing your plan

Every piece of work you submit for comment, marking or assessment by teaching staff can be treated as an important piece of key skill evidence that charts your progress towards your targets. When your work is returned to you this is an opportunity to review your progress and judge how well you are moving towards meeting your targets.

Make sure you share with the person marking your work what you are trying to achieve and ask them to give you full feedback on each area you have identified as needing improvement. Discuss any areas of the feedback you are unsure about and ask for further advice or comment on areas of work they may not have commented on.

Reviewing progress and achievements

You will need to review your progress every time you get feedback. This way you will be able to see how much progress you are making. Act on the feedback you get by making changes or adjustments to your learning.

Write up any new targets or changes made in a work journal or diary or alter your plan to show the changes.

Keep feedback and the marks for your course work or homework assessment as evidence of your progress. Even if the marks are not as good as you had hoped for, they can still form an important part of the portfolio. Combine them with your own notes on why you think you didn't get the marks you hoped for as well as notes on how you altered your LP strategy to try to improve.

Any follow-up discussion you have with your teacher should also be kept along with your thoughts on the discussion. You may even find it helpful to read your homework again after you have read the comments on it and discussed them with your teacher. Then you can give an honest assessment of your work yourself.

Outward bound courses and extra-curricular activities

Context

This idea aims to give you an indication of how you can use the 'Improving own learning and performance' key skill in other types of courses or challenges you may face. The context doesn't really matter too much, you should still be able to generate some LP evidence. Examples of outward bound or extra-curricular courses that could be used, include:

- Duke of Edinburgh awards
- Adventure Scout courses
- Life saving awards
- Survival challenges
- Music grade awards

The LP key skill can provide a useful framework for organising your extra-curricular efforts and help ensure success. As you work towards these goals, you will generate LP evidence along the way. So it should be a win–win situation.

Developing and understanding your targets

You should be able to merge the targets that you use to base your LP key skill activity around with the targets in your extra-curricular activity. Timescales should also be compatible. You are going to let the extra-curricular work take the lead and use the LP as a way of supporting this work. You need to have considered the following:

- Your targets
- Your plans, including backup plans
- People who can offer support and guidance
- How you will be assessed in your extra-curricular work

You will basically develop a learning and development programme to help you achieve your extra-curricular goals. If your activity is more practical based – for example, you may be taking a life saving award or a swimming course – you need to work out a training schedule based on supervised access to the pool. You may need to practise when the pool is quiet, while making sure that you don't interfere with other commitments. In order to make this process effective you need to set targets for practice and training. This applies to all the examples listed above.

Appropriate people to discuss your LP work with include not just your key skills assessor, but also the people involved in your extra-curricular activities. Both will be useful sources of advice when you come to set yourself realistic targets and can help you identify appropriate targets and ways to measure your performance.

Implementing your plan

You need to take the initiative and show you are capable of taking some decisions and responsibility for your own learning and improvement. However, part of this responsibility includes making sure that you are learning in a safe way, working under appropriate supervision and you must show that you can take account of the appropriate health and safety considerations.

Look to identify an appropriate stage to review your work. Either find a natural break in the learning programme or review your progress after you reach a target. Even if your activities are mainly physical and/or practical, you still need to review your performance and try to determine how close you are to achieving your targets. This also gives you an opportunity to make adjustments to your plan and/or training schedule, if necessary.

Reviewing progress and achievements

Your final extra-curricular assessment can be used to show your actual achievements. After completing your extra-curricular or outward-bound course assessment, look back on the whole process and consider the changes you would make to improve your performance in future.

Taking your driving test

Context

Learning to drive may be high on your agenda. You must be 17 years old to obtain a provisional licence to drive a motor car. The complete driving test for a motor car has two components: a theory test and a practical test. You need to pass the theory test before you can attempt the driving practical test. You will see, on the illustration of the DSA website, that there is a link to the practice theory tests and publication at the left of the screen. The LP key skill could be a useful way to prepare for the theory test and as you learn and improve your knowledge and understanding you will also

DSA webpage. Note the link to the practice theory tests and publications on the left-hand side of the screen

be generating evidence for your LP portfolio. The LP key skill will help you approach the challenge in a well-organised way. It will help you think carefully about how to organise your learning and how to monitor your performance.

The LP work will involve creating a learning programme designed to get you ready to take the theory test. Remember, although the desired end result (a pass in the driving theory test) is important, a record of how you approach the challenge will be needed for your key skill portfolio of evidence.

This type of idea is more ambitious than the key skill intended and could be more complex than you need. If you don't want to set such a large goal for yourself or you are worried that the process will be too complicated, then work with someone suitable to devise a learning programme that tackles only one particular part of the knowledge needed for the driving theory test. For example, at level 1 you could focus on learning to recognise what the different road signs mean. Alternatively, you could set your short-term targets for preparing to take the online test, rather than

EVIDENCE FROM OTHER ACTIVITIES | **221**

the actual driving test. That way you can limit what you need to do to a more appropriate time period.

At level 1 a lot of the organisation will be done for you and you will need to concentrate on checking that you understand your short-term targets. At level 2, you will be expected to take a little more responsibility in helping to set your targets and planning your work.

Developing and understanding your targets

Before you are able to set appropriate targets you need to gather information on how to achieve what you want to do. The types of information you need to collect and the issues you need to address include:

- Completion of documentation to obtain a provisional licence. You must hold a current licence to sit the theory test and can set the necessary administrative process in motion with a visit to the post office to pick up the appropriate form
- Getting acquainted with the procedures and regulations
- Locating your most convenient theory test centre where you can pick up the necessary literature about the test
- Studying the Driving Standards Agency (DSA) leaflet explaining the touch screen computerised theory test
- Checking out the DSA website (**www.driving-tests.co.uk**) which includes the range of publications and products available in book, manual and CD-ROM format
- Investigating the possibility of formal practical driving lessons from an approved instructor so as to enable you to develop practical skills and experience alongside theory acquisition
- Investigating the costs involved (provisional driving licence; theory test; approved driving lessons; learning resources)

Implementing your plan

You will need to find out ways to test your knowledge to help you measure how much you have learned and to judge how effective your learning programme is. One way to do this is to take practice theory tests.

You will find practice test questions in various teach-yourself type books and CD-ROMs and you can also take a practice test online using the web address shown above. The Driving Standards Agency has a CD-ROM that contains a question bank and gets you familiar with the types of screen you are likely to see used during the test. This is a useful resource to build into your learning programme.

The online test is a useful way of getting used to the form of questions you might face in the actual theory test and will help you get used to using computers to take a test. During the actual driving theory test you select your answers by touching the computer screen. Though you will get a brief practice session to get used to the actual system before starting your theory test, using the online practice tests will give you an idea of the type of thing to expect. Though there is no time limit when you take the online practice tests, you can begin to introduce the time as a factor. It is a factor in the actual test, where you are expected to answer 35 questions in 40 minutes. You must get 30 correct answers to pass the actual test. The online test will be automatically marked for you on completion.

Build in a few opportunities to take some form of practice test as a way to monitor your progress.

Reviewing progress and achievements

After you take a practice test, review how well you have done. Unfortunately, with the online practice test you don't get a chance to see which questions you answered incorrectly. If you can, take note of the questions you are having to guess or are not sure about as you answer them on screen. Then you know which areas need further attention when you start learning and revising again.

Hobbies and interests

Context

Investigate the possibility of using a hobby or personal interest as the way to generate evidence for the LP key skill. You need to discuss this with your key skills tutor. You should be able to generate evidence to show how you improved your performance by either studying or learning through a practical activity depending on your interest or hobby. For example, your interest or hobby could be anything from astronomy to athletics or bird-watching to basketball. It shouldn't really matter as long as you focus on learning and improving your performance and concentrate on meeting the requirements of the key skill.

Developing and understanding your targets

Try to find someone suitable to work with or to ask for advice. This should be someone connected with your interests, for example a club official, your coach or someone with the same interest as you but with more experience. They can help you learn more about your area of interest, while your key skills tutor can help you with the LP requirements. Both will be able to help you work on your targets and help you come up with a plan for meeting them. More experienced people and/or your key skills tutor could also be considered as appropriate people to help you review your progress.

Try to identify some area or topic within your hobby or interest that you want to learn more about and use this as the basis for identifying suitable targets.

You also need to think of how you can show that you have met your targets successfully. Think of good ways to demonstrate what you have learned or how your performance has improved.

Implementing your plan

It is your hobby or personal interest so you should find it easy to take some responsibility for decisions about your own learning. Because you are interested in the topic your pick, you should have the motivation to search for the information or practise the skills that you have targeted.

Spend time exploring where and how you can find information about your chosen subject matter or skills. Investigate the following ways to find out more about your chosen interest to help you improve:

- Specialist websites
- Local resources like libraries
- Self-help manuals
- Specialist CD-ROMs
- Specialist magazines

Reviewing progress and achievements

You need to sit down with your key skills tutor and/or the person you used to help you with your targets to review how well you have done in meeting your targets. Hopefully, you will have found a way to evaluate how well you have done in meeting your targets. You should put these into practice to determine how well you have done, once you have discussed the methods with an appropriate person. They may have their own ideas about how you could measure how well you have done.

What do you want to do next?

Context

At some point you may have to consider what your next move is to be in terms of the course or career you what to pursue. There are a wide range of opportunities and course choices available and as you decide on what opportunity to follow up you could be generating evidence for your PS key skill.

After your have completed the course or courses you are currently taking you will be confronted with a range of options that you could do next. For example, GCSE students have to decide what they intend to do after completing Key Stage 4. You may decide to do A-levels or Vocational A-levels, take other vocational courses, try to find employment, go to further education college, sixth form college or perhaps follow some other route.

There may be a chance to start thinking about your next move and generate PS evidence at the same time. The key skill can be used to help you organise your thoughts about what you intend to do next and can be a useful way of organising how you go about sorting things out.

Problems and options

Simply put, your problem is really 'What do I do next?'. The solution could be a clearer idea of what you would like to do along with ideas of how and where to do it. For example, you may want to go to university to study a particular course. If so, you need to identify what courses you should take to get you there. Part of the process might involve finding out which particular A-levels or Vocational A-levels would be the best options to take as a way to prepare. There may be other courses more suitable that you also need to consider.

You need to think about how you are going to reach your solution. Think about the strategies or methods you will use to find the information you need in order to make your choices. These will be your problem-solving options. Listing a range of possible courses that you might like to do and finding out more about them would not be identifying options. Remember, your problem is 'What do I do next?' so your options have to relate to how you will solve this problem. They are methods for finding out the answer.

Three possible ways to tackle this task, depending on your circumstances, are:

- You could consider looking at the type of university course you want to take and work back from there. This will mean exploring what would be the best university entrance qualifications to take next (for example, Vocational A-levels) and the grades you will need. This could be one option to help you solve the problem
- If you are intending to try to work in a certain type of job then you could explore what kinds of qualifications or training you will need before you start applying for those types of job. Then you could establish where you could go to get this training. These types of options involve finding out about what you want to do eventually and working back from there
- If you are less certain about what you want to do you could reverse the process and explore where different choices might lead. Look at the different range of options available to you and explore where they could lead

How are you going to find out what is available in your local area? Are you going to visit colleges and sixth forms? Write and ask for prospectuses? Visit your careers advisers?

Planning and trying out options

One of your best sources of advice and support will probably be your careers and guidance tutors. Careers tutors will also have access to a large amount of different information that can help you with your choices.

Choose which option you want to use for solving your problem and then try it out. Confirm with your key skills tutor or careers tutor what option you intend to use, taking account of any advice they have.

Try to record in a journal or notebook your thoughts on how things are going and what you are finding out. Record how you feel about the information you are finding out and how it changes your opinions on what you think your next move should be.

Checking if problems have been solved

Your teacher or key skills tutor may have ways or methods to assess your solution, but with something like this the only real way is by trying to work out how well your plan for what you should do next suits you. You also need to think about how realistic it is. This means looking at questions like:

- Are you likely to get the grades you need to progress on to your choice of courses?
- Is there somewhere that can offer you the options you want to take?

Fault finding

Context

It doesn't really matter what piece of equipment or machinery you are trying to use as the basis of your fault-finding exercise. The point will be to follow the correct processes that will allow you to safely detect the faults and either fix them or explain how to fix them. The types of things you could be working on include:

- Equipment or machinery you use in class or at work
- Motor vehicles (routine tasks like checking fluid levels)
- Computer hardware (for example, fault finding with a printer)

There may be a range of fault-finding options to follow in the manuals that come with the equipment you are working with. There may also be websites that the company making the equipment provides to help you with maintenance and fault finding.

You must limit your problem solving to routine maintenance or repairs. This means carrying out tasks that the manufacturer would expect you to do yourself. Do not attempt anything more complicated than this.

Problems and options

At level 1 you will be given the problem and you will need to check that you understand what is involved. Then work with an appropriate person to identify two options for solving it. At level 2 the key skill expects you to be able to identify the problem and options with less assistance from others.

By reading manuals and finding out what is already known about fault finding for your chosen equipment you will be able to identify where problems might exist and find ways to locate and fix them. Even if you are given the problem, reading the manuals or support materials available will help you check that you fully understand the problem. The more you know about the equipment the better prepared you will be to identify problems and come up with suitable options to help you solve them.

One extremely important aspect of any work of this type is that you fully understand the health and safety requirements and hazards involved in working with your particular types of equipment. Spend time identifying the health and safety issues involved. Then you can ask questions about how to ensure you work safely.

Planning and trying out options

Ensure that any options you intend to follow meet with the manufacturer's instructions or recommendations for repairing or maintaining the equipment. Think about how you could show the work that you need to do. You could consider using an action plan to show the series and sequence of tasks that you need to carry out. You could even show the decisions that you need to take and processes you need to follow in the form of a flowchart. Many manuals and equipment guides use flowcharts as a way of helping you pinpoint where problems might be in the equipment if something goes wrong.

Make sure that you have advice and support available if you need it.

Checking if problems have been solved

You will need to find some way of checking if the problem has been solved. Your method for checking the problem has been solved could be something as simple as the safe and smooth running of the equipment and demonstrating that it is able to run and function properly. Make sure you know how to operate the machine safely and responsibly.

Index

action plans   8–9
active listening   36–7
advanced searches   52–3
agendas   29–30
aims   3
appropriate people   56–7
arguments   26–8
Art and Design   142–6

bottom line   56–140
brainstorming   10–13
browsers   48,   49
Business   146–9

chairing meetings   30–1
conflict   26–8
Construction and the Built
    Environment   149–151
contingency planning   9
courses   142–202
    Art and Design   142–6
    Business   146–9
    Construction and the Built
        Environment   149–51
    Design and Technology   151–4
    Engineering   154–7
    English   157–8
    Geography   158–61
    Health and Social Care   161–4
    History   164–7
    Hospitality and Catering
        168–71

    Information and Communication
        Technology   171–6
    Land and Environment   176–9
    Leisure and Tourism   179–83
    Manufacturing   183–6
    Mathematics   186–9
    Media   189–93
    Performing Arts   193–6
    Retail and Distributive Services
        196–9
    Science   199–202

Design and Technology   151–4
discussions   34–6
driving theory test   220–3

Engineering   154–7
English   157–8
evidence   59
    group   72–3
extra-curricular activities   219–20

feasibility studies   5–6
feedback   19–21
flowcharts   14–16

general opportunities   203–27
    cooking   207–9
    driving theory test   220–3
    fault-finding   226–7
    gardening   209–11
    hobbies and interests   223–4

homework strategies
217–19
outward bound courses
219–20
producing publications   211–13
study groups   215–17
taking part in a club or event
213–15
web pages (creating)   204–7
what to do next   224–6
Geography   158–61
ground rules   23–4
group work   22–5
aims   3–4
arrangements   25
evidence   72–3
leaders   23
monitoring   25

Health and Social Care   161–4
History   164–7
holding meetings   28–9
homework strategies   217–19
Hospitality and Catering   168–71

Improving your own learning and
performance (LP)   91–119
Improving your own learning and
performance   level 1
91–101
confirming targets   91–5
reviewing progress and
achievements   98–101
using your plan   95–8
Improving your own learning and
performance   level 2
102–16
reviewing progress and
achievements   111–16
setting targets   102–16
using your plan   107–11

Information and Communication
Technology   171–6
Internet   46–54
Internet Service Providers (ISP)   47–8

language
racist   41
sexist   41
Land and Environment   176–9
learning curve   1–55
Leisure and Tourism   179–83

making decisions   42
Manufacturing   183–6
mapping   16–18
Mathematics   186–9
Media   189–93
meetings   28–9
chairing   30–1
minute taking   31
monitoring   9–10
group   25

objectives   4–5
group   24–5
offensive language   40
on-line services   47
outward bound courses   219–20

Performing Arts   193–6
plain English searches   51–2
planning   2–18
portfolios evidence   56–9
problems   43,   129–30
problem solving   42–5
techniques   43–5
producing publications   211–13
Problem solving evidence   level 1
119–28
checking problems have been
solved   126–8

confirming problems and
identifying options 119–23
planning and trying out options
123–5
Problem solving evidence level 2
130–9
checking problems have been
solved 137–9
identifying problems 130–3
planning and implementing
options 134–6

Qualifications and Curriculum
Authority 55
questioning 37–8

Retail and Distributive Services
196–9
reviewing and evaluating 19–21

Science 199–202
searching the Internet 49–54
search engines 48–50
self-managing groups 23
sensitivity 39
skills audits 43

spider diagrams 13–14
straightforward 57–8
study groups 215–17
SWOT analysis 43–5

taking part in club events 213
targets 4–5

webpages (creating) 204–7
Web access 47
what to do next 224–6
World Wide Web 46–54
Working with others 60–1
Working with others evidence
level 1 62–71
confirming what to do 62–6
identifying progress 69–71
working towards objectives
67–9
Working with others evidence
level 2 73–86
planning work 73–8
sharing information on progress
82–6
working towards objectives
78–82